CITIZEN BEWARE—

SOMEONE IS PLAYING GAMES WITH YOUR LIFE!

Everything we now eat has been treated with some chemical agent. Our air, our water, our food— all have been infused with some poisonous substance.

There are some who claim that these agents are negligible. They feel that a small amount of poison will do no harm.

But the staggering health statistics prove that these people are terribly wrong. Our life is declining with each small dose. . . .

THE POISONS IN YOUR FOOD

Focuses a powerful and long overdue floodlight on one of the most explosive issues facing you today!

Also by William Longgood:

THE SUEZ STORY—KEY TO THE MIDDLE EAST

THE PINK SLIP (with Ed Wallace)

TALKING YOUR WAY TO SUCCESS—
    the story of the Dale Carnegie Course

THE POISONS
IN
YOUR FOOD

NEW REVISED EDITION

WILLIAM LONGGOOD

 PYRAMID BOOKS • NEW YORK

THE POISONS IN YOUR FOOD

A PYRAMID BOOK
Published by arrangement with Simon and Schuster, Inc.

Tenth printing, October, 1975

ISBN: 0-515-02043-5

Library of Congress Catalog Card Number: 59-13880

Printed in the United States of America

PYRAMID BOOKS are published by
Pyramid Communications, Inc. Its trademarks, consisting of the word "Pyramid" and the portrayal of a pyramid, are registered in the United States Patent Office.

PYRAMID COMMUNICATIONS, INC.
919 Third Avenue
New York, New York 10022 U.S.A.

Contents

Acknowledgments

In preparing this book I was fortunate in having the encouragement and assistance of some of the most competent medical and research physicians in America. These men, out of their own sense of alarm about the health hazard posed by chemicals being used in foods, gave freely and generously of their time and technical knowledge. I am deeply grateful to them for their help.

I wish to pay tribute to Congressman James J. Delaney of New York, who has lived up to the highest ideals of public service by courageously leading the fight for strong laws that will assure the nation a pure and wholesome food supply.

I also wish to express my respect and admiration for the doctors and other qualified persons who have spoken out so forthrightly and courageously on this tremendously important problem. These men are quoted as length in the following pages. It is to them, the real authors of this book, that this work is dedicated.

—WILLIAM LONGGOOD

INTRODUCTION

THIS BOOK, originally published in 1960, has been brought up to date in all major respects for this reissue. In the decade since it came out there have been many changes in the methods of growing, processing and packaging food. Primarily these changes have led to an even greater dependence on chemicals by farmers and manufacturers. I have kept no detailed bookkeeping account of these changes, but certainly there has been no change of philosophy on the part of the Food and Drug Administration, which regulates their use, or on the part of industry as a whole.

The official line persists that a harmful substance can be reduced in amount until it ceases to be harmful. In other words, poison in small doses ceases to be poison. This concept takes a quantitative rather than a qualitative view of matter; it makes no allowance for the minute size of a human cell and its vulnerability to alien substances. Along with this view of poison persists the parallel concept that anything that cannot be isolated in a test tube or viewed through a microscope doesn't exist. It follows, by this line of reasoning, that since chemicals injected into the daily diet have not been proved to cause immediate death or chronic illness, therefore they are safe.

All of this is part of what has been called the "philosophy of poison." Contemporary life is dominated by this philosophy. Poisons are part of our daily existence. They are in the air we breathe, the water we drink, the food we eat, the clothes we wear, the goods and materials with which we surround ourselves in daily life.

Industry generally has refused to look upon this chemical onslaught as raising a question of human survival. Rather, it deals with it as a problem in public relations. Those who question or criticize the use in food of these powerful chemicals that are alien to the human body are shouted down with shrill cries of "Crackpot . . . Food faddist . . . Nut." Industry scientists use bizarre logic and semantic evasions to avoid dealing with the critical issue at stake. They quibble about the definition of poison as if the body could be deceived by the sophistry of the mind. Their favorite argument is that because a small amount of salt is necessary to health and large amounts can kill, it therefore follows that virtually every chemical is safe in small doses. It is on this semantic tight-rope that all of us walk perilously over the abyss of the unknown.

Webster defines poison as "any agent which, introduced into an organism, may chemically produce an injurious or deadly effect. . . ." Any injury to the cell impairs the health of the organ of which it is a part. The greater the damage, the less health the organ enjoys. This damage may be so subtle that it can be neither seen nor measured, or it may be total, which is to say death.

But it is remarkable how much damage an organ can sustain and still be able to function, although with reduced efficiency. However, what standard is there in our lives to enable us to measure optimum health? How many of us really enjoy optimum health, or anything even approximating it? Most of us are like the boy who couldn't see fifty feet in front of him, but didn't complain because he thought that no one else could see any farther. We settle for far less than our birthright. We are content to drag through life, calling ourselves healthy if we are free of pain and measurable pathology. We do not consider exuberance of spirit a vital part of good health.

Despite the great advances in medicine, doctors have not changed their concept of health. They continue to be oriented to catastrophe. They are still blind to the delicate nuances of flesh and spirit. Medicine has not recognized the shadowland between pathology and a vibrant sense of well being. How many people go to their physician to complain that they "just don't feel well;" they can't put their finger on anything specifically wrong, they just feel out of sorts, tired all the time, barely able to drag through their days. The doctor tests them, thumps them, and announces triumphantly, "There's nothing wrong with you. The tests are all negative."

It may well be. But small comfort for the suffering patient. An absence of discernible pathology should not be mistaken for health.

What role do the poisons in our daily environment play in this sly undermining of our pleasures in life? Is there a connection? Is man not the sum total of what he eats, breathes, drinks, thinks and lives? While we receive assurances that "there's nothing wrong" with us, that limited amounts of poison are safe, our disease rates soar. Cancer and many other ailments seem almost epidemic. Cancer in children is no longer a rarity, as this book points out. The dreaded word seems to leap from the obituary pages with alarming regularity and ever-increasing frequency, a respector of neither age, social position nor economic achievement.

Our response to this threat has been, characteristically, to step up the search for the magic bullet—some mysterious, still-elusive cure that will permit us to continue to live without regard for the biological limitations imposed on mortal creatures; when disaster strikes, we'll take a pill, a shot of this or that, a bolt from some super machine will throb through our suffering bodies, and—presto! we can continue to live in the wanton and unnatural patterns that have already cut down and disabled so many of us.

We are a people often reckless in our obstinacy, so conditioned to look for hidden meanings that frequently we fail to recognize the obvious. We refuse to consider the simple notion of eliminating the foreign substances that assault us in our daily life; instead we stubbornly demand definitive proof that these insidious chemical agents are responsible for human ailments. We still insist upon laboratory proof of that which nature has already demonstrated on our tortured bodies with scuh relentless ferocity.

The time is late. It is to our peril if we delay longer in demanding relief, in purging from our environment the products and by-products and the whole host of man-made insults that have debased the earth and helped bring about our ever-increasing miseries of the flesh and spirit.

William Longgood
New York, 1969

1

The Poisons
You Eat

We are natural beings and are trying to live in an artificial world. It cannot be done. There are certain fixed points in our problem which limit our action; we may not ignore them or disaster happens. The effects of action taken in their defiance, sometimes, in the early stages, supervene so slowly that the approaching disaster and its cause are not seen or not accepted.

—DR. LIONEL JAMES PICTON

THOSE APPLES you bought at the supermarket for the children's lunch today—you made sure they were red, succulent, unblemished. But did you suspect they were probably shot through from peel to core with some of the most powerful poisons known?

And how about that prepared cake mix for tonight's dessert? Does it contain real eggs and shortening, or were these replaced by an inexpensive chemical that offers no nutritional value and has caused extensive organic damage and even death to laboratory animals?

Take a close look at your supply of butter, oleomargarine, cheese and liquid oils. Is that their natural color? Or do they contain coal-tar dyes, which are highly toxic and are suspect as causes of cancer?

Next, taste the peanut butter. Is that its original flavor? Or was it smothered by the addition of hydrogenated oil (linked with heart disease in man) and replaced with an artificial peanut flavor?

Do not overlook that loaf of "fresh" white bread you count on to give your family health and energy. Did you

10

know that the most valuable nutrients were milled out of the flour, that it was chemically aged, chemically bleached, the dough treated with chemical softeners and preservatives to make it appear fresh, the starchy remains dosed with three or four synthetic vitamins to replace some twenty-five nutrients that were removed, and that the bread was then sold to you as an "enriched" product?

Then there's the milk you give the children to make them grow and have strong bones. You already know it contains Strontium 90 from H-bomb fallout. But did you know the odds are better than six to ten it has traces of poison, and one to ten it contains antibiotics? The odds are three to four the butter is contaminated with at least one insecticide, and one to two these toxic substances are in the cheese.

The frankfurters are almost sure to have sodium nitrite and nitrate preservatives, and perhaps are dyed to give them their bright red color. Sunday's chicken may have traces of antibiotics, arsenic and artificial sex hormones which add useless fat and water—that you pay for. The roasts or steaks probably have traces of hormones, antibiotics and the inevitable pesticide poisons that went into the cattle's diet.

The list is endless. Virtually every bite of food you eat has been treated with some chemical somewhere along the line: dyes, bleaches, emulsifiers, antioxidants, preservatives, flavors, flavor enhancers, buffers, noxious sprays, acidifiers, alkalizers, deodorants, moisteners, drying agents, gases, extenders, thickeners, disinfectants, defoliants, fungicides, neutralizers, artificial sweeteners, anticaking and antifoaming agents, conditioners, curers, hydrolizers, hydrogenators, maturers, fortifiers, and many others.

These are the tools of the food technician—a wizard who can beguile, deceive and defraud the housewife by making her think she is getting something she isn't. His alchemy can make stale products appear fresh, permit unsanitary practices, mask inferior quality, substitute nutritionally inferior or worthless chemicals for more costly natural ingredients. These chemicals, almost without exception, perform their mission at the cost of destroying valuable vitamins, minerals and enzymes, stripping food products of their natural life-giving qualities.

The food technician usually becomes the victim of his own art because he too must earn a living and must eat what he prepares. He may not set out to shortchange the consumer nutritionally or economically, but that generally is the ultimate result of his primary function: to prolong the shelf-life of food products by preventing spoilage or staleness. After the life-process of a foodstuff is reduced or destroyed altogether, he must try to mask the damage; his chemicals are supposed to give an appearance of vitality where there is none, restore missing aroma, "improve" the color, give flavor to tasteless, lifeless products.

Along with nutritional loss, a prime casualty of the orgy of chemical adulteration of foods has been flavor. Processing leaves a tasteless product that is made palatable only by use of more chemicals. But this factory-made flavor cannot be confused with the flavor of natural foods. To eat foods in their true state for the first time after one has known them only as the end product of processing is to discover a new—or forgotten—pleasure.

The deterioration in taste applies to many fruits and vegetables. It is not romanticizing the past that makes you lament that these things don't taste the way they did years ago. Varieties once prized for their flavor and texture have been dropped and replaced by others that meet today's criteria. The test now is: Will they produce bulk? Will they keep? Will they ship? Do they *look* appetizing? Flavor and nutritional values have been sacrificed to economic expediency. Chemicals used in the growing process have contributed to both loss of flavor and decline in nutritional content.

Traces of these chemicals used in the growing process remain on practically all foods we eat, along with others which get into foods accidentally during processing; the latter substances are known as *contaminants*. Other chemicals, intentionally injected into foods during processing, are known as *additives*. Finally the finished product is distributed packed in materials which may contribute more chemicals or cause the food to undergo chemical changes. Then the restaurant chef or housewife may add more chemicals still: tenderizers, flavor enhancers, preservatives, etc.

These are the chemicals we eat at every meal every day. They form what has become known as the chemicals-in-foods problem.

The most serious part of this problem involves the pesticides, because they are unavoidable. The Public Health

Service has stated that it is virtually impossible to get a meal in these United States that is not tainted with these poisons.

The chemicals-in-foods problem often is referred to as a controversy. This implies two schools of scientific thought, one for the use of chemicals, the other opposed. The real dispute, however, is between vested interests and consumer interests—and rarely do these two interests coincide. Few people understand what is at stake in this issue. It is a problem so fraught with danger that it can spell the difference between health and sickness, even life and death.

The problem has hurtled toward a crisis, for what had been a trickle of chemicals has swelled into a torrent since World War II.

According to one authoritative estimate, by Arthur D. Little, Inc., the use of additives in foods in the United States rose from 419 million pounds in 1955 to 661 million pounds in 1965—a 58 percent gain in ten years. The same firm estimates that the use of additives will soar to 852 million pounds in 1970 and to 1.03 *billion* pounds in 1975. The present rate of consumption comes to approximately three pounds of additives per person per year.

It has been variously estimated that there are up to a thousand different additives in use. Just prior to a new food law that became effective in 1960, the Food and Drug Administration, (FDA), using the most conservative estimate of five hundred, said that about one third were known to be harmless; another third were considered safe *in the amounts used*, and the remaining third were in a scientific no man's land—they were in use but *had not been adequately tested*. The FDA's then Commissioner, the late George P. Larrick, said, "Our scientists do not know whether they are safe or not, but they suspect some of them ought not to be in use."

A Congressional subcommittee that held hearings on the use of chemicals in foods from 1950 to 1952 decided there were 704 of these substances. Headed by Representative James J. Delaney of New York, the committee said only 428 were known to be safe, leaving 276 of unproved safety—and the consuming public was left to play the role of guinea pig.

Some of these chemicals are so poisonous they will kill human beings instantly if eaten in large doses. But industrial chemists have argued that they are safe because they are consumed in small amounts—an argument that is the heart of the problem.

Many of these violently potent new compounds never existed before in the history of the world until mixed in somebody's test tube. Consequently the human system has had no experience with them. Dr. William E. Smith, a noted cancer researcher, said: "The growing custom of introducing an endless series of biologically foreign molecules into the human organism for various commercial advantages is not unlike throwing a collection of nuts and bolts into the most delicate machinery known."

The late Sir Edward Mellanby, one of Britain's best-known research physicians, said that "our patients are consuming substances which, if they knew, they would never dream of touching," and "medical experts . . . are no less ignorant than their patients, in respect to many of the questionable substances being used in foods."

The problem is compounded because these powerful chemicals are consumed indiscriminately by young and old, healthy and sick, weak and strong, without proper consideration for individual differences. Laboratory experiments with animals are the basis for claiming these compounds are safe for human beings, but the ideal conditions found in the laboratory seldom are duplicated in the outside world, and—more important—man and animals are different species. While absence of evidence of harm should not be taken as proof that no harm exists, we still must realize that evidence of harm to any species of animal must, for our safety, be considered relevant to man.

This difference was pointed up by Dr. H. M. Sinclair of Oxford University, who recalled the following incident: During World War II a group of soldiers in Canada became sick from eating a new kind of soup ration developed in the United States; when the scientist who had prepared the product was told it had been found wanting, he indignantly replied, "Why, rats grew all right on it in the laboratory."

Another problem is that frequently the people who are in a position to decide the issue of whether a chemical is harmful are judges or lawyers with no real understanding of the biological subtleties involved, and, as evidence of harm to human beings they demand nothing less than a corpse. Even if such evidence exists there may arise the question of whether the substances under fire triggered the fatal ailment. Injuries from defective foods usually take a long time to develop and are difficult to pinpoint. The problem could be resolved only by turning man into a laboratory specimen—employing him in controlled experiments, then cutting him open and examining his organs for damage.

The law makes no objection to using Americans in its great chemical experiment, turning them into so many chemical laboratories, but it draws the line at sacrificing them to determine how their innards fared. Because of this restriction, animals are used in man's place. This is not very satisfactory because what is true for animals is not necessarily true for human beings, as Dr. Sinclair and others have pointed out; but it is the best arrangement possible in the circumstances.

There are various examples of the dire results of such a casual attitude toward testing.

At least two persons died and more than 200 others were made ill in New Jersey and Pennsylvania after eating fish dosed with a high concentration of sodium nitrite, a preservative, shortly before Lent of 1959. The poison was illegally used on flounder and fluke by a Philadelphia wholesaler.

Only a few months later, shortly before Thanksgiving, the Government warned that huge supplies of cranberries had been contaminated with aminotriazole, a weed killer that had caused cancer of the thyroid when administered to test animals in minute doses. The government had approved the chemical for use in 1958, but only after harvest. It was claimed that some growers incorrectly used the weed killer prior to harvest, well before 1959, as early as 1957.

Industry spokesmen asserted that cranberries are only a small part of the diet and therefore the chemical was harmless, but as emphasized elsewhere in this text, cancer experts have warned repeatedly that a carcinogen need be administered only in tiny amounts and not continuously to cause cancer in susceptible individuals.

It is difficult, in general, for people to appreciate the danger of consuming toxic chemicals which, when taken in small amounts, work slowly in bringing on sickness and death. For this reason it often is assumed that a product is safe because it has been in general use a long time; but this is not by any means incontrovertible evidence of its harmlessness. Repeatedly it has been shown that long-term use is no guarantee of safety.

Coumarin, an ingredient of imitation vanilla flavors, was used for seventy-five years in a wide variety of confections before it was found to produce serious liver damage in animals used for experimentation. Dulcin, an artificial sweetening agent, was used for more than a half-century as a sugar substitute before it was found to cause cancer in animals. Butter yellow, a food coloring, was used for several years before it was found to cause cancer of the liver. Mineral oil, long used as a salad dressing and substitute for food oils, was found to interfere with the absorption and utilization by the body of several vitamins, primarily vitamin A, in foods.

This by no means exhausts the list. These substances now are outlawed from use in foods—but how many people are in their graves or in ill health because they once were used? How many more people are dying now or will die in the future because our food laws are designed to protect commercial interests first, and people afterward?

It is generally believed that the public is protected by the Pure Food Law. But is wasn't until the summer of 1958— some fifty-two years after passage of the original law— that Congress finally got around to requiring that chemicals be tested for "safety" before they could be injected into foods, and then the new law was riddled with so many loopholes that it was largely ineffective as an instrument for consumer protection.

Further, it should be emphasized, the amendment to the food law does not touch upon the most serious part of the problem—the pesticides. Nor does it affect most of the harmful and suspect chemicals discussed in this book.

How many people have died and will die because of the failure of the law to provide real legal protection for the people will never be known. But the record shows that there have been deaths due to eating foods containing poisonous chemicals; and there are known cases of illness and narrow escapes from serious illness.

While the new law required that chemicals be tested and approved by the FDA before they can be injected into foods, hundreds in common use had never been adequately tested. Many of these additives were scheduled to be eliminated under the new law's cut-off date of March 5, 1960, but the FDA stated that some would be permitted to remain in use another year, as provided by law, while being tested. All of the chemicals were permitted by Congress to remain in use in food, while they were being tested, for eighteen months after the law was amended in 1958, so further extensions could be granted by FDA. These substances were tested only for toxicity, not for their ability to cause cancer.

The public, as usual, played its historic role of guinea pig to accommodate commercial interests.

This accommodation had a more ominous meaning than might at first appear. Of some 1,329 chemicals tested by the National Cancer Institute, about 25 per cent have been found to be carcinogens (substances capable of causing cancer in man or animals). Most of these never appeared in foods. But it is anybody's guess how many of the untested substances now in common use in foods will turn out to be carcinogens. The Public Health Service has said that on the basis of past results it can be assumed that approximately one out of four may be found capable of causing cancer. In other words, you have no assurance that some of the food additives and contaminants you ate this very day won't push you along toward a cancer.

In addition to the chemicals that still have a question mark after their names, several substances that now appear in the American diet are known to have caused cancers in experimental animals, and others have caused cancers in men. The use of these carcinogens is tolerated and excused by government officials and food technologists, despite urgent warnings from cancer experts, on the grounds that they are consumed only in small quantities.

Despite claims by the Food and Drug Administration that there are no carcinogens in the food supply, Dr. Wilhelm H. Hueper, formerly the government's top investigator in the field of environmental cancer research and an international authority in his field, has said:

"It is a well-established fact that an appreciable and growing number of chemicals, of which a few are known to enter the human food supply, are capable of causing and do cause cancers in man under proper conditions of exposure.

"This disconcerting situation is aggravated by the observation that many additional chemicals, some of which are incorporated into consumer goods including foodstuffs, elicit cancers in experimental animals when introduced in proper amounts and under suitable conditions."

In 1967, two years after Dr. Hueper retired as chief of the environmental section at the National Cancer Institute, he was quoted in *Medical World News* as saying that "several thousand different chemicals and chemical mixtures used additives and pesticides for a great variety of purposes are now incorporated into foods. Many of these have not been adequately tested for carcinogenic properties. There is practically no feasible escape route left for the captive population to avoid continued contact with unintentional food additives."

Dr. Hueper urged the government not to settle for vaguely defined tolerance levels but instead to outlaw any food additives, cosmetics and pesticides that cause cancer in animals. Further, he called on the FDA to make public all information on toxicity and carcinogenicity of food additives that are submitted to the agency with petitions for certification.

"The present FDA policy of strict secrecy in these matters is definitely against the public interest," he said. "It prevents an examination of the submitted evidence, as well as an independent appraisal of reasons for any approval by competent investigators not connected with interested industries or with governmental agencies involved in these decisions."

The anticancer clause in the food law does not require that food additives be tested for carcinogenic properties before they are considered for use in foods. "Moreover," Dr. Hueper said, "it limits the incriminating evidence to the demonstration that oral administration of the chemical produces a cancerous response."

This failure to require that chemicals be tested for carcinogenicity, of course, weakens the law's effectiveness. Instead of being protected by strong laws restricting the use of carcinogens in foods the public has been asked to trust to the FDA's and industry's sense of responsibility. This overlooks the fact that the public isn't eating somebody's sense of responsibility; every day, at virtually every meal, people are ingesting known poisons and untested chemicals—and the consumer's primary "protection" is official optimism that he isn't being harmed.

Industry's optimism outshines even that of the FDA.

For many years industry vigorously fought any law that would require chemicals to be tested before being used in foods. In one instance a journal devoted to food technology criticized those who "leaned a bit backward in the interest of safety." Most tests were designed to prove only that the substance in question was not instantly lethal.

It's a rare chemical that finds its way into the food stream because of the consumer's nutritional needs. Industry and the government alike have felt that it is enough for the public if substances aren't downright harmful. Seldom indeed does an additive *improve* the nutritional value of a foodstuff.

Many additives were never designed specifically for use in foods. They started as by-products of other chemical manufacturing processes or were employed in some capacity unrelated to foods. Through someone's ingenuity a use was found for them in foods. This marriage of convenience between the chemical and food interests usually benefited everyone—except the consumer.

It doesn't necessarily mean that a chemical that is used in industry, as well as a food additive, is harmful, but at times it doesn't exactly increase its aesthetic appeal. Typical of the foreign chemicals now used in foods are some that have migrated into various frozen confections. Piperonal, an inexpensive substitute for costly vanilla flavoring, is also fine for killing lice. A nutty flavor may be imparted by butyraldehyde, an ingredient of rubber cement and synthetic resins. That cherry taste probably is aldehyde C-17, a flammable liquid often found in aniline dyes, plastics and synthetic rubbers. Pineapple flavor may come from ethyl acetate, better known as a solvent for plastics and lacquers; its vapor is known to be irritating to the mucous membranes, and prolonged exposure to it can cause chronic pulmonary, liver and heart damage.

Before ice cream had its ingredients fixed by Federal standards, it had about ceased to be a tasty mixture of eggs, milk, sugar and fruit. Often it was little more than a hardened conglomeration of emulsifiers, artificial flavoring and coloring and other chemicals—nutritional sins that didn't have to be confessed on the label. Federal standards, it should be borne in mind, apply only to certain ice-cream products in interstate commerce; others often remain exotic chemical mixtures into which anything goes, including baking soda to deacidulate soured milk and cream, to make them palatable.

A space-age phenomenon is blueberry pancake mix without blueberries. Consumers who thought they were eating the luscious berries depicted so temptingly on the packages, put out by two manufacturers, really were eating nothing more than synthetic purple pellets, which contained chemical adulterants. One company's "blueberries," according to the FDA, were made "chiefly of sugars, nonfat dry milk, starch, coconut pulp, artificial coal-tar coloring, artificial flavoring, and a very small amount of blueberry pulp." The second firm's "blueberries" were of an equally startling composition: sugar, gum acacia, citric acid, starch, artificial coloring and flavoring, and some blueberry pulp.

As the Consumer Reports pointed out, the mixtures were ingenious, but they weren't blueberries. Both companies were forced to change their labels so the public no longer would be misled into believing they were eating blueberries; but the FDA generously permitted the companies to use up their old labels on packages already in retail stores.

Cheese is another foodstuff that has gone down the primrose path of chemical adulteration. Processed cheese is little more than a complex of chemicals—it is artificially thickened, stabilized, preserved, flavored and colored. Methyl cellulose, a thickener used in processed cheese, also is used to make cosmetics and adhesives; sodium carboxymethyl cellulose, a stabilizer, is also employed in resin-emulsion paints and printing inks. Even the cheese wrapper is treated. Recently some 6,000 pounds of cheese were seized because the chemical used in the wrapping had seeped into the cheese; the contaminant was described as tasteless, odorless and as poisonous as carbolic acid.

Industry likes to point out that many products in use today would not be possible without additives. Sometimes the list of ingredients reads like a chemistry inventory. In 1966 *Chemical and Engineering News* published an article listing the additives used in several foods; in part it stated:

"General Mills Rice Provence contains, among its many ingredients, mono- and diglycerides (emulsifiers), monosodium glutomate (flavor enhancer) butylated hydroxyanisole, butylated hydroxytoluene, propyl gallate (antioxidants), propylene glycol (carrier), and citric acid (sequestering agent). General Foods Whip 'n Chill dessert mix contains adipic acid (acidulant), propylene glycol monostearate (emulsifier), and sodium carboxymethylcellulose (stabilizer). . . ."

In former days, a strong flavor of butter in cottage cheese was a sign of quality; now it may be nothing more than diacetyl, a highly reactive, yellowish-green chemical that gives a deceptive aroma of butter. If water is added to cheese to swell its volume, the butterfat content of the cheese will be reduced; but a dash of diacetyl will mask that fact by giving a rich, buttery aroma. Until recently cottage cheese contained the preservative 8-hydroxyquinoline (also used in contraceptives and rectal suppositories), which has caused cancer when injected into mice.

Cheese spreads may contain alginic acid (to give uniformity of color and flavor), also used in making artificial ivory and celluloid. In making domestic Gorgonzola and blue cheese it is not necessary to use the expensive sheep's or goat's milk that appears in imported brands; plain cow's milk may be substituted and the resulting yellow mixture bleached white with benzoyl peroxide, a substance known to destroy every trace of vitamin A in the milk.

Candies, especially the cheaper ones, are frequently loaded with chemicals. Their test-tube ingredients include shellac (to give polish or glaze).

Probably no beverage escapes some form of adulteration. Beer and ale, for example, may owe their clarity (light-stability) and storage life to the chemical polyvinylpyrrolidone (PVP), a multipurpose compound also found in aerosol hair sprays. Aside from completely lacking nutritive value in itself, PVP is an adsorbing agent that can take up vitamins and other substances and render them less available for absorption. The compound is now being tested for use in wines, fruit juices (particularly grape and apple), fruit jellies, vinegar, cider and whisky.

Butter is another example of the food chemist's art. Winter butter is deficient in nutritive value, but its revealing paleness can be masked by adding a bit of synthetic yellow dye made of a cancer-causing substance. Dr. William B. Bradley, scientific director of the American Institute of Baking, testified that "this particular use of a chemical to cover up the deficiency of a food is sanctioned by law." If the butter is to be stored for a long time or shipped a great distance, it is washed so that it will keep longer, and before being offered for use a shot of diacetyl is added, restoring the butter aroma but not the missing nutrients.

To prevent spoilage, carrots, oranges, apples, lemons and limes are likely to be waxed with a coal-tar-derivative paraffin that is highly suspect as a cause of cancer. These products and vegetables also may be contaminated with phenolic and copper compounds, ammonias and other preservatives—all questionable substances, some of which have cumulative tendencies known to imperil certain metabolic processes.

Most chemicals are accepted for use in foods if they qualify to perform the technical job demanded of them—with no further questions asked. Will they keep the cake from falling? Will they quickly and cheaply add weight to meat animals? Will they kill insects? Will they stiffen the pickles and firm the tomatoes? Will they keep mold off the bread, make the hamburger appear fresh? Will they tenderize the steak and give it a charcoal flavor?

If the chemical is able to perform its job without proving immediately fatal to test animals fed substantial doses of the substance, it is assumed to be safe for humans in small, repeated doses. Is not lack of a corpse proof of safety? The primary consideration is to reduce costs and increase profits; secondary effects are ignored. Why look for trouble?

What this attitude means to the consumer public is illustrated by a few chemicals in widespread use.

Beta-naphthylamine, for example, is a high-voltage chemical which has caused bladder cancer in animals and men. It is chemically changed to make two coal-tar dyes commonly used to color butter and oleomargarine—and exactly what happens to this dye in humans is not known: whether it is passed out harmlessly, or if it resumes its original deadly form as beta-naphthylamine. Latest testing procedures indicate that it may resume its carcinogenic form inside the body.

Another example is the artificial sex "hormone" stilbestrol, which quickly and cheaply puts weight on cattle and other meat animals by chemically emasculating them. This chemical is so potent it is called biological dynamite.

There are also the ubiquitous pesticides—perhaps potentially more dangerous than radioactive fallout.

To recognize the hazard of using these chemicals would necessitate a tremendous upheaval in industry's entire approach to the production and distribution of food. It is easier to close the ears and eyes and concentrate on the immediate advantages of more food and less money. Food is treated like any other commodity of exchange: something to be produced as quickly and cheaply as possible and sold for maximum returns—good business but, almost invariably, bad nutrition. This kind of merchandising leads to cutting corners, sacrificing quality to quantity, selling appearance instead of content. As often happens, the greater the offense against a product, the more money is spent advertising its nonexistent virtues; the greater the food's deficiency, the louder the denial of its shortcomings.

In the endless drive for commercial advantage, the American housewife has been the target of an intensive barrage of advertising and propaganda that has seduced her into believing that black is white and white is black. She has been flattered into thinking she knows all about nutrition while, in truth, she has been kept in relative ignorance about the shortcomings of the highly refined, chemically treated devitalized foods she feeds her family; she has been given a false sense of security that she is protected by the nation's food laws. She has been indoctrinated with false information about what constitutes good foods. Generally, she does not know that it is possible to be overfed and undernourished at the same time.

Many crusaders have tried to sound the alarm but have run into stern resistance. A forthright appraisal of the situation was offered by Dr. Edward J. Ryan, former editor of the *Dental Digest,* when he said:

"Anyone who speaks against food adulteration in any of the many forms is subject to 'name calling.' The most common epithets are 'food faddist' or 'food fakir.' If you object to spraying foods with poisonous chemicals, picking fruits green and then applying a dye, to injecting or administering antibiotics to poultry and dairy herds, to removing minerals and vitamins from natural foods, to adding chemical adulterants to preserve foods from normal chemical changes, you are offending . . . some of our largest and most influential corporations . . . we can be certain that the public-relations counselors will go to work to change the situation—even if that requires a bit of character assassination directed against those who are in the opposition.

"Every time a natural substance is removed from a food, every time an adulterant is added to a food, the balance in nature is disturbed . . . The chemical and cellular processes within the body cells cannot react to the passing whims of chemists without disturbance in function. It took thousands of years for the body to adjust itself to changing environmental conditions. When these conditions are suddenly altered by the actions of men, the cells cannot make the adjustment—disease is the result."

As the chemical onslaught gains momentum, increasing numbers of scientists and informed laymen are expressing alarm about where it will end. Former Representative Usher L. Burdick of North Dakota and others have charged that the public has not been protected by the food laws, and such laws as there are have never been enforced. Mr. Burdick flatly charged in a speech read into the *Congressional Record* that there has been a conspiracy to dump poisonous chemicals into foods for the resulting profits.

Accusations that government agencies charged with protecting public health and welfare have given their primary allegiance to protecting industry profits are hardly new, but they have been effectively withheld from the public for several decades through economic pressures. Approximately three decades ago Dr. Harvey W. Wiley, renowned as the father of the Pure Food and Drug Act, wrote a book called *The History of a Crime Against the Food Law*, in which he charged that the law was intended to protect the health of the people was "perverted to protect adulteration of food and drugs."

The adulteration of foods that has taken place since then makes Dr. Wiley's era seem in retrospect an era of chemical innocence. But one thing has not changed: the insistence that it is safe to inject poisons into foods, because they are ingested in small quantities. It is generally overlooked that by the time the many individual foods that compose our daily diet have received their particular treatment, the total toxic dose the consumer gets is no longer small.

The optimistic viewpoint about the "harmlessness" of eating small amounts of poisons will be examined subsequently, but first let's see which chemicals might go into a typical American family's Sunday dinner. We do not claim that whoever ate this meal would get every chemical listed, but he would almost be sure to get many of them, along with others not mentioned.

THE MENU

Fruit juice	Bread and rolls
Roast beef with	with butter
gravy	Pickles
Sweet potatoes	Apple pie with ice
Peas (canned)	cream
Tossed salad with	Milk
dressing	Coffee

Fruit juices: Benzoic acid (a chemical preservative); di-methyl polysiloxane (antifoaming agent); DDT and related compounds; parathion or one of the other potent phosphorus nerve-gas pesticides; saccharin (chemical sweetener).

Roast beef: DDT and related compounds, methoxychlor, chlordane, heptachlor, toxaphene, lindane, benzene hexa-chloride, aldrin, dieldrin and other pesticides, particularly in the fatty parts; stilbestrol (artificial female sex hor-mone); aureomycin (antibiotic); mineral oil residue from wrapping paper.

Gravy: DDT and other pesticides that were in the meat; antibiotics; products formed from the interaction between the chlorine-dioxide bleach used on the flour and the flour nutrients.

Sweet potatoes: Pesticides such as dieldrin, heptachlor, chlordane, ethylene dibromide; coal-tar dye; sulphuric pre-servatives.

Peas: Magnesium chloride (color retainer); magnesium carbonate (alkalizer); DDT, parathion, methoxychlor, malathion.

Tossed salad (with dressing): Sodium alginate (sta-bilizer); monoisopropyl citrate (antioxidant to prevent fat deterioration); DDT and related compounds; phos-phorus insecticides; weed killers.

Bread and rolls: Products of bleach interaction in flour; ammonium chloride (dough conditioner); mono- and digylcerides and polyoxyethylene (softeners); ditertiary-Butyl-para-Cresol (antioxidant); nitrated flour or coal-tar dye (to give bakery products yellow color suggestive of butter and egg yolks); vitamin fortifiers (to replace nutrients lost in milling); DDT and related compounds; parathion and related compounds.

Butter: Nordihydroguaiaretic acid (antioxidant); oxidation products resulting from interaction with hydrogen peroxide (bleach); magnesium oxide (neutralizer); AB and OB Yellow (coal-tar dyes); diacetyl (artificial aromatic agent); DDT and related agents.

Pickles: Aluminum sulphate (firming agent); sodium nitrate (texturizer); emulsifier (to disperse flavor).

Apple pie: Butylated hydroxyanisole (antioxidant in lard); chemical agents in flour and butter or margarine; sodium o-phenylphenate (preservative); several or possibly all of following pesticides used on apples: DDT, dinitro-orthocresol, benzene hexachloride, malathion, parathion, demeton, lindane, lead arsenate, nicotine, methoxychlor, chlordane and others. Some of these pesticides also would appear in the lard.

Ice cream: Carboxymethylcellulose (stabilizer); mono- and diglycerides (emulsifier); artificial flavoring; coal-tar dye; antibiotics; DDT and related compounds. (If not under the regulations of interstate commerce, ice cream might contain other chemicals that are banned under Federal regulations.)

Oleomargarine (used in cooking): Mono- and diglycerides; isopropyl citrate; monoisopropyl citrate (stabilizer); AB and OB Yellow; DDT and related products.

In the table salt sprinkled on the food were calcium hydroxide (stabilizer); potassium iodide (nutrient supplement); calcium silicate (anticaking agent). If drinks such as old-fashioneds were served before dinner, they probably contained dimethyl polysiloxane (antifoaming agent); orange slices with dyed peel; sodium o-phenylphenate and ammonia (preservatives); maraschino cherries which had been preserved with sodium benzoate; texture-improved with calcium hydroxide, bleached with sulphur dioxide, injected with artificial flavoring, and then colored an appealing red with a coal-tar dye. Both fruits would have insecticide residue. In the children's milk there almost certainly would have been DDT or its chemical kin and antibiotics—or both, as in cream used in the coffee.

Consumers will never know exactly what chemicals they are being subjected to until industry is required by law to label each individual product, with information as to which sprays, additives and other chemicals were used on this product, and the amounts of such substances in weights and percentages. Without this basic safeguard the public will continue to be a guinea pig, unable to choose or reject a food according to its integrity, forced, instead, to choose by its appearance or advertising claims for it.

Until this protection is legislated by Congress, Americans will be forced to continue their hazardous game of nutritional Russian roulette, dependent upon luck and someone else's concept of what is harmless, for their safety.

The longer our lawmakers delay in recognizing that their first obligation is to the public welfare and not to corporate profits, the more chemicals will be dumped into the food stream, the harder it will be to eliminate these substances, and the greater the peril will be.

Paul Dunbar, former FDA Commissioner, warning that no one can tell what new diseases may grow out of the use of synthetic foods, stated the case with admirable clarity when he said, "When man starts competing with nature in the blending of food elements he should be sure that his formula does not bear the skull and crossbones."

2

The Nation's Health— Hospitals, SRO

We have not been capable of distinguishing the prohibited from the lawful. We have infringed natural laws. We have thus committed the supreme sin, the sin that is always punished. The dogmas of scientific religion and industrial morals have fallen under the onslaught of biological reality. Life always gives an identical answer when asked to trespass on forbidden ground. It weakens. And civilizations collapse.

—ALEXIS CARREL
(Man the Unknown)

(1)

THE AMERICAN PEOPLE have been assured so often that they are healthier and live longer than any other people in the world that this statement generally is accepted as a fact.

Credit for this enviable state of health and longevity is traced to many factors in the so-called American way of life. Cited most often is the alleged excellence of the nation's food supply; and this, in turn, is attributed to technological advances of the food and chemical industries, working harmoniously and selflessly toward the mutual goal of a stronger, more prosperous and healthier (usually in that order) America.

Primary emphasis is laid on our increased life span. Statistics—that invaluable aid of those with something to sell—show that the average American of today can look forward to living longer than his ancestors and that the life span is increasing all the time. This claim is presented, and generally accepted, as conclusive proof of the nation's collective health and is supported by the fact that each generation is growing progressively taller.

Since health has been equated with diet (and properly so), the American people repeatedly are told that they are indebted to the fabricators and purveyors of the nation's food supply for their prolonged and healthful existence on this earth.

The linking of food and health suggests that a closer examination of the statistical foundations on which our assumptions rest is in order. And the fine print suggests that all is not quite what it is said to be.

As of 1967, life expectancy in this country had reached an average of 70 years. White boy babies, according to insurance statistics, will live to be 67.6 years old (nonwhite, 61.1), and white girls 74.7 (non-white, 67.4). Since 1900, it is pointed out, life expectancy has increased about 22 years.

The primary reasons for these gains are attributed to the decrease in infectious diseases and the reduction of infant and maternal mortality. The dramatic difference these factors alone made in expected longevity are spelled out by a few comparative figures.

The number of deaths from infectious diseases dropped from 676 to 66 per 100,000 persons between 1900 and 1949; antibiotics and sulfa drugs alone saved 1,500,000 lives during their first fifteen years of use, according to the U. S. Public Health Service. In 1916, ten per cent of the babies born in America died before their first birthday, but now less than three per cent die in their first year.

In the same period, maternal deaths have dropped from 622 to 83 per 100,000 live births.

Many Americans assume that because the expected life span has been increased twenty-two years, they can look forward to that many more years of life. The unpleasant truth is that a man of forty today can anticipate living only about two years longer than a man of forty in 1900.

This small increase is all we have to show for the remarkable improvements during the last half century in medical care, better sanitation, housing, improved knowledge of nutrition and other technological and social advances we justly take pride in.

The late Dr. Norman Jolliffe, in charge of nutrition for the New York City Department of Health, wrote in the *New York State Medical Journal* (September 15, 1955):

"Although in America today life expectancy at birth is near the best of any civilized country in the world . . . at the age of 40 life expectancy is near the bottom."

While longevity forecasts for today's babies are cause for great rejoicing, they may be premature. These are chemical babies. They are being born into a poisoned world. As matters stand, every day of their lives they are destined to exist in an atmosphere poisoned by radioactivity; they must breathe poisoned air, drink poisoned water, eat poisoned and unnatural foods; they must contend with conditions human creatures never before in the history of the world had to contend with.

According to the Metropolitan Life Insurance Company, in 1968 the United States had an infant mortality rate higher than that of 12 other countries. Deaths of children occurred at the rate of 22.1 per 1,000 live births.

The optimistic predictions of infant life expectancy is based on the age at which men and women are dying *now;* this older generation was raised on a diet relatively free of chemicals, and large numbers got off to a good start in the healthful environment of a rural area rather than the polluted cities.

They also were raised in a "sink-or-swim" atmosphere that has now been so modified that it can be said no longer to exist. They were not protected by a multitude of vaccines, sanitary conditions, sterile water, hospitalization for minor ailments, wonder drugs and many other factors that shelter today's youngsters; if they were strong enough to meet the stress of life they lived, if they were weak they perished; it was a matter of survival of the fittest.

Today's children often begin their life's journey with built-in weaknesses. Considerable evidence points out that today's babies are being weakened not only by environmental influences but genetic ones as well; and the child of the future may have even less inherent resistance to disease and sickness, due to the very medical and technological achievements we tout so highly.

The nation's reduced death rate is cited as further proof of our improved health. While cause for pride among health officials, the death rate has little to do with health. A British writer once took this argument apart in a telling manner. Pointing out that "again and again this fallacy appears in the press," he questioned why it was assumed that a falling death rate connotes higher standards of health. To save a man's life by drugs or surgery does not necessarily make a healthy man of him, he noted. The national health is the sum total of the healths of individuals; it can be nothing else.

"If the reasoning 'low death rate, therefore good health' is sound, then if in an institution filled with incurables there is no death during the year, the death rate becomes nil, and consequently the institution is the healthiest place in England, though there is not a single healthy person in it.

"What we should like to know is the number of semi-invalids carried by the nation; why all hospitals and nursing homes, etc., are full. Why . . . the increase . . . of . . . illness? Why the enormous decline in quality of eyes and teeth?"

Even the fact that we are bigger and appear more robust than our ancestors is little proof of health Harry L. Schapiro, anthropologist at the American Museum of Natural History, rhetorically questioned where our trend toward getting large is going to end:

"Are we headed for ungainly dinosaurian proportions that will lead to our extinction?"

Harvard's famous anthropologist, the late Dr. Earnest Hooton, held that "American overgrowth may well have serious results."

The late Dr. Alexis Carrel, the celebrated physiologist with the Rockefeller Institute, mulled over the same biological question in his classic *Man the Unknown:*

"Are larger and heavier children better than smaller ones? Intelligence, alertness, audacity, and resistance to disease do not depend on the same factors as the weight of the body. . . . The progress of man certainly will not come from an increase in weight or in longevity."

Dr. Carrel observed that even as we get bigger we become more delicate and fragile; we lack the raw stamina and wiry energy of our forebears.

Despite the weakening of modern man, improvements in the environment have enabled more people to live to old age today; almost three-fifths of all Americans now live past the age of sixty-five. But even the fact that more people are living to old age is not proof of health. As the infectious diseases have been conquered, people have become subject to a new and more insidious enemy of health —the degenerative diseases. Often it is claimed that these have become so much more prevalent merely because people are living longer. This ignores the fact that these scourges attack not only the old but also the young—even babies—a medical phenomenon that is new to our time.

The changing nature of disease was characterized by Dr. Iago Galdston, executive secretary of the New York Medical Society, as converting mortality (death) into morbidity (sickness). "Fewer die young," he said, "more drag their ills for longer years."

By 1939 chronic diseases had replaced acute infectious diseases to such an extent that Dr. S. S. Goldwater, then Commissioner of Hospitals in New York City, warned that if the trend continued "America may someday become a nation of invalids."

Since Dr. Goldwater made his dire prediction the chronic diseases have gained momentum rather than slackened.

Organized medicine, for all its successes in combatting agents of acute infection, recognizes that it thus far has lost in the battle against the degenerative diseases.

The sound of the trumpets that heralded the wonder drugs in recent years is a feeble sound compared to the dirge that accompanies a recital of the mushrooming incidence of degenerative diseases.

More than half the population—babies included—is said to be suffering from some form of chronic illness today. The toll these ailments of progressive deterioration and ultimate destruction take in human suffering and expense is staggering.

In 1958, Surgeon General Leroy E. Burney said that chronic diseases kept 8 per cent of the population, ages 15 to 44 years, from work or school; 20 per cent of those aged 45 to 64; and 57 per cent of those 65 and over.

A breakdown of the numbers of Americans suffering from the various degenerative diseases is a melancholy tabulation of cold statistics that have little real relation to the misery they represent.

Cancer claims more than 225,000 lives a year, and an estimated one out of every three Americans will develop cancer sometime during his life; heart disease takes more than 817,000 lives annually and accounts for more than half the nation's deaths; more than 7,000,000 Americans suffer from arthritis and other rheumatic ailments; one out of every ten living Americans will spend some part of his life in a mental institution, and more than half of all the nation's 7,000,000 hospital beds are occupied by mental patients—with 250,000 more beds acutely needed to care for the backlog of mental patients needing treatment.

Dr. W. Coda Martin, former Chief of Geriatrics Clinic, Metropolitan Hospital, and Visiting Physician in Geriatrics for the Bird S. Coler Memorial Hospital, New York, who is now practicing in Los Angeles, says that "not only does half the population have some form of chronic disease, but only 13 per cent of the remainder are free of some type of physical defect."

In the United States today there are a total of 88,-959,534 registered cases of chronic illness, according to Dr. Martin. He said that a survey he made of national health organizations dealing with specific ailments included the following figures:

Allergic disorders affect 20,000,000 persons; diseases of the nervous system, 15,000,000; psychosis and psycho-neurosis, 16,000,000; arteriosclerosis and degenerative heart disease, 10,000,000; mentally retarded children, 3 to 5,000,000 (one retarded child born every 15 minutes); ulcers of the stomach and duodenum, 8,500,000; cancer 700,000; muscular dystrophy, 100,000; tuberculosis, 400,-000 (100,000 new cases reported annually); multiple sclerosis, 250,000; cerebral palsy, 150,000.

Sixty per cent of all Americans have defective vision requiring that they wear glasses; 10,000,000 suffer various degrees of deafness; in 1955 there were 334,000 blind persons (66 per cent, or 220,440, cases caused by diseases such as arteriosclerosis and glaucoma, and congenital conditions); 10 per cent of American marriages are sterile, affecting an estimated 15,000,000 persons.

In addition, there are 32,000,000 Americans who are overweight; 4,000,000 alcoholics, all potential victims of disease and early death; and 2,000,000 cases of juvenile delinquency, which increasingly is being recognized as a form of sickness.

These figures must be taken as rough estimates because no accurate statistics are available; there also is a likelihood that some persons suffer more than one chronic ailment. But even if halved, or reduced still further, they paint a dismal health picture for the most prosperous nation in the world.

Other figures indicate that the nation's health is steadily deteriorating, rather than improving. Dr. Martin pointed out that, despite lowered physical standards, the rejection rate of draftees increased from World War I through the Korean conflict. He then gave this summary of the health of the flower of the nation's manhood, as reflected in the experience of three wars:

In the First World War 21.3 per cent of the drafted men were rejected and 9.9 per cent were placed in a limited-service category. At that time physical standards were high. These standards were substantially those used early in World War II, but it soon became apparent that essential manpower could be obtained only by reducing the physical standards with respect to some defects. At this time, 1941-43, the total found unfit for general military service with the reduced physical requirements was about 41 per cent in the white group, or approximately 10 per cent higher than in 1918.

The rejection rates sharply increased with age. The total percentage of rejected men from age 34-44 years was 64.7 per cent.

Then came the Korean conflict, and again the percentage of rejections increased, even over those of World War II.

In the seven years from June 1947 to June 1955, 4,321,000 young men between the ages of

18 and 25 years were called for pre-induction examination; 2,248,000, or 52 per cent, were rejected for physical and mental defects—an increase of 11 per cent over World War II, or a total of 21 per cent increase in rejections since 1918, in spite of a marked lowering of the physical standards.

The psychiatric requirements were considerably liberalized. In fact, the bars were down. Psychoneurosis of any degree was acceptable if it had not incapacitated the person in civil life. Persons with a history of transient psychotic reactions were accepted if they had otherwise demonstrated stability. Such persons were not accepted during World War II.

Also, there were some modifications of the physical standards, such as perforated ear drums, paroxysmal convulsive disorders, if controlled by medication, moderate deformities of the extremities, etc. All of which were disqualifying defects during World War II. Therefore the figures for rejections during the Korean conflict are of no value in determining the general health of the draftees.

In 1955, 25 per cent of all draftees, ages 21-26, rejected in New York City were turned down for heart ailments, and of some 200 American soldiers who were killed in action and autopsied during the Korean conflict, approximately 80 per cent were found to suffer from heart disease. The average age of these boys was about 22 years. Many of them would not have lived long even had they not been cut down in action.

While virtually every statistic that purports to prove something can be disputed, usually with good cause, there can be little argument that our nation's health is on a toboggan; the question is, How fast is the toboggan going downhill and how steep is the grade?

The greatest scourge, as health officials repeatedly try to hammer home, is heart disease. At an ever-accelerating pace it is striking down Americans, especially males. Many of them are young men, and some are children. To hear of men in their thirties and forties who have died of a heart-attack is becoming commonplace.

The incidence of heart disease among Americans has

been compared to the black plague of the Middle Ages. Each year 230,000 men and 130,000 women in this country die from heart attacks, and about one million more are felled by severe attacks.

Dr. Paul White, who treated former President Eisenhower following his heart attack, and Dr. Jolliffe reported to Congress in 1955 that the United States is "one of the most unhealthy countries in the world" with regard to coronary heart disease. Dr. White has called heart disease "the modern American epidemic." Dr. Jolliffe said: "It is more dangerous to be a man between the ages of 45 and 65 in the United States than it is in any other country in the world." The nation's failure to show a real gain in life expectancy among middle-aged men is due to the increase in heart attacks, according to Dr. Jolliffe. This increase, he said, "has been especially significant among younger and middle-aged males."

Many medical men insist that there has not really been more heart disease; that there are merely better statistics today, better reporting of ailments by doctors and better diagnostic methods. Some thoughtful observers, however, categorically reject this contention. Among them, Dr. Jolliffe, who said:

"Whereas coronary artery disease was a rarity prior to 1920, it has now become the number one cause of death in the 45-to-64-year age group as well as after 65. This has been a real increase over and above that accounted for by fashion in diagnosis, by an older population, and by improved diagnostic methods. This increase has been especially significant among younger and middle-aged males."

The *Lancet*, whose opinion is respected throughout the medical world, editorially states:

". . . all cardiologists whose experience goes back 30 years or more seem to agree with the vital statisticians that the higher mortality rates reflect a real increase in coronary artery disease, and also that young people . . . are now affected more often than formerly."

The treachery of heart attacks is all the more frightening because—contrary to general belief—heart disease can be detected only rarely before an attack. A study of hidden heart disease by a group of investigators headed by Dr. L. S. Goerke, assistant dean of the Public Health School of the University of California, reported in 1957 that available medical techniques can spot only a small percentage of hidden heart disease in seemingly healthy people.

Among 1,652 people found by various testing procedures to be normal, heart disease developed, within 30 months, in 52 of them and potential heart disease in 46 others. Thirteen of the subjects actually died of heart trouble during the two-and-one-half year study that was reported to the California Medical Association.

As a cause of death in middle life, heart ailments are trailed only by cancer. Since 1937 cancer has been the second most common cause of death. In 1900 the death rate from cancer was 64 per 100,000 persons, but by 1950 it had shot up to 147 per 100,000, claiming about 250,000 victims a year. Cancer, as noted earlier, is no longer a disease restricted to older people; indeed, it is second only to accidents as a cause of death in children between one and fourteen years of age, according to Dr. Charles S. Cameron, former medical and scientific director of the American Cancer Society. In 1954 then President Eisenhower told Congress that 25,000,000 Americans now living would die of cancer unless the present cancer mortality rate was lowered.

Dr. Hueper in 1967 made the startling statement *(Medical World News)* that in the United States alone, between 20 and 25 per cent of the total population have cancer at any given time.

Leukemia and lung cancer account for most of the current cancer deaths. Leukemia's toll is approximately half of all the cancer deaths of children under fifteen years old, according to the Metropolitan Life Insurance Company's figures. In general, it was stated, the largest rise occurred among children and older people: ". . . the mortality at ages 1-4 is not exceeded until ages 55-64."

Lung cancer, according to the company's statistics, accounts for nearly 30 per cent of total cancer mortality among men in the 55-64 age range: ". . . this is at least three times the comparable death rate from cancer of the stomach, the next leading site."

The stealthy nature of cancer makes it often difficult to detect the affliction, and in some internal sites of the body it is impossible to detect until it is beyond successful treatment.

The number of unsuspected cancer cases among Americans has been disclosed by many spot checks of apparently healthy people. In a routine examination of 491 apparently well, actively employed men in New York City in 1958, six cancers and 136 lesions that could lead to cancer were discovered, according to Dr. Walter E. O'Donnell of the Strang Cancer Prevention Clinic. Dr. O'Donnell said that only one of the 142 men with cancers and lesions had any symptoms that might cause him to go to a doctor.

The same year, in another medical screening in New York City, 297 husbands and 290 wives, all apparently well, were found to have a total of 18 cancers. Twelve of the cancers were in the men, along with 89 precancerous conditions and 95 benign tumors. The wives, in addition to having 6 cancers, had 147 precancerous conditions, 119 of these conditions involving the breasts and pelvic organs; the wives also showed 80 benign tumors. Wives and husbands, in addition, were found to have a total of 362 noncancerous ailments.

In addition to turning up unsuspected cancers, screening tests have given a dark picture of the nation's over-all health. The Brooklyn Cancer Committee reported that more than half of a group of 4,306 persons examined during 1958 in Brooklyn's eight cancer-detection clinics had noncancerous conditions needing the services of a doctor. Additional meaning can be read into these figures, because the people probably wouldn't have participated in the test unless they were in some degree health-conscious.

Of the 4,306 persons examined, 2,380 had ulcers, diabetes, high blood pressure, hernias, heart disease and other ailments; there were 659 persons with benign tumors, 74 with conditions suspect of cancer, and five had proven cancers. "Cancer was completely unsuspected by the five individuals found to have it," commented Dr. Saul F. Livingston, chairman of professional services for the Cancer Committee.

The general health of New Yorkers is indicative of the health of people throughout the nation, according to the results of similar studies elsewhere. In a recent study of five hundred business executives at the Health Research Center of Chicago, more than half of the men examined had some unsuspected disease. Only 8 per cent of the executives had no apparent disease, and these were invariably under forty years old. The physician in charge, Dr. Charles E. Thompson, said that one of every ten of the executives examined had a previously undiscovered heart disease; one out of nine had insufficient thyroid gland secretion, with an excess of fatty elements in the blood, believed to be a factor in hardening of the arteries. The findings also disclosed that 2 per cent of the men examined had cancer.

Along with the appallingly high incidence of physical disorders, there is an equally alarming amount of mental disease, with the curve soaring ever upward. Mike Gorman, executive director of the National Committee on Mental Health, recently upped the estimate that one American out of twelve would spend part of his life in a mental hospital—to one out of ten. "And it's getting worse," he said. "We're in more trouble than we thought."

He described mental disease in the United States as "an epidemic sweeping the land." By calling it an epidemic, he said he meant "our inability to stop it . . . the way it sweeps in its path all kinds of people . . . the increasing numbers of people affected . . . particularly among children."

Other figures reflect the underlying disaster of mental disease. A Metropolitan Life Insurance Company bulletin (September, 1955) noted that from 1931 to 1951 the rate for first admissions of patients rose from 85 to 111 per 100,000 population, and for patients resident in mental institutions it increased from 301 to 382 per 100,000. More significant, the bulletin stated: "About half of the males and females admitted for the first time in 1951 were under 45 years of age." The publication further observed that one tenth of all the patients were under age twenty-five.

And there are still other serious chronic illnesses suffered by more than half the population. In 1957 alone, according to the National Institute of Health, more than 100,000,000 Americans suffered from respiratory illnesses during the winter months. Many of the victims were hit several times.

This was the year of the Asian flu epidemic, but that merely dramatized a permanent condition—the lack of resistance to infection. Most of us have such a narrow margin of resistance to disease that we are felled by the slightest extra stress.

Respiratory ailments in 1957 caused an "over-all aggregate of 190,000,000 bed days of disability." During one period 6,000,000 persons were disabled each day. Pre-school-age children were a prime target of respiratory viruses and the grippe-like illnesses they caused.

Countless numbers of Americans drag along from day to day, exhausted, suffering from indigestion, constipation, minor aches and pains. How many people have told their doctor they are tired, completely bushed, that they feel like they can hardly drag along from one day to the next, only to be told by their worthy medical adviser, "Hell, I'm tired too. Everybody's tired."

The cost of medical care in the United States today represents 4 to 5 per cent of the average family's income, according to the Health Information Foundation.

While 58 per cent of Americans have medical expenses of less than 5 per cent of their income, 7 per cent were shown to have bills amounting to 20 per cent or more. In 1954 medical costs put eight million families—16 per cent of the population—in debt for two billion dollars, and of that amount $1,100,000,000 accounted for direct charges for treatment and the rest was owed to financial institutions and individuals who had lent the money. The average family's debt for such service was placed at $137.

Illness absences alone, by the most conservative estimates, cause the loss of service and production of one million workers annually, an approximate five-billion-dollar loss, according to the Research Council for Economic Security. The council said the average absence from work due to prolonged illness is more than 10.8 weeks, indicating a national annual loss of 453,000 man-years, equivalent to a total productive time loss of $1,777,000,000.

From 1909 to 1955, the number of general hospital beds increased some 200 per cent, while the population in that period increased only 80 per cent. It could be argued with justification that to some extent this reflects a different attitude toward hospitalization, but hospitals have become big business. They employ 1,300,000 people—approximately one out of every fifty working people.

In 1956 there were 22,089,719 hospital admissions—a 5 per cent increase over 1955, indicative of the burgeoning amount of hospitalization required by the American people.

The Federal Government spends $2,500,000,000 annually on health, and in 1958 Professor Wilbur J. Cohen of the University of Michigan, former technical adviser to the Social Security Administration, said that the United States "must spend from $5 billion to $10 billion more each year to take care of its senior citizens."

In addition to the staggering amounts spent every year for formal medical care, fortunes are spent for various remedies that are consumed by the ton to alleviate discomfort and pain, and to try to stop the relentless onslaught of disease and sickness. These figures seldom are included in health statistics.

Every year Americans spend fortunes for drugs to calm their nerves, settle their stomachs and ease headaches and other assorted aches and pains. *Drug Topics,* a trade publication, disclosed that in 1967 Americans spent $95,-060,000 retail for aspirin alone, and $324,920,000 for all aspirin compounds (Anacin, Alka Seltzer, Bufferin etc.). More than $100 million is spent annually on sleep-inducing drugs; Americans consume three billion sleep pills a year. In some parts of the country barbiturates and benzedrine can be found for sale in hotels, night clubs, gas stations and even grocery stores, although such sale is prohibited by law.

Dental decay, which is discussed in Chapter X, is so rampant that it affects 95 per cent of the population.

There are approximately twelve million surgical operations performed annually, and approximately 7 per cent of the population has some type of surgery every year.

What the future portends for the nation's youth is suggested by studies made by Bonnie Prudden, who served as a member of President Eisenhower's Advisory Committee on Youth Fitness. Miss Prudden, working with Professor Hans Kraus of New York University, tested more than 7,000 children in the United States, Italy, Austria and Switzerland. They found that 57.9 per cent of the American youngsters failed in one or more of six basic strength and flexibility tests, while only 8.7 per cent of the European children flunked.

Almost six out of ten American children were found to be physically unfit, compared to less than one out of ten in Italy, Austria and Switzerland. "President Eisenhower was shocked by these figures," according to *Reader's Digest* (July, 1956), "and slated a national conference to deal with the situation." If this account of the nation's health needed a postscript, it was supplied by the *Digest,* when it added that the physical condition "of our young people is even worse than it was during World War II, when almost three million young men drafted for military service were rejected for physical reasons."

And that's the state of the nation's "health."

(2)

It is characteristic of American optimism to think in terms of health rather than sickness. Despite evidence to the contrary, we cling with unshaken faith to the idea that we are a healthy people. Surgeons zealously remove tons of diseased organs; we spend fortunes to build and maintain more hospitals; we visit the doctor more frequently, we buy mountains of drugs and medications; the dentist's drill tries to keep up with the eroding force of tooth decay, and ever-increasing numbers of people fall prey to the degenerative diseases—but still we remain unshaken in our conviction that this is health.

The basic problem is that we do not think in terms of health. We talk health and think sickness. Our semantic seduction has been so complete that we boast of the number of hospitals and doctors in the United States as a measure of our health. We have forgotten that health is not made in hospitals; a hospital is a place where one goes when health has broken down, and a doctor is a symbol not of health but of sickness.

We no longer believe that health is a natural way of life, and that disease and sickness are abnormal. We take bad health so much for granted that hospital and medical-insurance plans are provided for in the family budget like food and clothing. Nearly 70 per cent of the population carries some form of health insurance.

We are resigned to old age, physical deterioration, sickness, even death at an early age. Biologists say a mammal should live to be five times as old as the time it took to reach maturity. This would mean that man should live to be around a hundred and twenty. But we are content to settle for much less; we feel fortunate if we live to be seventy.

We try valiantly to mask the effects of premature aging and physical degeneration with creams, powders, lipsticks, supporting garments, surgical procedures—even as we strive for this biological deception we prepare for what we consider the inevitable by financially crippling ourselves with excessive life insurance, medical insurance, "health" disaster insurance and other plans and schemes.

All this in the name of health.

Our confusion between sickness and health stems from the fact that most of us exist somewhere between the two extremes. We are not quite sick most of the time, but neither are we quite well.

Few of us enjoy perfect health. Most of us fall far short of that ideal. We may not be bedridden or unable to function; we may not be in pain or even discomfort most of the time, and generally we are not even aware of our shortcomings in health because we have never known anything else. We take it for granted that we will have a certain number of headaches, backaches, colds, virus infections and maladies without names every year; we philosophically suffer a succession of annoying but generally not disabling ailments; we tire easily, and frequently are nervous and ill-tempered; we do not hold up well under stress; and any resistance we have to serious disease usually is due to vaccines rather than natural immunity.

We confuse physical development with good health, seldom realizing that muscular prowess is not in itself insurance against fatigue or ill health; when the bloom of youth passes, our muscles lose their natural elasticity, our tissues weaken, and we must look to medical science for "health."

But the doctor is no more oriented toward real health than his patients. Probably even less so. While he also talks about health, he is dedicated to sickness. His sphere is one of disease and ill health. From the time he enters medical school he is trained to deal in pathology; he learns to recognize and treat physical abnormalities.

Curative medicine rarely lifts its goals beyond trying to return the stricken individual to a state of painless mobility. This is considered normal. But what is normal? It is a resumption of daily living within the shadowland between sickness and health—often an area of conflict between doctor and patient because there is no pathology the doctor can recognize as sickness and no euphoria the patient can enjoy as health. The clash frequently is exaggerated because the crude instruments of the former frequently will not confirm the vague complaints of the latter. No allowance is made for the no-man's land between optimum health and evidence of sickness.

The subtle difference between clinical and optimum health is illustrated by the story told of a veterinarian who one day went hunting high in the mountains. He followed the trail of game higher and higher, where civilization had not penetrated; finally he shot a deer and dissected it, later to exclaim, "I was startled by what I'd found. Until then I had never seen the organs of a healthy animal."

It is the same with the physician. His standard of normal is the abnormal: his criterion of health is the absence of clinical proof of disease. Dr. D. T. Quigley, veteran Nebraska physician, expressed the thought aptly when he observed, "We have been afflicted by mass disease for so many decades that the average layman and the average doctor, and quite obviously the average dentist does not know what is normal."

3

A Little Poison

It was all very well to say "Drink me," but the wise little Alice was not going to do *that* in a hurry; "No, I'll look first," she said, "and see whether it's marked '*poison*' or not"; for she had read several nice little stories about children who had got burnt, and eaten up by wild beasts, and other unpleasant things, all because they *would* not remember the simple rules their friends had taught them, such as, that a red-hot poker will burn you if you hold it too long; and that, if you cut your finger *very* deeply with a knife it usually bleeds; and she had never forgotten that if you drink very much from a bottle marked "poison," it is almost certain to disagree with you, sooner or later.

—*Alice in Wonderland*

WE HAVE OBSERVED the adverse state of the nation's health. Now let us see to what extent this can be blamed on the poisons used in foods.

Many arguments are advanced to justify the use of small amounts of poisons in foods. All claim to be based on the scientific method. Anyone who objects to eating these poisons—regardless of the quantity consumed—is accused of being hysterical, a crackpot, a food faddist, unscientific or something else. But the basic objection remains unanswered.

As Dr. Wiley repeatedly pointed out, the nature of the chemical is not changed by reducing the quantity. Regardless of how small the dose, it is still poison—just as salami remains salami, no matter how thin you slice it. Poison is harmful to the human organism, Dr. Wiley emphasized. When it is ingested by a human being there is damage. The more poison, the more damage. The smaller the amount, the less damage. The fact that the dose may be reduced until damage no longer can be seen or measured by man's instruments does not mean that the damage no longer exists; it merely means that it no longer can be seen.

The vested interests that profit from the sale and use of chemicals in foods are scornful of this attitude. They say it is not scientific. As "scientific" proof of the alleged harmlessness of eating small amounts of poisons in foods, they solemnly point out that it is possible for a person to cram enough salt or water down his throat to kill himself. This is supposed to prove that everything is harmful and even fatal if taken in large enough jolts; it is typical of the efforts of food adulterers to confuse and divert the real issue, which concerns the long-term effects of consuming small amounts of poisons in foods.

The argument is patently false for many reasons—primarily because it compares unrelated substances. What this strange logic claims is that because a little salt is innocent and a lot is harmful it follows that all other substances that are harmful in large amounts are safe in small amounts.

Of course salt or water and the hundreds of poisons used in foods cannot be equated in this way. Salt and water are necessary to life, while virtually none of the food chemicals is necessary or even useful to life; with only rare exceptions, these chemicals are antagonistic to living tissue. The question is not whether they harm those who consume them, but the extent of the harm.

Equally as fallacious as the salt-and-water argument is the contention that because certain poisons may be found

in certain foods in their natural state, it is therefore safe
to add not only a little more of those particular poisons but
also a host of other toxic substances. This too has been
submitted as scientific proof that it is safe to use small
quantities of poisons in foods.

Dr. Wiley pointed out that poison is poison, whether it
is produced by nature or propounded by man. Because
traces of certain toxic substances do appear in a few foods,
he said, this should not be interpreted as a warrant to add
more of these poisons, "but, on the contrary, as a highly
accentuated warning to avoid any additional burden."

Dr. Wiley and other scientists who share his views recognize that nature is a more skillful and subtle chemist than
man, and when she puts a toxic substance in a food plant
she also may supply—either in the plant or the body of
the person eating it—the antidote that can make it harmless, although the limitations of man's chemistry may not
be able to discern this subtlety.

They feel that natural foods, like the human body, have
a delicate chemical balance that was established by nature
for a purpose. These naturally occurring chemicals exist in
their specific proportion for a specific purpose and this
balance evolved over millions of years. If a larger or
smaller quantity were desirable, the amount established by
nature through the evolutionary process would have been
larger or smaller.

Anyone who considers this attitude unscientific should
consider that nature created and sustained life for untold
thousands of years before science came into being, only a
couple of centuries ago. Man has not only been unable to
duplicate or initiate life, he does not even understand what
life is, either biologically or philosophically. He can isolate
and mix the components of protoplasm, but he cannot inject life.

This is not to detract from the achievements of man. He
has made remarkable progress in understanding his physical
world, especially during the last century, but he is not yet
ready to challenge nature as the master chemist—or biochemist. The true scientist appreciates this fact. He is a
being of humility and wisdom; he recognizes his limitations
just as he recognizes his achievements, and he also respects
his ignorance as he does his knowledge.

The true scientist does not scorn the lessons of nature;
he accepts her as his teacher. He does not try to conquer,

pervert or deceive her with biological tricks and chemical cunning; rather does he seek to understand her laws and work harmoniously with them. He understands and appreciates fully the lesson Alexis Carrel propounded when he said that biologically, in man, the things which are not measurable are more important than those which are measurable—and for him these things can have momentous consequences.

Such an approach to the problems of man must be contrasted with that of the food technologist. The food technologist is an employee of a corporation that is in business to make a profit, and the more profits he can help bring about, the greater his own financial rewards. His job is to find ways to substitute cheaper ingredients for more expensive natural ones, to develop money-saving shortcuts, to reduce spoilage, to entice the consumer into buying his firm's products. He is not hired to make the public healthier, happier or more prosperous; if any of those happy ends came about it would be through chance rather than design.

By means of propaganda, modern advertising techniques and a host of provocative names for toxic substances people not only have accepted poisoned foods but even consider them superior to natural products. They have accepted the false thesis that poisons cease to be harmful simply because they are taken in "small" quantities. Many people can understand that using cheap and impure fuels for a car will cause certain parts to wear out prematurely, although no apparent damage may be seen in daily operation of the vehicle; but they cannot conceive that their own bodies suffer similarly from the daily use of adulterated foods.

In considering the biological effects of small amounts of chemicals injected into foods, it is essential to bear in mind one basic fact: the food we eat is the stuff which makes up the blood, brain, bone and flesh that constitute a human being. If the ingredients that make up man are poisoned and synthetic, what is man himself? Can the whole be more than the sum of the parts? Can a person be expected to have a strong nervous system and enjoy mental health when his system is bombarded daily by nerve poisons and other toxic substances? Are we to believe that nature is so easily deceived about the inherent nature of a poison merely because the amount is reduced?

Dr. Wiley, when confronted a half century ago with the argument that small amounts of poison are safe, testified before Congress that there can be no excuse to justify the use of a harmful substance even in small quantities. "The character of the offense is not so much the amount of the material used as its nature," he said. He warned about the fallacy of thinking that merely because a substance "doesn't hurt you so that you can measure it, it is not harmful." That does not follow at all, he said. If only an infinitesimal amount of poison is added to the diet, "we may not be able to note any injury coming from it, but there is a subtle injury which will tell in time."

He pointed out that if any substance is added to food that places a burden on the organs, they wear out prematurely, the general vitality of the body is reduced, the aging process is speeded, the body becomes susceptible to sickness and disease, and inevitably death must result. This change is taking place, he emphasized, whether it can be measured or not.

The late Dr. Anton J. Carlson, internationally famous physiologist of the University of Chicago, and other scientists not beholden to food and chemical interests have repeatedly warned about the effects of toxic substances in foods today. Dr. Carlson warned that poisons can cause many changes in the body that cannot be detected. "Most of the organs in the body can be injured a great deal before we become actually sick," he said.

The science dealing with the complex subject of poisons is known as toxicology. The modern practice of toxicology, permitting the use of "small" quantities of poisons in foods, is based upon the ability of the body, primarily the liver, to detoxify and eliminate poisons which are not consumed in lethal doses. Instead of recognizing the liver as a safety valve and protecting it in every way possible from overwork and damage, the food technologists have exploited it by dousing foods with poisons and untested chemicals—in "small" amounts—for commercial profit.

Because people usually do not drop dead immediately after consuming these allegedly small amounts of poisons, it has been possible for industry to convince many legislators and the public generally that these substances are safe.

To determine how small the quantity of a poison must be to avoid killing people outright, each newly formulated chemical substance is subjected to what is known as an LD-

50 test. This is the method used to find the lethal (L) dose (D) for half (50 per cent) of the animals experimented upon; then this amount is used to fix what is believed to be a safe dose for humans.

A major shortcoming of the LD-50 method is that it is based upon the *average* resistance of all the animals being tested and it makes little allowance for the most susceptible. A few people may suffer ill effects or possibly die after taking only a tiny amount, or percentage of the LD-50, while others can stand twice as much or more without obvious ill effects.

Some people may not die or even become ill, but, doctors point out, the slightest exposure to foreign substances may trigger allergic disturbances ranging from simple ailments like sinus, nose, throat and ear irritations to more complex respiratory, liver, kidney and metabolic disabilities.

The tremendous difference in susceptibility among individuals has been emphasized by doctors, who note the scientific truth of the adage, One man's meat is another man's poison. Susceptibility is influenced by countless factors, such as diet, liver, kidney, metabolic disease, allergy, age, sex, physical condition and other considerations.

Animals are used to prove the alleged harmlessness of various chemicals used in foods, but how can an animal report what subtle effect a compound may have on his general state of health? He cannot report that he has spots before his eyes, headache, backache, dizziness, upset stomach and similar complaints which ordinarily would not be picked up by routine testing procedures. Nor can humans who suffer such indispositions trace them precisely to any of the hundreds of chemicals they eat.

The instruments science has to measure damage or functional efficiency in man are fantastically crude compared to the delicacy and sensitivity of the life process. Yet it is these instruments which must be used to determine harm from poisons used in foods.

Dr. Morton S. Biskind, a noted research physician, observed that "in clinical medicine there is at present a deplorable tendency to assume that when objective physical findings and laboratory reports are substantially negative, there is nothing wrong with the patient, no matter how severe his symptoms. But a patient is a whole human being, and how he feels is to him the most important aspect of his existence. The patient is the only unimpeachable authority on this subject and no amount of contrary objective data can alter that fact.

"A new principle has, it seems, become entrenched in the literature," he added. "No matter how lethal a poison may be for all other forms of animal life, if it doesn't kill human beings instantly it is safe."

The threat food chemicals pose is increased by the effects they may have on one another. One chemist is concerned with proving the "harmlessness" of small amounts of a poison insecticide, a second with artificial sex hormones, a third with antibiotics, a fourth with emulsifiers, a fifth with dyes, a sixth with various preservatives. But almost nothing is known about what happens when this conglomeration of powerful substances is mixed together in the human gut. There have been practically no experiments along this line.

The problem was brought into sharp focus recently by Dr. Henry van Zile Hyde, former chief of the international health division of the U.S. Public Health Service, who said:

"Thousands of industrial plants discharge chemical wastes into the rivers and streams that provide our drinking water. Hundreds of chemicals that have not been adequately tested for their effect on man are added to food in order to preserve, color and flavor it. Industry and motor vehicles pollute the air of our cities. Each year we are swallowing 14 million pounds of aspirins. . . . People who do not appear to be happy either asleep or awake are taking tranquilizing drugs to keep them in between. How dangerous is this chemical miasma?"

Dr. David E. Price, assistant surgeon general of the U. S. Public Health Service from 1952-1957, questioned whether all the pollutants man has produced might not lead to his wiping out his own species.

Some medical researchers point out that poisons in foods have the following effect on the human body:

Every poison taken into the body, if it cannot be excreted rapidly in its original state, must be detoxified. This places a heavy and continuing burden on the liver and various other organs. In the process of detoxification certain vitamins are used up, primarily the B vitamins and vitamin C. The detoxifying organs, in order to get the extra vitamins necessary to do the extra work demanded

*of them, take vitamins from other parts of the body. This
can cause a vitamin deficiency. Eventually it can set off
a chain reaction; certain organs may break down from this
burden and become unable to do their job, which would
lead to serious ailments, degenerative diseases including
cancer, and even death.*

Dr. William Smith, cancer researcher, has said that the
attitude some technologists have about chemicals today is
about the same as that held by many scientists about germs
a century ago. These scientists compared the size of a
germ to the size of a man and insisted that a little thing
like a germ couldn't harm a huge creature like a man. Today that sounds ridiculous, in the light of present knowledge that germs so tiny they can't be seen by the naked eye,
or micro-organisms so infinitely small they remain invisible
under the most sensitive microscope, can hastily dispatch
a man into the hereafter.

The mysterious and fascinating world that exists beyond
the eye of the microscope is discussed by Douglas Mars-
land, professor at New York University, in *Principles of
Modern Biology,* a widely used college textbook. He states:

"The microscope provides many clues to the functions of
the different parts of the cell. But below the reach of the
microscope there lies a realm of smaller things: the world
of molecules and atoms, which compose the ultimate
structure of all matter."

A human being is the multiple of the cells in his body
and his state of health or sickness depends upon these
individual cells.

The true scientist who works in the field of biology is
aware of the profound complexity of the human mechanism
and its sensitivity to subtle injuries. It is only the pseudo-
scientist and the charlatan who deceive and cheat the public in the name of science.

Dr. Carlson once was asked by a member of the Delaney
Committee if crookedness played a part in the results of
some experiments on food chemicals that were said to
prove the harmlessness of harmful substances. The vener-
able psychologist replied, "Actual crookedness is a minor
factor. It does occur occasionally, I am sorry to say, but it
it stupidity on the whole rather than crookedness. It is
stupidity."

F. J. Schlink, president and technical director of Consumer's Research, testified before the Delaney Committee

that toxicology is one of the weakest branches of modern science, and relatively poorly grounded scientifically.

A complicating factor, he noted, is that education in the field of toxicology is on a very limited scale in this country in spite of the importance of this science to the maintenance of public health, and very few toxicologists, other than those working in criminal investigation, are available. He added:

"Besides, toxicologists who do work on food, beverage, and drug problems are so accustomed to receiving their assignments from the industry that they tend to be weak in respect to what might be called an attitude of concern toward those who will be called upon to consume the finished products. Chemists are peculiarly at a disadvantage in this respect in that for the most part they are not aware even of the terrible hazards involved in some of the materials which they use in their work, and since they are accustomed to handling poisons in their daily activities in the laboratory, they do not acquire proper respect for them, nor are they aware of the dangers to laymen who will have no conscious need at all to be on guard against avenues of entry of poisonous materials into the body.

"Most chemists have little or no background in biology and toxicology and, worse still, the people who employ them for development and improvement of chemical additions to foods and beverages do not know the limitations of chemical knowledge, are not even aware that chemists are not qualified to pass on questions of wholesomeness and safety of the food supply."

The evidence that is piling up in alarming "health" statistics presents a powerful indictment against the use of harmful chemicals in food—even in "small amounts." For, as Alice pointed out in her excursion in Wonderland almost a century ago, if you continue to take poison, "it is almost certain to disagree with you, sooner or later."

4

Bug Killers
in Every Bite

(1)

THE MAJOR SOURCES of poison in our daily diet are the chemicals that are used in growing foods. These substances generally are known as pesticides. They have a number of functions, but their primary job is to kill bugs that attack farm crops and animals.

This would seem like a noble mission, except for one drawback: at the same time man is poisoning his insect enemies, he also is poisoning himself by being forced to eat traces of these substances that remain on his food. The Public Health Service has said it is virtually impossible to find a meal that isn't laced with these poisons.

Unlike the pesticides used before World War II, DDT and other fantastically potent new poisons in use today cannot be washed off foods. They not only remain on the outside but penetrate fruits, vegetables and grains, and concentrate in the fats of the animals we eat.

DDT and its chemical cousins also have the unpleasant habit of accumulating in the body fat of people. There probably is not a person alive in the United States who does not have some DDT in his body cells. DDT has, in fact, become part of our very being. Babies are born with DDT in their bodies, and this poison is in the milk of nursing mothers.

A study reported in *The New York Times* (January 1, 1966) disclosed that pesticides were found in the tissues of stillborn and unborn babies in concentrations approximately as high as those found in the mothers and young adults of comparable age.

Despite its tremendous toxicity, DDT has been so widely advertised as harmless for humans that it is used recklessly, appearing in everything from wallpaper paste to dry cleaning fluid. Each time we are exposed to it a little more accumulates in our bodies. For this reason it is known as a *cumulative poison,* and toxicologists recognize it as one of the most treacherous poisons ever developed.

DDT's cumulative nature underlines the warning of Dr. Otto Warburg, a famous German medical researcher and Nobel Prizewinner, that any poison which interferes with the respiration of the cells causes irreparable damage and inevitably leads to deterioration in the form of degenerative diseases, including cancer. Because some of the newer poisons do not accumulate in the body, their manufacturers claim that they are harmless for man. This ignores a basic fact of toxicology: a poison need not be cumulative to have a cumulative effect; the effect of each dose adds to that of the previous ones.

The menace of all the newer poisons has been so skillfully underplayed that they have enjoyed tremendous success. DDT's rise has been little short of meteoric. By 1956, total production of this wartime product and its kin had reached 506,370,000 pounds—more than four times the total reported for 1947. The amount of money spent nationally on all pesticides leaped from $40,000,000 in 1939 to about $260,000,000 in 1956—with the profiting chemical industry predicting sales of one billion dollars by 1975, a 284 per cent increase.

Potent as DDT is, it has been outdistanced by some of the poisons that followed it; many of these now have a nightmarish toxicity. Some of the organic phosphates—related to the war nerve-poisons—are so lethal that a single drop in a person's eye will cause death within seconds. Farmers who apply these poisons must protect themselves by dressing like space men. Many who got careless have paid with their lives.

Even within its own family group DDT has been left behind by its chemical blood brothers. Chlordane, for example, is rated by the Food and Drug Administration as at least four times as toxic as DDT. The FDA found that pigeons could not survive in a small room treated with chlordane, even after it was thoroughly scrubbed with alkali and subsequently aired for several weeks.

Dr. Arnold J. Lehman, chief pharmacologist of the

FDA, told the Delaney Committee in 1950 that "I would hesitate to eat food that had any chlordane on it whatsoever." Despite this warning, the Department of Agriculture has continued to recommend the use of chlordane on a multitude of food crops, including sweet corn, sugar beets, sugar cane, beans, broccoli, cabbage, carrots, radishes, strawberries, turnips, potatoes and apples. Fourteen years after Dr. Lehman's statement it is still being used.

DDT's formal name is dichlorodiphenyltrichlorethane. Among chemists it is known as a chlorinated hydrocarbon, composed of chlorine, hydrogen and carbon. DDT's prominent relatives, in addition to chlordane, include aldrin, dieldrin, benzene hexachloride (BHC), endrin, heptachlor, lindane, methoxychlor, TDE and toxaphene.

DDT was discovered in Germany in 1874 but did not become popular as an insecticide until World War II. After the war it was introduced to agriculture and was in use several years before its hazard to man was suspected. By then a tremendous vested interest had been built up in it, and the government was in the embarrassing position of having released it and endorsed its safety without adequate testing.

Economic and political expediency dictated the policy that subsequently was followed. Anyone who challenged the wisdom of eating foods garnished with DDT and other poisons was assailed as a crackpot, crank, faddist or quack. A gigantic advertising and public-relations program smothered all criticism and completely sold the public on the harmlessness of eating poisoned foods.

One of the most outspoken and articulate foes of DDT has been Dr. Morton S. Biskind, who formerly was a member of the headquarters staff of the Council on Pharmacy and Chemistry in the American Medical Association and in charge of the endocrine laboratory and clinic at Beth Israel Hospital in New York. Dr. Biskind told the Delaney Committee:

"Somehow a fantastic myth of human invulnerability has grown up with reference to the use of these substances. Because their effects are cumulative and may be insidious and because they resemble those of so many other conditions, physicians for the most part have been unaware of the danger."

Dr. Biskind noted that although there was a large body

of information available on the toxicity of DDT, "the evidence has been treated with disbelief, ignored, misinterpreted, distorted, suppressed, or subjected to some of the fanciest double talk ever perpetrated."

Dr. Lehman reinforced this warning by testifying that it was his "honest opinion" that the potential hazard of DDT had been underestimated for some time.

The AMA Council on Pharmacy and Chemistry, in a warning about the use of insecticides in electric vaporizers, pointed out that it is not reasonable to expect that humans can avoid injury if they are exposed year after year to a toxic agent in concentrations that kill insects in a few hours—a warning that applies to exposure in any form. The AMA said *"the resultant injury may be cumulative or delayed, or simulate a chronic disease of other origin, thereby making identification and statistical comparison difficult or impossible."*

Dr. Malcolm M. Hargraves, internationally known blood specialist at the Mayo Clinic, testified, in a legal proceeding in Brooklyn Federal Court in 1958, that he was *positive* that DDT and the solutions that carry it in sprays cause leukemia, aplastic anemia, Hodgkin's disease, jaundice and other blood disorders, many of them fatal. Of more than two hundred patients he treated for those maladies during the last four or five years, he said, all had histories of exposure to chlorinated hydrocarbons. Dozens of those patients are now dead, he added.

Emphasizing that he could speak only for himself, Dr. Hargraves said that the majority of the hematologists he worked with at the Mayo Clinic shared his beliefs about the dangers of DDT. He said there has been a definite increase in the incidence of the diseases he mentioned since DDT came into common use after World War II, and this increase could not be accounted for by better reporting or superior diagnostic techniques. The greatest incidence of leukemia was in five western states that have the most cattle and consequently do the most spraying, he said.

He and other medical witnesses emphasized that people vary greatly in their reactions to poisons, just as one person may get drunk from a single beer and another remain relatively unaffected by a quart of whisky. Dr. Hargraves stated that people with allergies are the most sensitive to the chlorinated hydrocarbons; he agreed that such persons form a minority, "but . . . when you consider that there are one hundred and seventy-five million people in this country," this minority represents a sizable number. He also pointed out that a person might go a long time without apparent effects from DDT and then be exposed to a slight additional amount that would suddenly bring on symptoms of poisoning.

Dr. Hargraves stated: "With many noxious agents intermittent exposures, or exposures repeated after variable lapses of time, may permit the susceptible individual to develop a marked degree of sensitivity so that the next exposure may precipitate a disastrous consequence. Our periodic spray program would be an ideal mechanism to precipitate such a disaster."

FDA experiments have demonstrated that rats fed only small amounts of DDT developed liver damage, and after larger doses tumors appeared. While there is no definite proof that DDT causes cancer in man, Dr. E. H. Lucas, a cancer researcher at Michigan State University, observed that "to state with authority that DDT is harmless is impossible, and there is no scientist in the United States or anywhere else who would dare to stick out his neck by making such a statement."

As far back as 1951 the Public Health Service described DDT as a "delayed action poison," explaining:

"Due to the fact that it accumulates in the body tissues, especially in females, the repeated inhalation or ingestion of DDT constitutes a distinct health hazard. The deleterious effects are manifested principally in the liver, spleen, kidneys and spinal cord.

"DDT is excreted in the milk of cows and of nursing mothers after exposure to DDT sprays and after consuming food contaminated with this poison. Children and infants especially are much more susceptible to poisoning than adults. . . .

"A recent report from the National Cancer Institutes discloses that the inhalation of petroleum mists or fogs (used as carriers for DDT in sprays) has been incriminated as a major cause of lung cancer and laryngeal cancer. These types of cancer occur with overwhelming predominance in men. . . ."

Less easily masked than the chronic effects of DDT are the effects of acute poisoning; these are well established and easily recognized. There may be gastroenteritis, nausea, vomiting, abdominal pains, coughing and sore throat, similar to the symptoms of certain virus infections or the common cold. Other symptoms of acute poisoning include pains in the joints, general muscular weakness and fatigue. Congestion of the lungs and pneumonia also are common findings.

In chronic poisoning other symptoms may develop: hypersensitive skin areas and numbness, tingling sensations, itching and headaches; the patient may develop twitching of the muscles and nerve involvement which interferes with walking. The brain also reveals signs of intoxication, such as loss of memory, inability to concentrate, dizziness and "foggy" brain. Mental depression and emotional instability are not relieved by psychiatric help. There is a distaste for work and all forms of effort. But probably the most common complaint is a feeling of anxiety and apprehension; many victims have used the identical expression: "I felt like I was going to die." Dr. Biskind has raised the possibility that DDT is implicated in many of the new viruslike ailments reported since World War II. Other investigators have traced the viruslike "X-disease" in livestock to chlorinated hydrocarbons that appeared in crankcase oil that was ingested by cattle when they tried to lick grain off farm equipment, or when they ate feeds that were processed on machines lubricated with this oil. These poisons were chemical cousins of DDT. The disease could also be produced by feeding the cows batches of commercial feed; the poison was found in their milk.

However, it is not the clinically apparent effects of DDT poisoning that are the primary concern of doctors who are familiar with the pesticide problem. It is the effects of long-term exposure which cannot be identified or measured with present medical diagnostic tools. In this respect they resemble injuries due to fallout or X rays; although the damage often cannot be seen or proved, it is nevertheless, there; it may take ten, twenty, thirty or more years to appear, depending on the individual.

Virtually nothing is known about the long-term effects of DDT. It is an acknowledged delayed-action poison, so everything about it has been studied except its delayed effects. The AMA's Council on Foods and Nutrition, noting "the appalling lack of factual data" on the effects of the new pesticides when ingested with foods, stated: "The chronic toxicity to man of most of the newer insecticides is entirely unexplored."

Two California investigators, the late Dr. Francis Pottenger, Jr., and Dr. Bernard Krohn, testified that "the reported cases of insecticide deaths were the spectacular ones, involving swift death from massive exposure. Pathological diagnosis was made at autopsy. But many other patients may die slowly from insecticides without the true cause of their death being recognized."

These researchers observed that rats fed chlorinated hydrocarbon insecticides showed higher mortality than did the controls. "Yet the tissues of the animals showed no changes at autopsy, demonstrating how easily such toxicity might escape notice. In short, one could not prove the diagnosis of insecticide toxicity in these animals by clinical or laboratory methods. But their lives were shortened by insecticides. We shall never know how many humans suffer similarly."

Various other studies with rats, mice, rabbits, guinea pigs, cats, dogs, chicks, goats, sheep, cattle, horses, monkeys and fish have shown that DDT causes functional disturbances and degenerative changes in the skin, liver, gall bladder, lungs, kidneys, spleen, thyroid, adrenals, ovaries, testicles, heart muscle blood vessels, voluntary muscles, the brain and spinal cord and peripheral nerves, gastrointestinal tract and blood.

While animals and humans differ in their response to poisons, it was pointed out in the *Yearbook of the American Journal of Public Health* that "contrary to previous beliefs, it now seems likely that a substance which is poisonous to one form of life is very apt to be found to some degree toxic for other animals, including men."

The implications this statement holds for man were dramatized by an experiment conducted by Dr. Robert F. Mobbs when he was plant physician for a North Carolina factory that mixed DDT and BHC. A child who lived about three hundred feet from the factory became sick and died in convulsions. Dr. Mobbs, suspecting the insecticides as the cause, placed six rabbits in the plant; within a short time all the rabbits were dead—their tissues showing changes identical to those of the child.

DDT also has been shown to destroy vitamins and inhibit the body's delicate enzyme systems. "The fact that a very small amount of a biological poison is ultimately able to effect a relatively enormous weight of animal tissue shows that the poison interferes with an essential link in a chain of vital processes," according to Dr. John J. Miller, Chicago biologist.

DDT also has been implicated in the phenomenal rise in liver ailments in recent years. Dr. W. Coda Martin, who has done extensive pesticide research, says that by damaging the liver DDT brings on the "slow, progressive, internal deterioration of the tissues and cells of the body." The old methods of detection and control are not applicable to the present situation, which is assuming epidemic proportions, he believes.

Cirrhosis of the liver became one of the country's top ten killers in 1957, and cases of hepatitis reportedly have shown a 100 per cent increase between 1955 and 1957. A New York Hospital study group recently stated its belief that a direct relationship existed between hepatitis cases and DDT in food. The University of Minnesota Medical School has expressed puzzlement over a "striking increase" in the prevalence of hepatic necrosis in the ten-year period from 1946 through 1955. The DDT-happy U.S. Army also has been concerned about the rise in hepatitis cases.

DDT is absorbed by the body through the mouth, lungs and skin, accumulating in the fatty tissues in many times the amount that would be acutely fatal if injected into a vein in a single dose. Of twenty cadavers examined at random in California by the FDA, organic pesticides of the DDT type were found in nineteen. Liver damage was found in sixteen of the twenty cadavers. The patients died of such diseases as cancer, heart disease and pneumonia. It is not possible to blame DDT positively, in whole or in part, for these deaths, but neither can it escape a cloud of suspicion.

The amounts of DDT we consume and store in our bodies are measured in parts per million (ppm). In common terms one ppm equals about one teaspoonful of DDT in ten tons of food. This poison is so potent that FDA tests showed that rats fed only 5 ppm DDT in their diet suffered liver injury. Dr. Biskind has pointed out that "it is a rare food that escapes contamination with amounts [of DDT] often greatly in excess of that known to produce liver damage in animals."

In a series of tests run on New Yorkers in 1955 it was

found that more than 25 per cent had over 5 ppm DDT
stored in their bodies, the highest concentration being in
the body of an infant. In a U. S. Public Health Service
study of 113 subjects, DDT content ranged up to 68 ppm,
averaging 6.41 ppm. Two DDT handlers had 91 and 291
ppm respectively. The Public Health Service has estimated that the national average of DDT storage in fat is
about 5 ppm, but some objective investigators believe it is
closer to 9 ppm—and rising steadily.

The *Journal of the American Medical Association* has
pointed out that DDT in the fatty tissue is not like butter
stored in an icebox, but that the cell has a constant turnover; there is a rich blood supply and the use of the fat
is regulated by endocrine, enzyme and nerve influences.
The *JAMA* said it appears to be a reasonable assumption
that fatty tissue which has "these many important functions can be influenced by the presence of cumulative poisons such as the chlorinated hydrocarbon insecticides."

Further, the *Journal* warned, the level below which adverse long-range effects are absent is unknown, and the
influence of the stored compounds may not be limited to
the fatty tissue but may influence the ability of the body
to manufacture hormones and utilize vitamins.

Incredibly little is known about what happens to these
poisons in the body. Some are known to break down into
more toxic substances; others have been found to have
what is called a synergistic effect—they make one another
more poisonous than they originally were. As Dr. Lehman pointed out, chemicals also may combine with the
food they are in to form new poisons, and time may
change chemicals compositions.

A little known hazard of DDT storage is that any sudden weight loss, due to reducing or illness, would burn up
the fat rapidly, releasing large amounts of DDT into the
blood stream, possibly causing an attack of acute poisoning—a special threat to children because of their high fat
content and sudden weight drops due to childhood sick-
nesses. Doctors generally are so uninformed about this
hazard that in such cases few would consider the possibility of DDT poisoning.

Since DDT produces symptoms that resemble many ailments, it is known to mask other diseases; some researchers claim it produces a condition easily mistaken, during
epidemics, for polio. Because DDT is a nerve poison it

may damage cells in the spinal cord, increasing susceptibility to polio and other ailments.

Despite the voluminous evidence pointing to the harm-
fulness of DDT, its champions still insist it is safe for
humans. Their primary claim is based on an experiment
in which human volunteers demonstrated they could tol-
erate substantially large daily jolts of the poison over several months without apparent ill effects.

This study, as the *Journal of the American Medical Association* noted, was "the first experimental study of the
storage, excretion, and possible clinical effects in man of
DDT given in many small doses." The experiment was
made in 1955—*10 years after DDT had been in widespread use in foods.* It was conducted by the U. S. Public Health Service, which had released DDT for use on
the food of America's millions a decade earlier without
first learning what the chronic effects would be on multi-
tudes of people.

At that late date (1955), the PHS could hardly afford
to have the test show that it had made a mistake ten years
earlier. The PHS, sitting as judge and jury to evaluate
evidence supplied by its own investigators, completely
vindicated its decision to permit the use of DDT in foods.

The highly publicized test was conducted in a Federal
prison where a group of volunteers ate up to two hundred
times as much DDT as appears in the ordinary diet for up
to eighteen months, allegedly without harm. Results of
the study were published in the *Journal of the American
Medical Association*, and this report has been widely
quoted as proof of DDT's alleged harmlessness for man.
Since it is the primary study on which the safety of the
American people must rest, it demands critical examination.

The experiment was conducted by Dr. Wayland Hayes,
former head of the toxicology section of the Technical
Development Service, Communicable Disease Center of
the U. S. Public Health Service. After getting his medical
degree in 1946, Dr. Hayes entered the Public Health Service. His attitude toward DDT was expressed before the
Delaney Committee when he testified that DDT causes
definite changes in the livers of rats fed it, but he would
not characterize these changes as damage. Just changes.
"Its interpretation is going to require further scientific
study," he stated.

Dr. Hayes's celebrated feeding test began with fifty-one prisoners. At the end of a year only fourteen men were still in it. At the conclusion of the study after eighteen months there were just *four* men—hardly a representative cross section of the American people.

Because this handful of men allegedly withstood large doses of DDT for a relatively short time without perceptible harm, it was concluded that it is safe for some 175,000,000 Americans to ingest small portions of this *cumulative* poison in their food three times daily, year after year.

The report implies that DDT is harmless as a component of the human diet, stating that after about a year DDT storage in the body reaches a maximum "and thereafter (people) store no more of the material despite continued intake."

Analysis of the report suggests that its conclusions have been quoted more than they have been analyzed. Dr. Hayes's own charts do not seem to bear out his own findings.

Of eleven controls in the experiment, eight showed more DDT stored in their bodies when they left the experiment than when they began. One subject showed a rise of almost 30 ppm of DDT after only four months' participation. Other controls also showed substantial gains.

The controls were men who ate the regular prison diet without extra doses of DDT. The fact that they continued to build up DDT in their bodies throughout the experiment supports the findings of independent researchers who say that Americans generally are constantly storing more and more DDT, depending on the amount ingested, without any leveling-off point.

Dr. Pottenger testified in a 1958 court action that he believes Americans today have three to ten times as much DDT stored in their body fat as in 1950. One of his patients, he said, had 5 ppm in 1949, and in 1953 the same patient had 23 ppm. Another patient's DDT content rose from 3.8 ppm in 1949 to 173 ppm in 1955.

To assume that it is safe to have DDT in the cells of the body, even if storage does level off, is like saying that because there is always alcohol in the blood of a heavy drinker it is not harmful.

Dr. Martin cited the medical argument against the presence of DDT in the body of man when he testified: *"DDT affects the enzyme system which controls the supply of oxygen to the individual cells. The greater the concentration, the greater the damage. There isn't a cell in the body that isn't affected by DDT."*

Every private physician I know of who has published papers on the effects of DDT has emphasized that a person may go along for many years without a sign of DDT poisoning. Then, suddenly, he will have accumulated his individual toxic limit. Disease or even death may follow—without anyone's being able to pinpoint the real culprit. The fact that a person dies of a heart attack or cancer doesn't tell what brought on the fatal ailment. Is the DDT in the body a direct or indirect cause of disease or death? Who can say?

No short-term feeding test like the Hayes study could even begin to answer the complex questions posed by the use of DDT and other poisons in the daily diet. Twelve or eighteen months is a short period in the life of a man; it is not long enough to tell what happens to the person ingesting these substances, nor does it tell what happens to his descendants—but animal experiments indicate there may be severe repercussions.

Probably the sharpest critic of the Hayes study has been Dr. Biskind, who called it "an intricate, carefully contrived and ingeniously composed document, perhaps a classic of its kind."

He pointed out that the study ignored the tremendous differences in the way individuals react to poisons, burying individual findings in group averages; certain comparable medical data on the subjects at the beginning and end of the experiment were lacking, and complaints of the subjects which could not be confirmed by laboratory tests were dismissed or called psychoneurotic in origin.

The experiment, Dr. Biskind noted, was said by its authors to have shown that "no volunteer complained of any symptoms or showed, by the tests used, any sign of illness that did not have an easily recognized cause clearly unrelated to exposure to DDT."

The Hayes report, Dr. Biskind observed, does not state that these signs and symptoms could not have been caused by DDT but only that they could "easily" find another explanation. "For instance, one of the subjects complained of 'pain every day in every bone, occasional headache, and tearing of the right eye.' Say the authors, 'His complaints obviously were of psychoneurotic origin.' " Dr. Biskind pointed out that British scientists who exposed themselves to DDT complained of symptoms almost identical to the complaining subject in the Hayes test. "Were their complaints also of psychoneurotic origin?" he asked.

Other objections to the study were that it ignored the fact that Federal prisoners have a more carefully regulated life (and diet) than most of the population, which would make the prisoners less susceptible to the effects of poisons; it ignored the fact that all the subjects were males, acknowledged by the Public Health Service in an earlier statement to be considerably more resistant to the effects of DDT than women, children and infants; it ignored the fact that the public is made up of the strong and the weak, young and old, healthy and sick; it ignored the fact that the subjects began the experiment with DDT already stored in their bodies, so the initial impact could not be measured; it ignored the fact that even the controls had DDT stored in their cells and they ingested it daily in their regular meals throughout the experiment; and that the study was concerned with DDT and DDE (a derivative of DDT) *only*, at a time when DDT had been largely replaced by even more toxic compounds, and the average person's daily diet certainly contained residue of a dozen or more pesticides other than DDT.

The experiment, according to Dr. Biskind, also omitted pertinent medical data on the prisoners' condition and ignored what appeared to be adverse results in some of the subjects. It presented no medical follow-up on what later happened to the experimental group. There is no guarantee that some of the subjects ultimately will not be doomed to serious ailments as a result of having participated in the tests.

Also noteworthy is the fact that the physical examinations on the prisoners were made by Dr. Hayes personally; his assistants were technicians. By his own admission, his previous clinical experience with patients was limited to a one-year internship in a government hospital; he never engaged in private practice. No other physician checked his findings, as far as is known.

Dr. Hayes's failure to find physical damage from the DDT fed to the prisoners, regardless of how thorough his methods or good his intentions, is no proof that the damage did not take place. It only means that he and his associates did not find such damage, according to their report.

The point that failure to find injury is no guarantee that injury did not occur is nicely made by Dr. Ian Stevenson, a physician, who wrote in *Harper's* Magazine (April 1949) that there are three states of ill health: "The first is a functional impairment or misuse which is often impossible to detect and may not be noticed by the patient or his physician; the second brings definite symptoms of illness; the third brings structural changes. . . .

"To try to learn about an ailment under such circumstances is something like trying to learn about chess by watching only the last moves of a game between experts, unaware that the outcome is frequently decided in the first moves."

The late appearance of structural changes is food for thought in view of the "changes" DDT produces in the livers of rats fed much less DDT than most people have stored in their bodies. Dr. Stevenson, unlike Dr. Hayes, apparently did not think that such physical alterations needed interpretation. To him, tissue changes were the most drastic manifestation of ill health.

A more subtle form of damage that can elude the researcher was cited by the late Dr. Ehrenfried Pfeiffer, a biochemist. He said that one weakness of feeding tests like the one conducted by Dr. Hayes was that experimenters look out for poisoning effects in terms of common toxicology. "The minimum lethal dose is determined and gross poisoning effects are looked for," he said. What counts, however, and what passes unnoticed, are the often unnoticed dynamic and systemic changes which cannot be easily discovered."

In brief, the Hayes study did not prove that it is safe to eat DDT in repeated doses, small or large, over a lifetime. It proved nothing except that a small group of men, who had already demonstrated their ability to withstand repeated small doses of DDT in their regular diet, could withstand substantially large amounts without immediate disastrous consequences.

(2)

Congress legalized mass poisoning of the American people by granting the FDA the right to determine how much poison residue may remain on marketed food—a right granted under the Miller Pesticide Act of 1954. The permitted amount of residue is known as a poison's tolerance. DDT, for example, had a tolerance of seven ppm on single items of food. Chlordane's tolerance is 0.3 ppm. Some pesticide poisons are so lethal they carry a zero tolerance—not even a trace is supposed to remain when they are marketed.

These tolerances were established on the basis of amounts known to produce injury in animals.

Through odd circumstances, however, the tolerance level for DDT was recently lowered. In 1968 West Germany, after an extensive testing program, established a tolerance for DDT of only one part per million—just one-seventh as high as that of the United States. Were Germans seven times more fragile than people in the United States, or were our scientists seven times more optimistic? The Germans also cut the tolerance of other pesticide residue drastically below U. S. figures, establishing zero tolerances for chlordane and dieldrin; both of these can remain as residues on some food products in the U. S.

Soon after the Germans announced their new tolerances, the U. S. sent a delegation to Bonn to ask them to reconsider. The U. S. wasn't as concerned about the health aspect as about what the lower tolerances would do to trade: American exports would be stopped by Belgium and the Netherlands, which had tolerances similar to those of the Germans. But the Europeans wouldn't relent. Consequently the U. S. cut its tolerance of DDT to 3.5 parts per million on most crops—one half of what it had been previously, and to one and 1.5 on a few other crops.

Before the Miller Act was passed, FDA had virtually no control over the production or use of pesticides. Manufacturers were not required to test their products to prove their "harmlessness" for humans before using these poisons on crops and animals eaten by humans. The Miller bill was designed to give some control over the use of these substances.

The FDA, after considerable prompting, sent me some figures to show how effective the Miller Act has been. Of 536 domestically grown fruits and vegetables tested during a 13-month period, ending in 1956, 11.9 per cent exceeded their tolerance. Of 912 imported fruits and vegetables tested, 8.6 per cent were above tolerance. Of samples tested for DDT, 9 per cent were over tolerance. Of those tested for endrin—so powerful it has a zero tolerance—44 per cent were over tolerance.

The number of tests was disturbingly small, but the percentage of violations is even more alarming. The report covered analysis of fruits and vegetables only and included just sixteen major cities throughout the United States.

Despite the number of violations, only 21 seizures were made for excess residue. Six were for too much poison on wheat and barley. The figures released pertain to excess residue on vegetables and fruits only, but *almost one third of the seizures were for excess residue on wheat and barley*. In the first two months of 1957, according to the government report, there were 14 seizures—13 of them for contaminated wheat and oats. Why did the FDA fail to state the percentage of highly-treated grains found to be over tolerance?

The public is not always so lucky as it was when, on January 6, 1956, the FDA reported that two freight cars loaded with 30,816 heads of lettuce containing excess pesticide contamination were seized in a *spot check*. On another occasion, a shipment of mustard greens was seized after several Californians who ate them became ill; tests showed the green contained nicotine residue of 70 to 90 ppm. Nicotine has a tolerance of 2 ppm. In a 1955 seizure, 83 of 140 samples of frozen vegetables were found to have "high residues" of a "highly toxic dust" (unidentified) that was not even supposed to be used on such crops. Consequently, 190,000 pounds of frozen broccoli and kale had to be destroyed.

When the late Dr. L. G. Cox of the Beech-Nut Packing Company appeared before the Delaney Committee, he testified that the firm was spending $100,000 a year trying to control the pesticide-residue problem and he recited numerous cases in which crops were rejected because of dangerous amounts of residue. Was this highly contaminated produce destroyed? It was not, according to his testimony. Instead it was sold in the open market or to less particular processors.

Excessive residue found by Beech-Nut have been confirmed by numerous other private analyses. Recent DDT tests conducted by the Laboratory of Industrial Hygiene, Inc., in New York showed egg yolks containing up to 50 ppm, cheese 70 ppm, and butter up to 10 ppm. Dr. W. Coda Martin reported that private analysis showed DDT residue of 150 ppm on cheese, and butter might run as high as 2000 ppm.

When the Public Health Service analyzed DDT residue, during a four-day testing period, in the ordinary meals in the Federal prison where the Hayes feeding tests were conducted, it caught stewed dried fruit with 69 ppm DDT content and bread with 100 ppm. Contamination in the bread was blamed on the lard, but private investigators calculated that if all the contamination was in the lard, it would have amounted to 2500 ppm DDT.

Another indication of what might be slipping past inspectors was supplied by John M. Dendy, head of the analytical division of Texas Research Foundation, who tested milk and meat samples for their DDT content. He testified before the Delaney Committee that all milk and meat samples his organization bought in supermarkets were found to be contaminated. Contamination ranged from 3.10 ppm DDT in lean meat to 68.55 ppm in the fat; and in milk it ranged from less than 0.5 ppm DDT to 13.83 ppm.

When DDT was released in 1945, the USDA recommended its use on cows and in dairy barns. Four years later, however, the recommendation was withdrawn—after investigators belatedly learned that even if DDT was used merely in the barns, with feeding troughs covered, and the cows kept outside while it was being applied, the poison would appear in the milk within twenty-four hours.

For many years the FDA took the strong position that no pesticide residue whatsoever could be permitted in milk; this made it illegal for milk containing *any* DDT to pass from one state to another.

The FDA's Frank A. Vorhes, Jr., has pointed out that processing eliminated some residue from most products, but "once incurred in milk . . . a residue will ordinarily be consumed in its entirety." He said milk constitutes not the average 25 percent, but a preponderance of the diet of that segment of the population to which potential harm from pesticide residues is probably the greatest. "For the weak, the sick, the very young, and the aged, milk can represent close to 100 percent of the nutrient intake, and supplant most of the water intake as well."

This forthright statement notwithstanding, many observers found it impossible to understand why DDT was safe in foods and dangerous in milk in any degree whatsoever. Certainly the weak, the sick, the very young, and the aged are all going to get some food, and virtually all of it contains DDT and related poisons. Babies are getting some DDT in baby foods, despite any precautions taken to hold down the amount, and infants are getting contaminated milk from their mothers; in one series of tests private investigators found 116 ppm DDT in mother's milk.

FDA, however, stuck to its unwavering opposition to pesticide residue in milk. Early in 1958 it denied tolerances to two substances—malathion and methoxychlor— both considered less toxic than DDT. FDA flatly stated that residues were unacceptable in milk in *any degree whatsoever* and the tolerance level for both substances would remain zero.

Despite this forthright action on behalf of pure milk, FDA disclosed that tests of 800 milk samples from all parts of the country showed residue in 62 per cent of the milk examined; other dairy products also showed a high percentage of contamination, with residue in 75 per cent of the butter and 50 per cent of the cheese sampled. In similar tests, from 1948 through 1951, DDT was found in 25 per cent of the milk sampled.

Other tests were said to reveal contamination ranging from traces of poison to serious amounts present. But FDA admitted that none of the poisoned milk was seized and there were no prosecutions. An educational campaign was said to be continuing—although farmers had been getting educated to keep DDT away from dairies and cattle forage since 1949. Since the educational program began, violations had shot up 37 per cent.

In 1968 the government finally realized the hopelessness of trying to keep pesticides out of milk and set a tolerance for DDT, DDD and DDE: 0.05 ppm for whole milk and 1.25 ppm for milk fat. There is still no tolerance for other pesticides in milk, including the less toxic methoxychlor, which is less likely to appear and thus can be excluded. Since tolerances were set FDA has condemned large quantities of milk. But is too optimistic to hope that most milk on the market is within tolerance; it is almost beyond hope to look for a glass free of all contamination.

Most of the contamination of milk allegedly comes from feeding cattle sprayed forage, a practice FDA repeatedly has condemned. But farmers, after spraying their corn, are reluctant to waste the stalks. In 1955 the California Department of Agriculture reported that 10,000 tons of silage made from sweet corn stalks and leaves contained

DDT residue as high as 250 ppm. What this might mean
to the person drinking milk from cows fed this fodder was
indicated by a witness before the Delaney Committee. He
said that hay made from sprayed alfalfa with an average
DDT residue of 7-8 ppm was fed to dairy cows; after the
first few days of feeding, the DDT content in the milk was
about 2.3 to 3 ppm. Butter made from the milk, because
of the concentrated fat, contained 65 ppm DDT.

At the same time that the sharp rise in contaminated
milk was taking place, Paul A. Clifford of the FDA noted
that many pesticides other than DDT were coming into
common use. He observed that "residues of lindane,
technical BHC, methoxychlor, rhothane, heptachlor, toxaphene, chlordane, members of the aldrin group perthane,
dilane, lethane, and others might be encountered in milk."

Mr. Clifford made the remarkable admission that "for
most of these no specific test method exists." This means
the government has no way of knowing what to look for
or how to measure the amount present, except with crude
tests based on the number of flies killed. When specific
tests could be made, Mr. Clifford revealed, as many as four
individual insecticides were found in single milk samples.

In addition to the DDT compounds, there were residues
of the super-powerful organic phosphate pesticides. More
than one third of the contaminated butter samples were
said to contain the parathion-type insecticides, members
of this family. Mr. Clifford said "a further complication
was recognized from the start" because "little is known
about the metabolism of most of these products; some or
all might degrade to unknown products of unknown
toxicity."

The problem is neatly illustrated by heptachlor, a chlorinated hydrocarbon, which in 1950 was given a tolerance
of 0.1 ppm on thirty-four raw argicultural commodities,
including fruit, vegetables, grain and forage crops. In late
1959, however, the FDA discovered that, largely as a result of weathering, the chemical was converted to heptachlor epoxide, which is even more toxic than the parent
heptachlor. The FDA noted that when heptachlor epoxide was fed to cows (as it would be on forage) it was
"deposited in their milk and meat."

FDA claimed that heptachlor epoxide had not been
identified on crops sooner because no detection method
was available. Unmentioned was a 1953 report FDA re-

searchers published stating that heptachlor was transformed to heptachlor epoxide in animal bodies. Why wasn't the detection method used on animals applied to crops?

In its 1959 statement the FDA said that additional studies showed that the combined residues of heptachlor and heptachlor epoxide "were likely" to exceed the 0.1 ppm tolerance and there was no evidence that such residues would be safe. The FDA then proposed a zero tolerance for heptachlor, after the public had been consuming it and its more toxic derivative for more than a decade.

The same problem that existed with milk plagued the FDA with meat for several years. It was against the law for poisons to be in meat, but contamination was universal. Finally this embarrassment was neatly resolved: contamination was made legal. In 1957 FDA fixed a tolerance of 7 ppm for DDT in the fat of cattle, hogs and sheep. There still is no tolerance for poisons in lean meat, although it would be impossible to find any that is uncontaminated.

One factor that makes DDT so effective as an insecticide also makes it so treacherous for man—its amazing persistence. In an extraordinary feeding demonstration, researchers applied DDT to hay growing in the field, fed the hay to beef animals, slaughtered the cows and fed their flesh to pigs, which in turn were slaughtered and analyzed; after these two complete digestions the DDT was found to remain intact. It has been sprayed on the outside of boxes of raisins, and the fruit inside became contaminated. Baggage cars sprayed with it have contaminated subsequent food shipments. Grains suffer heavy contamination from treated elevators and storage areas.

How tenaciously DDT clings to human flesh was shown by a Public Health Experiment with two men who worked with insecticides. When originally tested they showed 91 and 291 ppm DDT in their body fat. The report said that "even after prolonged rest from their occupations (in the first case two years) the DDT levels in the fat were still 30 and 240 ppm."

The poison is equally stable in soil. Seven years after DDT was applied to test plots, 80 per cent still remained. Each year's spraying builds up the amount of poison in the ground; in orchards it has been found in amounts up to 113 pounds per acre under trees. It has been demonstrated that chlorinated hydrocarbons in the soil are absorbed by crops grown in that soil. Some plants absorb poisons in greater concentration than their concentration in the soil. Investigations have shown that heavily treated soils produce crops of inferior quality and taste, and such impairment may take place before growth and yield are affected.

Dr. Ehrenfried Pfeiffer cited recent tests in Germany which showed that following DDT spraying "the protein nitrogen of Boston lettuce was reduced from 75 per cent of the total nitrogen to 64.9 per cent. The sugar was increased from 21.59 per cent to 24.51 per cent; ascorbic acid (vitamin C) was reduced from 606 mg. per cent to 442 mg. per cent, as against the untreated control."

This biochemist also referred to other experiments in Germany, in which sprayed vegetables (carefully washed to remove all possible outside adhering DDT) were fed to animals: "During the first year, only the weight curves of the male animals were lower than the one of the control. During the second year, the weight curves of the male and female animals were lower than the controls, which got untreated vegetables. After the second year of the feeding test autopsies of the animals showed significant changes of liver and spleen. The liver showed shrinkage. . . . The spleen showed an even more pronounced decrease in weight." Similar tests have not been carried out in the United States.

The threat to crops and humans alike has been discovered only belatedly in many pesticides that were introduced to the sound of trumpets. Among them was benzene hexachloride (BHC). It was heralded as deadly for all kinds of harmful insects but "relatively harmless for humans." Annual sales hit 98,000,000 pounds before government researchers found BHC appearing in the brain tissues of laboratory animals and producing abnormal cancerlike cell growth elsewhere. Having a tolerance of 5 ppm, it is, despite this evidence, still used on many citrus fruits and vegetables. BHC is so stable that it retains up to half its original strength in the soil after three years, migrating into crops grown in the contaminated earth. Many processors have objected to it because it gives an off flavor to certain foods, if for no other reason. Benzene hexachloride and chlordane have been found to be active in soil twelve years after they were applied to it.

In 1953 Dr. Mobbs testified before a Congressional committee that previous testimony given to the FDA and the Delaney Committee about the dangers of BHC was ignored. He said the testimony pointed out that BHC destroys an important vitamin, inositol, which he said has, perhaps, a more beneficial effect in preventing hardening of the arteries than any other substance. Dr. Mobbs added:

"One thing that shocked me was the fact that the American Cancer Society not too long ago gave a grant to the professor of biochemistry at Columbia in which he used benzene hexachloride to produce abnormal cell formation or cancerlike changes and then used inositol to try to overcome those things, and yet at the same time we are using BHC . . . in a fashion in which it contaminates crops, gets in the milk supply, it is now used in many restaurants and in home vaporizing devices." During the Korean war, he said, "BHC was used to dust troops and prisoners."

While the public plays its guinea-pig role to determine the effects of chronic poisoning by pesticides, it must depend on the farmer to follow instructions carefully if it is not. to be exterminated suddenly, along with the bugs, by an unintentional overdose of the things. To stay within legal tolerances, for whatever protection this may offer, the farmer must use the exact concentration prescribed, apply the material as directed, and wait the required number of days after applying the poison before marketing his crops. This assumes that the farmer will read the directions on the label and that he can and will follow them. This is the public's "margin of safety." But what if a farmer doses his crops and only a couple of days later there is a particularly favorable market for his produce? Will he pass up the sale and wait the specified number of days or weeks, risking a lower profit or even a monetary loss?

And what assurance has the public that the spray is properly applied? When the late Charles Wesley Dunn, general counsel for the Grocery Manufacturers of America, Inc., was supporting the tolerance concept for pesticides, he testified that he had heard his own farm manager in Vermont "say any number of times, when he came to the problem of using an insecticide in growing our own crops, 'Well, if it is good in the quantity that it is recommended, it ought to be twice as good if I use twice as much,' and so he would use an excessive amount." Are we to believe that human nature has changed since passage of the Miller Act?

In many instances farmers have used the wrong insecticide at the wrong time. A California grower was caught "dropping a spoonful of parathion dust" into the crowns of plants to control mites even during the picking season. In another case, reported by FDA, a lettuce farmer used chlordane, endrin, dieldrin, DDT, toxaphene, malathion, cryolite and rotenone on his crop "and still had 11 days to go before harvest." A third example concerned a farmer who used some four times as much nicotine spray as directions specified because the stuff was old and he supposed it had lost its potency.

Another source of contamination that can send poison residues soaring is indiscriminate use of insecticides in retail markets. A New York doctor was recently in an exclusive food store when an employee began firing a DDT bomb all over the produce. The doctor wrote a letter of protest to the management. In reply he received an apology—along with the assurance that in the future the spraying would be withheld *until after the store was closed for the night.*

Still another threat is revealed in recent charges that newly developed pesticides which proved "too hot" for the American market are being shipped abroad to countries that have taken fewer precautions—or none—to control pesticides. How many of these "hot" compounds may return to America via contaminated food imports? In a parallel case involving preservatives, the chemical thiourea was banned in the United States after it was found to be highly toxic, but in 1956 it was found on oranges shipped into the United States from Mexico.

Still another source of contamination is from mass aerial sprays unleashed by the government. Pests hit from the air have included gypsy moths, fruit flies, mosquitoes, fire ants and grasshoppers. The intensive grasshopper offensive in Colorado and other western states in the summer of 1958 added untold amounts of poisons to those normally used on the oceans of wheat produced in the area.

In 1957 some three million highly populated acres in New York, New Jersey and Pennsylvania were soaked with three million pounds of DDT in an all-out assault to "eradicate" gypsy moths. In the wake of the spraying there were unnumbered dead animals, dead fish, dead birds, dead bees, damaged paint jobs on cars, food contaminated far in excess of legal limits, highly poisoned milk, outraged citizens, lawsuits—and live gypsy moths.

Robert Cushman Murphy, retired curator of birds at the Museum of Natural History in New York and an internationally famous naturalist, said the evidence builds up of "criminal negligence in damage to the natural environment and a threat to human health. . . . In all our history there is no more flagrant case of a bureaucratic attitude signifying 'The Public be damned!'" He called the $5,000,000 program of mass poisoning of man and his environment a gigantic boondoggle.

U. S. Department of Agriculture officials were taken to court by Mr. Murphy and other irate plaintiffs, who sought an injunction to prevent future sprayings. It was proved beyond question that in the sprayed area milk had been contaminated in direct violation of Federal law up to 14 ppm and forage was poisoned so the contamination would be continued for many months. Dr. Hayes himself testified that it would be impossible to conduct such a spraying without contaminating milk produced in the area. But because the plaintiffs could not produce a human corpse to prove that the spray was harmful to humans, the Federal judge ruled against the plaintiffs.

Government witnesses revealed an incredible ignorance about what the effects of the spray might be on man, wildlife or the environment. Two weeks before the spraying program started, another government agency had requested a Congressional appropriation to study the effects of such sprays. Even as government officials were admitting that virtually no research had been done to determine such effects, the USDA was starting an even more ambitious and deadly aerial spray program in the South—it blanketed 27,000,000 acres in nine southeastern states to try to eradicate the fire ant.

The poisons used were dieldrin and heptachlor at the rate of two pounds per acre. Both substances have a food tolerance of 0.1 ppm. Heptachlor is said to be ten to fifteen times as poisonous as DDT, and dieldrin is considered about twenty times more toxic. John H. Baker, former president of the Audubon Society, warned that "insecticide hazards may well rank in seriousness of adverse effects with the dangers of radioactive fallout." He said "the use of toxic chemicals for the purpose of protecting agricultural and forest crops has now skyrocketed to the point where cumulative secondary poisoning of human beings and wildlife, which already exists to some extent, may become catastrophic."

After making its own ten-month investigation of the program, the Audubon Society said it resulted in "an alarming prompt kill of many species of wildlife," and dead livestock; it was begun without adequate information about the immediate or chronic effects of the poisons on people, crops, fire ants, livestock, wildlife, soil organisms or other life forms, and it upset the entire balance of nature within the sprayed area.

Further, charged the usually conservative Audubon Society, reports about the serious damage the ants allegedly caused to crops, livestock, wildlife and people were erroneous; and the ant, in fact, had a beneficial effect by eating harmful insects. The Society accused the USDA of making untrue and misleading statements for propaganda purposes to get huge appropriations from Congress.

While these massive chemical toxic storms have swept the earth, wiping out lower forms of life and poisoning the food supply, human beings have been subjected to additional doses of insecticides in the course of their everyday life. DDT and other insecticides fairly drench hotels, motels, trains, theaters, golf courses, gardens, hospitals, public buildings, homes, public parks, textiles, dry-cleaning fluids, even the public highways, leaving toxic vapors that remain for weeks and months, to be sucked into the lungs and to add to the toxic burden of the body.

These direct and indirect sources of poison have made a farce of efforts to regulate the poison intake of humans. The Miller Act, concerned only with pesticides ingested in foods, offers phantom protection at best.

To enforce its tolerances and patrol its realm of some 96,000 food and drug installations, the FDA has only about 300 inspectors, which enables it to send inspectors to visit each plant only about once every five years. Further, the FDA is responsible only for foods passing from one state to another. Most states do not have separate laws setting tolerances but leave the job of food protection up to the FDA. This means that in most states there is little or no supervision of foods not in interstate commerce. Some states—especially in the South—make virtually no provisions for enforcement of food laws, and practically none have the facilities to do their own testing.

(3)

Not only do pesticides threaten the health and lives of humans, but there is increasing evidence that they have failed in their basic bug-killing mission. Former Secretary of Agriculture Charles F. Brannan noted in the *1952 Yearbook of Agriculture* that the problem caused by insects seems to be bigger than ever. "We have more insect pests although we have better insecticides and better ways to fight them," he said.

The pest problem becomes increasingly acute because insects build up resistance to the newer pesticides—one problem that never rose with the pre-World War II insecticides. Some flies now can take, without adverse effects, a thousand times the dose of DDT that killed their ancestors. In 1956 the World Health Organization stated that there were thirty-six pests of public health importance with insecticide resistance, compared to one in 1946.

Warning about the "most alarming" increase in the number of resistant insects, the World Health Organization said: "The world may soon face an emergency because the resistance problem is intensifying day by day." Dr. Lehman of the FDA pointed out that, as the insects get more immune to the various poisons, "we have to continue making the poisons stronger."

Among the arsenal of progressively more powerful poisons are the systemic insecticides. These are made of the organic phosphates which are so fantastically potent that a single ounce in a thousand gallons of water can rid an acre of pests. One manufacturer of these compounds warns that after application workers should keep out of the treated fields for thirty days unless wearing protective clothes and masks—a warning that prompted Dr. Biskind to ask what happens to birds and other wildlife that can't read.

The technique applying the systemics calls for soaking the seeds of food plants in the poison so they absorb the stuff and it spreads through the entire plant as it grows; then when insects suck on the foliage they are killed; the plants thus are said to "bite back." Theoretically the plant is supposed to convert the poison into a nontoxic substance after a period of time, but it is not known what new chemicals the poison actually does break down into. The *Farm Journal* warned about one of these compounds that it "is short-lived, but when you put it on, it's strong enough to kill humans and animals, so be sure to follow the precautions on the label."

The primary drawback to all insecticides, other than their toxic effect on man, is that they disrupt what naturalists call the balance of nature. All living things in this world exist together in a series of interrelated balances, checks and counterchecks, just as the moon and the stars and the tides and the winds and the seasons exist in a profound harmony beyond man's understanding. Nature preserves this biological balance by having different forms of life prey on others. When poisons are used to kill some forms of life, the natural delicate balance is upset.

In some cases insects that were of no consequence have, as a result of sprayings, assumed serious economic importance. Typical of the kind of disastrous chain reaction that can be touched off when such a biological balance is upset is what happened when DDT began to kill off the natural predators that used to control mites. Mites were formerly of little economic importance, but after repeated DDT sprays destroyed their natural enemies, they themselves became a serious problem. To keep mites in check, a pesticide called Aramite was developed. This compound holds such disastrous implications for human health and life that it is dealt with separately in the following chapter.

Many naturalists feel that the only real solution to the pest problem must rest on a base of what is called biological warfare—introducing and encouraging natural enemies of pests to fight them; this would include insects, birds, viruses and fungus diseases. But, as G. C. Ullyett, a Canadian biologist, pointed out, entomologists have ceased to be biologists and, in the majority of cases have become, in effect, mere testers of poisons or insecticide salesmen. Dr. Cox said that they have become chemical specialists. They have tried to apply a chemical solution to a biological problem.

Instead of solving the bug problem, it has been pointed out, pesticides have only intensified and perpetuated it. They have wiped out astronomical numbers of beneficial insects, birds and other natural enemies of harmful insects. At the same time the pests have become poison-resistant.

This has left man in an unfortunate position; he has killed vast numbers of his allies, surrounded himself with indestructible enemies, and, in his frenzied effort to escape this trap he got himself into, he is gradually poisoning himself to death with ever more potent chemicals. The more desperate his plight becomes, the more feverishly he plunges ahead with single-minded determination to create an antiseptic world, he is deaf to logic, blind to the evidence of his folly, smothering all opposition in new clouds of stronger poisons.

Continuance in the present direction inevitably must end in disaster. There is now too much vested interest in error for government officials to admit their mistake and back down; the only alternative is to keep plunging ahead with stronger and stronger poisons. As pointed out, the antidote for one poison is more poison.

One entomologist was moved to ask if man, in frustration at the failure of all his efforts to wipe out every form of life that isn't sympathetic to him, hadn't perhaps lost his sense of judgment.

But all appeals to reason are drowned out by a chorus of government and chemical propagandists predicting that we would all starve to death and insects would take over the world if it were not for sprays. In the frenzied effort to increase the sale of pesticides, no opposition is tolerated; those who suggest other ways to combat the pest menace feel the lash of ridicule and scorn.

One of the few encouraging signs pointing toward a possible end of this poison mania was the withdrawal, in 1957, of the Thompson Chemical Corporation of St. Louis from the manufacture of DDT. William Thompson, the firm's president, stated that the ingestion "of presently employed insecticide residue by humans and other warm-blooded animals is a correlative problem of a *highly serious* [Mr. Thompson's emphasis] nature. The industrial hazards inherent in the indiscriminate wide-scale application of chemicals of such highly toxic nature also causes concern."

Mr. Thompson said that continued use of present agricultural insecticides could deal a damaging blow to the nation's farm economy. He warned that the use of nonselective poisons—those that kill friend and foe alike—is upsetting the balance of predator-parasite insects and "could easily cause heretofore unimportant insects to increase to the status of economic pests."

He pointed out that the effectiveness of the poisons against many pests was at best only temporary, and the whole problem was "becoming serious, economically very serious." He said his decision to quit the production and sale of DDT insecticides was based on a twelve-year study of their effects. But the immediate decision followed an inspection trip he made through farm country. In some areas in the South, he said, the resistance problem was so bad that several farmers were forced out of business and were compelled to turn their farms into grass in an effort to restore them.

And what was the reply of other pesticide manufacturers to Mr. Thompson's commendable action? A promised 284 per cent increase in pesticide sales by 1975—a bold announcement that the American diet will become progressively more toxic.

No one can say with certainty what the ultimate outcome of this progressive poisonous onslaught will be on human beings. A frightening possibility is suggested by an incident recalled by Dr. Mobbs. An eighteen-year-old North Carolina boy who worked in a pesticide-manufacturing plant was, in the course of his job, accidentally doused with toxaphene, one of DDT's kin.

Dr. Mobbs said: "He had won an award three weeks before as the outstanding athlete in the local high school. This boy developed virus-like symptoms, then anemia, hypertension, paralysis; and eight months following his original illness he died. . . . I think his case could be a preview of what could happen to some of the rest of us as we eat food that is contaminated by insecticides and gradually store it in our tissues."

And welded to that ominous forecast is this somber warning from Dr. Biskind: "Unfortunately, our culture is dominated by a simple-minded test-tube approach to biology. The laws of biology are intricate. All living beings on this earth exist in a system governed by an incredibly sensitive complex of checks and balances. We can learn the laws of nature and adapt them to our needs, or we can defy them and perish."

5

Cancer

and Human

Guinea Pigs

EVEN MORE SINISTER than the common insecticide poisons are a number of other compounds that force the American public to assume the role of guinea pig in a life-and-death experiment.

These are the carcinogens—cancer-causing substances that appear regularly in the nation's diet.

Almost a score of these chemicals are now in use, and several others have been eliminated after having been used for many years; a third group narrowly missed getting into foods only because, accidentally, their cancer-causing properties were discovered.

Because the law does not require testing food chemicals for carcinogenicity, it is unknown how many chemicals now appearing in foods may be capable of inducing cancer. Based on the statistical results of previous tests, scientists estimate that up to 25 per cent may be found to have this power.

An excellent illustration of the risk the public has been subjected to is the story of Aramite. Aramite is an acknowledged carcinogen that was permitted in the nation's food until it was recently banned by the Food and Drug Administration. Previously, the FDA had permitted its use even knowing that when rats ate the substance they developed cancers.

The fact that Aramite no longer can remain on food crops *in interstate commerce*—at least not legally—can be little comfort to people who have consumed it for several years. Because of the insidious nature of carcinogens, their effects may not be felt for twenty or thirty years—long after person who were once exposed to them have forgotten that they were formerly part of their diet.

The permitted use of Aramite dramatizes the approach many scientists, food technicians and government officials have toward the powerful chemicals employed in foods today, and the direction in which their sense of responsibility lies.

Aramite is a pesticide that bears the awesome chemical name beta-chloroethylbeta-(para-tertiary-butyl-phenoxy)-alpha-ethyl-methyl-sulfite. Specifically, it is a miticide, designed to kill mites. Aramite is under jurisdiction of the Miller Pesticide Act, which makes no provision for barring carcinogens from foods.

The Aramite story began in 1951 when the substance was developed by Naugatuck Chemical Division, United States Rubber Company, after a five-year developmental program that cost the company about $500,000.

There was a ready market for the product. Mites had become a serious problem for farmers. DDT and its fellow chemicals had killed off insects and birds that normally kept mites under control by eating them. The United States Department of Agriculture referred to the problem in its 1952 Yearbook of Agriculture, stating: "Never before have so many pests with such a wide range of habits and characteristics increased to injurious levels following application of any one material as has occurred following the use of DDT in apple spray programs."

Aramite was introduced on a limited test sales basis in 1951 and licensed for sale by the USDA in 1953. The following year, 1954, the Miller Act was passed by Congress, requiring the FDA to set a tolerance for each pesticide chemical used on raw agricultural crops.

In 1955, Naugatuck Chemical Company petitioned the FDA for a tolerance of 2 ppm residue of Aramite in or on certain fruits and vegetables, and a tolerance of 5 ppm on certain other raw agricultural commodities. The FDA does not safety-test every chemical used on food. To do so would require an army of scientists. The FDA's scientists did, however, test Aramite. They showed that rats fed the substance developed liver tumors. The FDA ruled that because of Aramite's carcinogenic nature it would grant a zero tolerance. This meant that no Aramite could remain on crops when they went to market.

The company withdrew its original application and submitted a new petition requesting a tolerance of 1 ppm; it also requested that the new petition be referred to an advisory committee of experts for study and recommendations—a procedure guaranteed by law.

A five-man committee of scientists, with one member absent who expressed his views by telephone, met in Washington on July 25, 1955, and after a morning and afternoon session issued three recommendations:

1. That a residue tolerance of 1 ppm be established for Aramite.

2. That the petitioner be advised to secure acceptable data on the chronic toxicity and carcinogenicity of Aramite at feeding levels between zero and 500 ppm in the mouse, rat and dog.

3. That the entire problem be reviewed by this or another committee in 1957, when further laboratory and other data would be available.

The committee recommended tests at zero to 500 ppm to find out if tumors would be produced at those levels, which were lower than those previously studied.

Congressman James J. Delaney later pointed out that "these surely were strange recommendations for scientists to make. They admitted that they felt that the data which they reviewed were insufficient and incomplete, and, in particular, suggested that more information be secured regarding the cancer-inducing propensities of Aramite. Yet, at the same time, they were perfectly willing that the public be exposed to a certain amount of it.

"It is all the more strange when we consider that the committee had before it reports of tests which showed that Aramite, when fed in certain concentrations, produced liver injury and malignant tumors in test animals." Once again, as so often in the past, the public became a guinea pig.

After its one-day session in which it recommended introducing a known carcinogen into the lives of 175,000,000 Americans, the committee dissolved, responsible to no one.

The FDA accepted the recommendations of the advisory committee, withdrew its previous ruling, and published a tolerance of 1 ppm for Aramite.

The publication made no mention of the cancer hazard.

A casual reader could only have learned that a tolerance had been set to permit sale of food containing what was just one more new chemical. Americans went on eating without realizing that someone in Washington had made a decision that could affect their lives and the lives of their children.

The significance of the Aramite decision was not lost upon cancer-researcher Dr. William E. Smith, now director of the Nutrition Research Laboratory at Fairleigh Dickinson University in Madison, New Jersey. In 1954, Dr. Smith served as chairman of the Symposium on Cancer Prevention at the Sixth International Cancer Congress in Sao Paulo. There, cancer experts from all over the world united to caution against use of carcinogenic chemicals in food, and their resolutions were forwarded to the FDA.

Dr. Smith called Congressman Delaney's attention to the fact that the Aramite decision established a precedent for granting "tolerances" to chemicals found to induce cancer. Dr. Smith pointed out that this precedent accommodated chemical manufacturers, but consumers were left to the mercy of somebody's guess that human beings might be less sensitive than test rats or mice. He suggested that our food law should expressly ban chemicals found to induce cancer.

Mr. Delaney paid tribute to Dr. Smith, reading into the Congressional Record that he "has had a brilliant research career and at various times has been on the staffs of the Harvard Medical School, the Rockefeller Institute for Medical Research, the Sloan-Kettering Institute for Cancer Research. . . . Dr. Smith is a dedicated scientist and a courageous man who has not hesitated to tangle with the industries in attacking practices which he has felt might endanger the public health."

Dr. Smith noted that the FDA's advisory committee's report showed that the committee had before it the following FDA interoffice memorandum:

"An experiment with any lower dosage level will not remove the onus that Aramite is a known carcinogen. The Division of Pharmacology cannot recommend that such a substance be used on human food."

Mr. Delaney, pointing to this communiqué, said that "at the time of its original ruling, the Food and Drug Administration had on hand evidence to show that Aramite, so far as the public health was concerned, was at least a suspicious product. Under the law, FDA was not required to accept the recommendations of the advisory committee and grant any tolerance to the chemical." Why, then, did the FDA's Commissioner ignore the advice of his division of pharmacology?

The FDA order permitted residue of Aramite on apples, blueberries, cantaloupes, celery, cucumbers, grapefruit, grapes, green beans, lemons, muskmelons, oranges, peaches, pears, plums, raspberries, strawberries, tomatoes, watermelons and sweet corn, but not forage thereof. Dr. Smith noted that "the last phrase indicates that members of Congress and their constituents can be obliged to eat this substance, but a cow cannot."

The decision to permit use of carcinogens in foods was at complete variance with a recommendation of outstanding cancer experts throughout the world. The International Union Against Cancer, made up of cancer specialists from fifty nations, has twice passed a resolution against the concept of establishing "tolerance" doses for carcinogens.

The IUAC has held that any substance found to induce cancer in any species of animal in *any dose* by any route of administration should not be approved for use in food.

Cancer experts explain that ordinary poisons are different from carcinogens. The latter produce changes in cells that are irreversible, and they have a cumulative effect that may result in cancer, sometimes in only a few months, sometimes in three or four decades.

Dr. Smith noted that single, small doses of carcinogens eaten by young individuals may have no immediate effect but could result in cancer much later in life. For this reason, he said, a carcinogen introduced into the nation's food supply tomorrow could, even though subsequently reconsidered and withdrawn, induce cancer many years later in individuals who consumed it.

As a rough example, it has been asserted that a man of fifty exposed to certain cancer-inducing substances would not normally live long enough to develop cancer. But a youth of eighteen, if exposed to the same influences, would probably die of cancer before he reached the age of fifty. And a child exposed to carcinogens from the day of birth might die of cancer before he even reached thirty.

Dr. Smith observed that "many scientists have induced cancer late in the life of animals by giving them when young a single dose that could be put on the head of a pin."

Dr. Francis E. Ray, head of the Cancer Research Laboratory, University of Florida, emphasized the danger to children by pointing out to a Congressional committee that "our experiments show that the younger the animal is when he is treated with a carcinogen, the more certain is the production of cancer. And so, we may be initiating cancer in the children of today by the addition of chemicals, and they are very susceptible to that. We will not know, perhaps for a generation or two, what the effects will be."

Repeated warnings have been given by cancer experts about the irreversible, cumulative effects of carcinogens. Dr. Ray explained that very small doses produce in the cell an irreversible change, and other small doses push that change along into active cancer. "The production of cancer by chemicals is considered to be divided into two stages—initiation and promotion." He said certain chemicals initiate changes in cells that will lie dormant for years, waiting for some promoting factor to push the dormant cancer cells into active cancer production.

Another warning about the danger of small amounts of cancer-causing properties comes from Professor Hermann Druckrey, chairman of the Food and Dye Commission of the German Research Council, and a member of the International Union Against Cancer. He pointed out that "we now know that cancer can be caused by chemical substances and is therefore clearly a toxicological problem."

When the dose of a carcinogen is reduced, he added, cancer develops more slowly, but if the dose is given early in life and the animal lives long enough, cancer eventually develops. Professor Druckrey said the carcinogenic action depends on *the sum of all single doses*, independent of the time over which they are distributed. A recovery factor does not operate, he emphasized, but the effects of small doses remain irreversible throughout life.

It has been shown that cancer can be induced by chemicals, physical injury and viruses. Dr. Smith explained that cancer cannot be thought of as a disease with one specific cause, but, rather, must be considered a type of cell or body reaction that is in the same category as an inflammation. "Everyone accepts the fact that a few bacteria can enter the body, multiply, and cause disease," he said. "We are concerned now with the fact that a few chemical molecules can enter the body, stimulate a body cell to multiply, and as that cell and its descendants go on multiplying we eventually get a mass of cells that we call cancer."

Despite repeated protests from Mr. Delaney and the warnings of Dr. Smith and other cancer experts, Aramite remained in the nation's diet for thirty months with the expressed approval of the FDA. It was not withdrawn until the spring of 1958, after the feeding tests recommended by the original advisory committee were concluded. The tests showed that Aramite would not only incite tumors in the livers of rats at lower dosages than originally studied but would also produce liver damage and malignant tumors in the liver and bile ducts of dogs.

FDA then ordered a zero tolerance for Aramite, and the U. S. Rubber Company promptly announced it would appeal the decision.

Mr. Delaney said FDA was to be commended on "admitting its mistake" and publishing the revised tolerance. "However," he added, "that does not remove the possible effect that Aramite may have had on the public during the period in which its residues have been permitted."

It is important to note that in lowering the tolerance of Aramite, the FDA indicated concern only over the chemical's potency and in no way revoked the principle it had supported in permitting people to eat cancer-causing chemicals in "safe doses."

Although the 1958 amendment to the pure food law bans carcinogens as chemical additives in interstate commerce, this proviso applies only to *additives*—not to pesticides and certain substances covered by the meat laws. The wording of the clause leaves loopholes big enough to drive a hearse through, as shall subsequently be brought out.

While residues of Aramite are not supposed to remain on foods that cross state lines, other carcinogens remain in the nation's food supply, at least for the moment, with the blessings of the FDA. All the objections that apply to Aramite also apply to them; Aramite merely received more publicity because it established the precedent of "safe doses" for carcinogens.

The concept of safe doses has been attacked by cancer experts on many fronts. Dr. Hueper, formerly of the National Cancer Institute, which, like the FDA, is part of the

Department of Health, Education and Welfare, has warned that in addition to the cumulative and irreversible nature of carcinogens, the differences between animals and people are so great that it is extremely hazardous to fix "safe doses" for humans on the basis of laboratory experiments; he also pointed out the vast differences among people in their response to carcinogens. No one can know exactly what his individual limit is, short of the actual appearance of a cancer.

Moreover, said Dr. Hueper, the general population is composed not only of normal individuals but also of a considerable proportion of metabolically defective and sick individuals who possess varying susceptibilities to carcinogens.

He also noted that present experimental methods of determining the relative carcinogenic potency of chemicals do not permit an adequate determination of factors necessary to establish an allegedly "safe dose" of a carcinogen.

Further, he continued, "the claim of an allegedly 'safe dose' of a dietary carcinogen disregards completely the important fact that the entire population becomes exposed during its lifetime to an appreciable number of known and unknown carcinogenic influences which are in part identical with those carcinogens recommended for inclusion in the general food supply, and which doubtlessly may accentuate the action of dietary carcinogens. . . . The inclusion of nonessential carcinogenic agents in any amounts in the daily diet would violate a fundamental principle of cancer control."

Finally, he said, "consideration should be given to the fact that the inclusion of carcinogenic additives in foodstuffs even in allegedly safe doses necessitates the institution of complicated and expensive control measures which would be paid for by the general taxpayer. Since the use of such carcinogenic chemical additives is not in the interest of the taxpayer, he should not be forced to provide funds for his own protection against hazardous and nonessential chemicals added to foods for the financial benefits of the manufacturer of the chemicals and the producers and processors of the foodstuffs.

Frequently the Government and apologists for industry excuse the use of carcinogens in foods by asserting that they have only a "weak" cancer-causing action. The advisory committee that recommended the use of Aramite in food noted the presence of two so-called weak carcinogens now in use as part of their justification for recommending a 1 ppm tolerance for Aramite. They referred to the pesticides DDT and methoxychlor.

Their report stated: ". . . concentrations of DDT at 200 ppm produce hepatic hypertrophy (excessive development of the liver from overuse) and have a 'minimal carcinogenic tendency'; a tolerance of 7 ppm of DDT is permitted on raw agricultural products designed for human consumption. Methoxychlor also produces similar effects and is permitted a tolerance above zero."

The hazard of "weak" carcinogens for cancer-susceptible people was spelled out by Dr. Smith. As an example, he said, take a chemical that induces cancer in, say, only 1 per cent of the exposed individuals. Such a compound would have nine chances out of ten for receiving a certificate of harmlessness when tested on a group of ten animals. If fifty animals were used, the odds would be even that its hazard would go undiscovered. Yet, if such a chemical were put into the general food supply of the nation, and human beings were one hundred times *less* sensitive to it than any animal, a one per cent toll could mean 15,000 cases of cancer.

Again, said Dr. Smith, consider the possibility that a dose is found that fails to induce cancer in one hundred animals of each of several species tested. What does this mean in groups too large for laboratory study? A single such substance in a dose eliciting only one cancer per 100,000 individuals can mean 1,500 unnecessary deaths in the population of the country.

Another warning about the risk of depending on animal tests to detect carcinogens was sounded recently by Dr. David D. Rutstein, head of the Department of Preventive Medicine at Harvard University. Taking to task persons who made light of the threat to health from the contaminated cranberries mentioned earlier here, and supporting the forthright stand taken by Arthur S. Flemming, Secretary of the Department of Health, Education and Welfare, in banning the tainted berries despite tremendous industry pressure, Dr. Rutstein stated:

"Animal testing is difficult to do because a substance may cause cancer in one species and be harmless to another. But one fact is clear: a substance is more likely to

produce cancer in man if in any dosage it produces cancer
in test animals.

"A further difficulty is introduced by the fact that large
amounts of the cancer-producing substance, the carcinogen, may be needed to produce its evil in one animal and
yet smaller amounts may produce the safe effect in another species." Dr. Rutstein added that consideration also
should be given to the fact that a carcinogen also may be
more harmful to humans than the animals on which it was
tested.

There are many other risks involved in the "safe dose"
concept because of the enormous number of variables that
influence human biology. This factor is so complex that a
substance may even be harmful to a person at one time in
his life and harmless at another.

The problem is further complicated, Dr. Hueper has
explained, because of the possibility that carcinogenic
chemicals may be formed from noncarcinogenic ones under
the influence of heat, and additives and contaminants
which were originally noncarcinogenic may interact with
each other or with food constituents and form, in the foodstuffs, new compounds possessing carcinogenic properties.
He said they may be produced under the influence of processing procedures or during the preparation of food in
the kitchen. "Plastics used as wrapping material, sausage
skins and coating material of fruits, cheese, meat, butter,
and can linings may carry a similar hazard," he said.

The eminent Government cancer researcher also warned
that merely because chemicals have been used for many
years without becoming suspect as carcinogens, this is no
guarantee that they are innocent. Butter Yellow, a dye
(never widely used in butter), was used in other foods
before it was found to be carcinogenic; Dulcin, a synthetic
sweetening agent, was in use more than fifty years before
it was found to be a carcinogen; the FDA report stated that
when the substance was fed to rats in amounts comparable
to those used in foods, it inhibited growth, adversely affected the blood and produced liver tumors. Other substances also have been found capable of causing cancer
after having been widely used in foods for many years.

Dr. Hueper said present investigative methods make it
difficult if not impossible to prove that cancerous effect in
members of the general population are due to any particu-

lar chemical additive "once this substance has been put to general use."

Appearing in foods at the present time, according to Dr. Hueper, there are more than a dozen categories of chemicals which he classifies as carcinogens "according to the widely accepted definition that carcinogens are agents which when applied under certain conditions to man or animals elicit the subsequent development of cancers which would not have appeared otherwise."

Among the chemicals which Dr. Hueper has named as carcinogens are:

● Certain food dyes—he lists the triphenylmethane dyes, Green No. 2, Blue No. 1 and Green No. 3; also the beta-naphthylamine azo benzol dyes, Yellow AB and Yellow OB, used to color butter, margarine and baked goods. These will be discussed in Chapter 6.

● The preservative 8-hydroxyquinoline, used in cottage cheese as a coagulator; also present in contraceptives and rectal suppositories. (Recently eliminated.)

● The synthetic mucilage carboxymethyl cellulose. The Food Protection Committee of the Food and Nutrition Board, National Academy of Sciences—National Research Council lists this compound as a stabilizer in processed cheese, French dressing, salad dressing, ice cream, sherbets, ices, ice milk, chocolate milk and chocolate-flavored beverages, pressure-dispensed whipped cream, sirups for frozen products and various frozen mixtures; also as a bodying agent in beverages and canned fruits sweetened with nonnutritive sweeteners.

● Arsenicals found in foodstuffs as pesticide residue and as an additive of animal feeds of poultry and livestock.

● Estrogenic chemicals used for promoting fattening of poultry and livestock.

● Chlorinated hydrocarbon pesticides, "especially Aramite" (since eliminated) and DDT present as residues in foodstuffs.

● Polycyclic aromatic hydrocarbons with carcinogenic properties contained in soot adherent to smoked goods or generated on foodstuffs by the application of excessive heat during roasting and grilling procedures.

● Wrapping and coating materials composed of polymerized carbon and silicon compounds.

● Paraffins and mineral oils if insufficiently refined and

employed for the coating of foodstuffs such as cheeses and
fruits and for the impregnation of food containers.

● Radioactive substances either attached to the surface of
foodstuffs from radioactive fallouts or entering plants and
animals through absorption from contaminated water and
soil.

● Potential carcinogenic contaminants: these may be introduced into foodstuffs if vegetables, fruits, fish, oysters
and livestock are grown on soil or in water polluted with
known carcinogens, such as arsenicals, selenium and polycyclic hydrocarbons contained in ship fuel oils, since these
chemicals may be taken up and stored by the vegetable
and animal matter growing in such contaminated media.

Selenium also has been used as a pesticide. Like Aramite, it was a miticide, and was used on citrus fruits, apples
and grapes from about 1933 until the early 1950s. Dr.
Lehman of the FDA testified before the Delaney Committee that "using very small amounts in the diet [of ani-
mals], we find about three parts per million will produce a
liver disease known as cirrhosis of the liver . . . The animals eventually developed cancer of the liver and the
amounts necessary are very small, down to three or four
parts per million."

He noted that selenium built up in the soil and could
migrate into the growing plant and eventually appear in
the fruit. Residues were rather high, he said, approaching
1 ppm on an unwashed apple.

"Selenium will penetrate the skin of an apple and appear in the pulp . . . Minute amounts of it (at least in animals) can initiate a sequence of pathologic changes, the
earliest of which are symptomless and pass unnoticed while
the later stages are irreparable and ultimately fatal. . . ."

What did the FDA do about this? Dr. Lehman said,
"We called this to the attention of the manufacturers of
Selocide and through a number of years we have had correspondence with them advising them against the use of
the product."

Despite this action, he said the product had continued
to be manufactured and used, and it was still being used
when he testified in 1950.

An FDA report stated that residues also appeared on the
skins of oranges sprayed with the substance and "washing
as ordinarily practiced removed little or none of the selenium. . . . It would probably have been impossible to estab-

lish that the quantities of selenium in or on these oranges was dangerous to health. It is also far from certain that the selenium absorbed by the tree from the contaminated soil and transported to oranges is 'added' within the meaning of section 402 (a) (2) of the Federal Food, Drug, and Cosmetic Act. Far greater levels of selenium are, of course, found in various crops grown on naturally seleniferous soils. . . ."

There is no indication that the Government ever tried to force the issue by banning the pesticide and makes the manufacturer fight to get it back. So the substance remained in use a dozen years, until given a zero tolerance under the Miller Act.

One of the biggest problems with carcinogens is that, unlike ordinary toxic chemicals, they usually do not produce warning symptoms of poisoning; yet subtle changes occur in the exposed cells, and cancer eventually develops. Dr. Hueper has cautioned that there is no relationship between the toxicity of a substance and its ability to produce cancer. In fact, he said, "only occasionally have chronic toxicity tests revealed in the screening of chemicals for toxic qualities their carcinogenic character. As a rule, the minimal carcinogenic dose is distinctly lower than the minimal chronic toxic dose."

This has an ominous meaning for man because the cancer-causing properties of a chemical can easily be missed in ordinary toxicity-screening tests. The ease with which a carcinogen might get on the market was illustrated by Dr. Hueper when questioned by Vincent A. Kleinfeld, chief counsel to the Delaney Committee:

Q. Was the discovery that acetylaminofluorene [a proposed pesticide] produced cancer an incidental or accidental one, or was an attempt being made to determine the fact?

A. The authors made it quite clear in their communication that it was accidental.

Q. In what part of the organs of the body did it produce cancer?

A. It would produce cancer of the liver, the stomach, the breast, the thyroid, the pelvis, the kidney, the bladder, the female genital tract, the external auditory canal and occasionally the brain.

Q. After the discovery that this proposed insecticide did produce cancer it was discarded for that use, was it not?

A. That is right. It was never used for that purpose.

Q. If the fact that it did produce cancer had not been ascertained in the accidental fashion which you mentioned, it might now be used as an insecticide; is that correct?

A. Doubtlessly it would have been.

Q. After the discovery was made with respect to acetyl-aminofluorene, did you know whether a general program was started by anyone to test other insecticides then in use for their possible tumor-producing or cancer-producing properties?

A. Not that I am aware of.

Despite the obvious disadvantages the guinea-pig approach holds for the public, it has been stoutly defended by some scientists. An insight into their thinking is afforded by the testimony of W. M. Hoskins, professor of entomology at the University of California Agricultural Experiment Station. He said he probably made the first DDT produced in California and "it was unbelievably toxic to flies, ants, and other common insects . . . and the persistent effects were beyond our previous experience."

He pointed out that long-term tests for chronic effects of chemicals often are more important than short-term tests for acute toxicity. Since man is the species whose well-being is of most concern in this matter, he said, only by long continued and extensive tests on humans can really unchallengeable data on toxicity be obtained.

"How can this be done?" he said. "It is already being done in an unplanned way with every new agricultural chemical."

Under questioning by the startled Delaney Committee, he was asked if that couldn't be "fairly called the human guinea pig approach."

A. I presume so.

Q. How do you think these human guinea pigs feel about it?

A. Why, I believe they would object. . . . No drug is ever given a clean bill of healthonthebasis of animal testing. It is taken from animal quotas into the clinic and tried on humans. Many don't know they are being used as guinea pigs.

Q. I imagine these humans are asked whether or not it should be used.

A. They don't know whether they are in the control or test group.

Q. Do they not consent to the experiment?
A. Yes.
Q. Do you not think that is important?
A. Not especially.

It must be presumed that Mr. Hoskins speaks for himself as an individual, and his views can be binding on no other person or institution. The FDA has insisted that its position is that no person is expendable under the food laws. This is a noble creed, but one that seems to ring somewhat hollow when it is realized that the public's margin of safety in the matter of chemical carcinogens in foods is an assurance based on the tenuous thread of the definition of what constitutes a carcinogen.

6

Dyes—

the "Innocent"

Carcinogens

(1)

WHEN IS A CARCINOGEN not a carcinogen?
The Food and Drug Administration repeatedly has asserted there are no cancer-causing chemicals in the nation's food supply.

In a speech before Housewives United, November 30, 1956, Wallace F. Janssen, then assistant to the FDA commissioner, stated: ". . . it is . . . a fact that we do not know of evidence that there is any chemical or food color in use in this country today that is carcinogenic, and . . . if we had any such evidence we could, of course, take appropriate action under the Federal Food, Drug, and Cosmetic Act."

On August 7, 1957, Dr. Hueper told the House Subcommittee on Health and Science: "It is . . . a well established fact that an appreciable and growing number of chemicals, of which a few are known to enter the human food supply, are capable of causing and do cause cancers in man under proper conditions of exposure."

Who is telling the truth?

The answer is tricky, and a bit complex, but it illustrates the chemical "brinksmanship" the American people are being subjected to in the matter of chemical additives. The problem is best illustrated by the way dyes are used in the nation's diet.

These compounds are unique among additives because not even their strongest supporters can claim they are useful to anyone—except to their manufacturers and to food processors. Against this questionable advantage, the dyes make it possible for the public to be deceived and cheated by masking inferior products and creating nutritional illusions, and they are among the most poisonous chemicals that go into foods.

A majority of the synthetic dyes approved for use in foods have been shown to cause cancer in animals; among them are chemical cousins to highly potent cancer-causing substances that actually have caused cancer in man. Some dyes, though not carcinogenic, are harmful to animals, even in tiny doses; on different occasions large numbers of children have been made violently sick from eating artificially colored foods.

America leads the world in using synthetic dyes to color food. From 1955 to 1965 the use of these dyes in the United States shot up from 1.69 million pounds to 2.6 million pounds.

A synthetic dye is one which is put together by man. It is mixed in a test tube out of artificial compounds. The synthetic dyes certified for use by the FDA are coal-tar products.

Dyes appear in everything from sweet potatoes to frankfurters. They are used in some processed breakfast cereals and in flavored straws designed to beguile children into drinking their milk. In recent years dyes have even been used as coloring matter in many household detergents; these dyes come from a chemical family that has produced cancers in rats.

The use of dyes has shot up in recent years with the greater consumption of ready-prepared, canned, bottled and packaged foodstuffs, which are shipped great distances and stored and stocked for months.

Most products must state on their labels if dyes are present, but ice cream—in which dyes are almost universally used—was granted an exemption under the 1938 Pure Food Law.

The dyes themselves have an interesting history. For many years there were vast numbers in extensive use without having been tested. Then it was decided to limit the number, test the selected ones carefully and use in foods only those found to be harmless.

Under the 1938 Food, Drug, and Cosmetic Act, nineteen dyes were certified. Since then eight have been decertified, leaving eleven approved for use in foods.

When a dye is certified, it means that it is "pure." Mr. Janssen has pointed out that "under the law, the colors are supposed to be certified as completely safe—so that no matter how much color is used it would not be harmful. No legal action is possible against anyone for using an excessive amount of a certified color."

Despite this legal assurance, Dr. Arthur A. Nelson of the FDA reported in 1957 that ten out of thirteen certified dyes tested—all in wide use—had produced cancers in rats when injected under the skin.

Dr. Nelson would not estimate how much color the average person gets in his daily food, but science writer Earl Ubell said that from Dr. Nelson's figures "it was estimated that some must get twice as much by mouth as some of the rats got under the skin. . . ."

The oil-soluble colors reportedly were "in general so poisonous when injected under the skin that the mice died before the scientists had a chance to see if cancer developed in many cases. Only reduced doses brought out the cancer-producing proclivities of two of the colors."

The International Union Against Cancer said that not one dye had been proved safe for use in food. The cancer experts listed twenty-nine food dyes as "unsuitable or potentially dangerous, which should not be added to food or drink for man or animals." The list included nine dyes that were commonly used in foods in the United States. Despite the warning, only two of the colors subsequently have been taken off the government's "approved" list.

The nine U. S. certified dyes listed and the foods they appear in are:

ORANGE No. 1—Fish pastes, carbonated beverages, jellies, confectionery, custards, blanc-mange powder, biscuits, cakes, ice cream, cordials, cordial extracts and crystals, ice cream toppings, milk bar sirups, sausage casings, puddings, frozen desserts, solutions for home use, soft drinks. (Now decertified)

ORANGE No. 2—Cheese, margarine, candies, edible fats, external coloring of oranges. (Now decertified)

YELLOW No. 1—Confectionery, macaroni, spaghetti, other pastas, baked goods, beverages.

YELLOW No. 3 (Yellow AB)—Edible fats, margarine, butter, cakes, biscuits, candy.

YELLOW No. 4 (Yellow OB)—Same as Yellow No. 3.

GREEN No. 1—Cordials, jellies, soft drinks, candy, bakery goods, frozen desserts.

GREEN No. 2—Candies, essences, cordials, biscuits, cake, jellies, maraschino cherries, frozen desserts.

GREEN No. 3—Candies, jellies, desserts, bakery products.

BLUE No. 1—Icings, cordials, cordial extracts and crystals, jellies, ice cream, ice-cream toppings, milk bar sirups, candies, cake decorations, frozen desserts, soft drinks, puddings, bakery goods, solutions for home use.

Subsequently the government withdrew approval of several of these dyes—Orange No. 1, Orange No. 2, Yellow No. 1, Yellow No. 3, Yellow No. 4 and Green No. 1. But because of the nature of carcinogens, no one can give assurance that many years from now, long after it has been forgotten that they ever appeared in foods, they won't cause cancer in someone who ate them.

Two of the dyes whose cancer hazard has been repeatedly emphasized are Yellow AB and Yellow OB, widely used to color butter and margarine. They are made from a potent chemical called beta-naphthylamine. In explaining the treachery of carcinogens, as compared with ordinary poisons, Dr. Hueper said that beta-naphthylamine possesses a "remarkably low toxicity while being one of the most carcinogenic substances known."

In fact, he said, beta-naphthylamine had such a high cancer hazard that most of the large chemical manufacturers stopped its production because it had caused bladder cancer in from 50 to 100 per cent of the exposed workers.

It long has been feared that when dyes containing beta-naphthylamine are ingested and broken down in the body, the carcinogenic capacity is restored to the chemical. Dr. Hueper and Dr. Ray, cancer expert of the University of

Florida, have expressed that belief, based on animal experiments. Dr. Hueper said that when Yellow AB and Yellow OB were fed to rats at high levels, some of the animals developed liver cancer.

In addition to this evidence, the FDA, in 1953, reported that Blue No. 1, Green No. 2 and Green No. 3 had caused cancers when repeatedly injected under the skins of animals.

An advisory committee from the National Academy of Sciences said, in 1956, that with the FDA's present facilities and personnel it didn't see how the work necessary to obtain adequate toxicity data on all the dyes could be completed by the FDA within a twenty-five-year period.

The committee observed that some dyes produced cancer when painted on the skin of rats but had no apparent effect when taken internally, and some which produced cancer when swallowed appeared harmless when painted on the skin.

It added: "Demonstration that a dye is harmless when administered by one route cannot be construed as indicating that it is harmless when administered by any other route."

This is the key to understanding the conflict between Dr. Hueper and the FDA over whether there are carcinogens in the diet. It's a question of definition.

Dr. Hueper subscribes to the definition of the International Union Against Cancer, which holds that a carcinogen is a chemical that causes cancer in any living organism, regardless of how it is administered.

The official IUAC definition states: "A carcinogen is a chemical, physical or animate agent which is capable of producing cancers in any organ or tissue of any species following exposure to it in any dose and physiochemical state and when given by any route either once or repeatedly."

Dr. Lehman and Dr. Nelson of the FDA, however, at the Rome Cancer Conference, said they did not accept this definition of a carcinogen, although they admitted that if it were accepted it would apply to some chemicals presently used in foods. They further hold that the mere fact that a chemical would cause cancer when injected under the skin should not rule out its use if the chemical was normally taken by mouth.

The assumption that a chemical which apparently starts

cancer only when injected under the skin is safe to eat is based on the observation that some dyes are not readily absorbed in the intestinal tract.

Dr. Hueper has pointed out, however, that some dyes which ordinarily are not absorbed in the intestinal tract may be absorbed if taken along with detergents, which appear in foods as additives and unintentional contaminants. If such dyes have started cancers when injected under the skin, he says, they also may start cancers when absorbed through the intestinal tract. In such cases detergents may act as co-carcinogens or cancer promoters, he explained.

A co-carcinogen will not start a cancer by itself but enhances the cancer-causing power of other chemicals. Co-carcinogens need not be administered at the same time as carcinogens but can be applied months later and still produce cancers. Dr. Ray pointed out that some chemicals that cannot be shown to cause cancer may trigger the ailment in people who have an inherited or unsuspected tendency to develop cancers.

Cancer researchers also have noted that carcinogens may start cancers even when not absorbed in the intestinal tract but merely by contact. The length of exposure to unabsorbed carcinogens—such as some of the certified food dyes—may depend on a person's state of health, diet, how long the food remains in the digestive tract and many other factors over which the average individual has little or no control.

The cumulative, irreversible effects of carcinogens always should be borne in mind; once they appear in foods, the damage cannot be undone by removing them. For example, said Dr. Smith, "O-tolylazo-2-naphthol (Orange No. 2), a dye long thought safe and used by the thousands of pounds annually in food in the United States, has been found in recent years (by British researchers) to induce intestinal polyps and cancer when fed to animals. . . . Last year's [1956] discontinuation of the use of this dye offers no assurance that it will not cause cancer years later in children who have already eaten it. . . ."

The threat to children is repeatedly stressed because of the number of years they have ahead of them after they get their dose. Dr. Hueper has warned that the tissues of the young are as susceptible to carcinogens "if not more so, than those of the old." He said "it is likely" that at least some of the cancers observed at birth or in infants and children can be attributed to the mother's exposure to carcinogens before or during pregnancy and while she is nursing. He said experiments have shown that carcinogens penetrate the placental barrier to the fetus, and other findings suggest that they can be excreted in the mother's milk. Dr. Hueper also noted that when pregnant rats were injected with certain dyes their offspring were born with "congenital anomalies" such as clubfoot, heart and genitourinary ailments, no eyes, displaced hind limbs and other defects.

The danger carcinogens in foods pose to children is dramatized by the increasing number of cancers observed in infants and children. A few decades ago they were a medical rarity; now they are commonplace. This cannot be explained away by the usual excuse of alleged better reporting, better diagnostic methods, etc.; it is a real increase. Only recently a special 280-bed hospital was dedicated in Boston for the treatment of cancer in children, and already it is overflowing with patients. Cancer takes a greater number of lives among children aged four to fourteen, in the United States, than any other disease (one out of every four deaths from disease in this age bracket). *Among children, deaths caused by cancer are nearly 50 per cent greater than a decade ago; half of these deaths are due to leukemia.*

Sir MacFarlane Burnet, director of the Royal Melbourne Hospital in Australia, a Nobel Prize Winner in 1960, pointed out that "in all countries the recorded deaths from leukemia at all ages are rising in approximately logarithmic fashion, the incidence doubling in fifteen to twenty-five years, or rising at a rate of 4 per cent or 5 per cent per annum.

"To a slight extent this may be due to improved diagnosis and reporting of cases but the increase has been steady. . . . Some of it is undoubtedly due to the fact that the proportion of older people has been steadily increasing, but when this is allowed for, the increase is still striking at all ages."

He said, "The findings in childhood are of particular interest. In the United States, the United Kingdom, and Australia, the incidence curve has developed a peak in the three-four year age bracket. . . . No other disease shows this type of age incidence of death."

Another researcher sees the increasing incidence of leukemia as a warning that certain foreign agents may be causing irreparable genetic changes in people. Dr. M. Burnet, writing in the *South African Practitioner* and quoted in the *Journal of the American Medical Association* (April 11, 1959), issued this warning relative to the "production of chemical substances outside biologic experience."

It is disquieting, he stated, and "it raises the lurking fear that anything that is increasing the incidence of leukemia may also be breaking through the other barriers that in the past have protected the germ cells from mutagens. I think one would be wise to pay even more attention to leukemia than its intrinsic interest and lethality demand just because it is possibly the best indicator one can have of the last and greatest danger to civilization, active and avoidable genetic deterioration. . . . The exposure to physical and chemical mutagens should be reduced as much as possible . . . . On the chemical side a beginning has hardly been made."

The difficulty of trying to trace any specific cancer-causing agent in the public at large has been pointed out by researchers because of the creeping treachery of these compounds. Dr. Ray noted that "very small amounts, not sufficient to affect the general health, are sufficient to initiate cancerous growth." Dr. Smith observed that powerful carcinogens could be distributed to the general population in large quantities for many years before their effects would take place. He added that detection of carcinogenic effects of any one of the many chemicals in use—including the dyes—would be extremely difficult to pinpoint, and could be recognized "only after multiple thousands of cases of cancer had occurred to provide statistical samples of the necessary size."

Even as the incidence of cancer continues to rise among the general population, these 1,500,000 pounds of dyes still continue to be produced and consumed annually on the biologically shaky premise that man is not a mouse and he eats his carcinogens instead of injecting them under his skin. Meanwhile, the tests go on.

Dr. Smith said consumers have been required to wait several decades for decisions by juries of test rats and dogs as to the safety of dyes which these consumers have eaten in their food for some twenty years; during that time half a million pounds of two dyes were certified for use in food although they were primarily composed of beta-naphthylamine, a molecular compound known to cause cancer of the bladder in factory workers who make it.

In 1953, alone, he continued, "100,000 pounds of dyestuffs known to cause cancer in animals were approved by the United States Food and Drug Administration for use in foodstuffs to be consumed by human beings." This, he said, was "the same as dumping 50 tons of cancer-causing substances down the gullet of the American people."

(2)

Apart from the question of the cancer hazard from many food dyes is the problem of their toxicity. It is ironical to note that when the dyes were certified in 1938, the tests that demonstrated their "harmlessness in any amount used" obviously were then considered adequate to protect the safety of the American people. This proof of harmlessness turned out to be unwarranted optimism, as has happened so often in the history of food additives.

In 1955, a few months after 200 children were made ill from eating dyed popcorn at a Christmas party, the FDA announced decertification of the three dyes involved: Red No. 32, Orange 1 and Orange 2. In announcing the ban, the FDA told food and beverage manufacturers they could legally use up previously certified stocks of the colors, but cautioned them that foods containing excessive quantities of these colors "can cause illness to consumers."

The law protecting the manufacturers was stressed to protect them from financial loss, but the law guaranteeing the safety of the dyes when used in any amount was ignored, leaving the public to take the risk.

How slowly the law grinds in getting a harmful chemical out of the diet is indicated by the timetable that governed the decertification proceedings. The original "notice of hearing" was published in the Federal Register on December 19, 1953, but the ban didn't go into effect until February 15, 1956. All that time the public continued to eat substances that had been found to be too poisonous for human consumption, even by the government's generous allowances.

The list of damages caused in animals by the three dyes reads like a catalogue of biological horrors—and the amounts used were small. The dyes caused everything from loss of appetite to death.

The report stated in part:

> When FD&C Red No. 32 was fed to rats at a level of 2.0 per cent of the diet, all the rats died within a week. At a 1.0 per cent level, death occurred within 12 days. At 0.5 per cent, most of the rats died within 26 days. At 0.25 per cent approximately half of the rats died within 3 months. All the rats showed marked growth retardation and anemia. Autopsy revealed moderate to marked liver damage. Similar but less severe results were obtained with rats on a diet containing 0.1 per cent of FD&C Red No. 32. In addition to liver damage, however, autopsy also revealed enlargement of the right side of the heart in this latter group. Subcutaneous injection of approximately 10 milligrams per week caused death within 8 weeks to most rats on the experiment. These rats exhibited anemia, hemorrhage, and reduction in the size of the liver. Dogs taking 100 milligrams per kilogram of body weight per day showed moderate weight loss. A level of 0.2 per cent of FD&C Red No. 32 in the diet of dogs caused rapid deterioration and weight loss and sporadic diarrhea, moderate atrophy of vital organs, and muscular dystrophy; 0.01 per cent in the diet caused weight loss and the death of one out of four dogs. A single oral dose gave diarrhea in the majority of the dogs tested. . . .

An idea of the small amounts of dye necessary to bring about these adverse effects may be had by pointing out that 100 milligrams weighs about the same as two postage stamps.

The report also reveals that the results of tests of Orange No. 1 were similar to those of Red No. 32. Red No. 32 had been used to color cheese, edible fats, oils, candy, bakery goods and the skins of oranges.*

When the FDA ordered the ban on Oranges 1 and 2 and Red No. 32, industry vigorously countered by insisting the dyes were not harmful to human beings when used in small amounts and claimed that without them certain in-

---

*Red No. 32 subsequently was outlawed as a dye for oranges and replaced by Red No. 2 which also is of questionable toxicity.

dustries would be ruined. Florida and Texas orange growers insisted that if they waited for their fruit to turn orange it would be overripe and ruined. An industry spokesman said that more than half the Florida orange crops was run through a dye bath to give green oranges an orange color.

The hearing disclosed that canned and frozen orange juice often contain dye; this was said to come from previously colored "packing house rejects" that were bought by the freezing and canning industry.

When the Government first tried to ban the use of Red 32 to dye oranges, industry spokesmen argued that the dye is just in the peel, which usually is discarded, although it was conceded that orange peels are used in many ways: as candied orange peel, marmalade, and in drinks such as orangeade and old-fashioneds, and also, extensively in baking cakes and icings.

Another use for orange peel, noted by Dr. Clive McCay, was in controlling diarrhea in babies. In such use, he said, peels "might be ingested by babies for a long time period and the added chemical (artificial dye) might be very important."

Although industry spokesmen claimed children throw away the peel when eating an orange, a state health official who discussed this subject in connection with another matter gave a different picture. Dr. Geoffrey Martin, of the Kansas State Board of Health, in a government publication, commented on a case involving preservatives on fruit:

"Children, and particularly young children, are a special group in the population whose eating habits are different. In eating an orange, for example, a child frequently goes about it in such a way that he scrapes off and consumes the outer layer of the peel—together with the chemicals that have been added to it. Children are also unmoderate eaters; a child may happily consume rather large numbers of oranges each day in this way while adults would generally eat one or two. Children are less apt than adults to wash and clean an orange before eating it. . . ."

He said that whatever harm there was in the chemicals present "would probably be realized in children." At the same time, he continued, "children, as growing organisms, are obviously variable in weight, and in addition—because they are growing—may handle synthetic chemical substances in a manner different from that of adults. . . ."

Along with the dye in an orange peel, there may be various preservatives. Oranges and other fruits, such as apples, lemons and limes, are likely to be waxed with a coal-tar-derivative paraffin (highly suspect as a carcinogenic substance); and they also may be contaminated with phenolic compounds and other preservatives previously mentioned—questionable substances which have cumulative tendencies and are believed to interfere with metabolic processes that are essential to health. All of these chemicals could be consumed in the skin of an orange.

Despite the recognized toxicity of several of the dyes now used in foods it appears certain that Congress, with the blessing of the FDA, will set tolerance levels so that they can be used in small amounts.

In anticipation that such tolerances may be granted to all or some of the coal-tar dyes, a comment by Dr. G. Martin is pertinent. Dr. Martin addressed himself to what he described as "the so-called absolute protection afforded by FDA tolerances." Noting that certain chemical substances in use had been tested by the FDA and found to be safe for human consumption, he said:

"In our opinion, this 'protection' is almost wholly illusory. If a substance is found to be 'safe,' the safety is only in terms of present knowledge and tests and may be completely upset by better knowledge and further tests, and . . . in general synthetic chemicals may only be considered as safe when used within established tolerances—and the FDA does not have the money or the people to give any guaranty to the public that the limits of tolerance are being observed by commercial processors.

"There are numerous examples which will be known to you of synthetic chemicals which have been considered safe for human consumption, and then found to be unsafe and reduced to zero tolerances. It is also well known to you, I am sure, that the job of policing tolerances calls for a large staff which the FDA has not had, does not have, and perhaps never will have."

(3)

The risk the public is forced to assume by ingesting the synthetic dyes is underlined by the irony that it also may be cheated nutritionally and financially by the use of these substances in foods.

Dyes have been used in baked goods to suggest the presence of missing ingredients. *Consumers' Research* observed that "if the consumer buys dyed store cake on the assumption that the yellow means the cake contains egg yolk, he is being cheated. for very often bright, attractive color indicates nothing except the presence of a coal-tar dye of uncertain safety that makes a nutritionally skimped food resemble a food of better quality." The Delaney Committee report stated that "there are indications that the use of artificial coloring matter is increased when quantities of whole eggs or egg yolks are reduced in commercial cake formulas."

Another instance of using dye to deceive the consumer is the addition of color to make pale winter butter look like summer butter, which is more nutritious.

But dye is not the only chemical used to mask deficiencies in butter When butter is stored a long time or shipped great distances it must be washed to preserve it. The long storage periods of our great butter surpluses is a well-known fact. Washing removes the aroma of butter and is believed to destroy its vitamin A. So, before the butter is used, a dash of the chemical diacetyl is added. Diacetyl has been described as "a very reactive substance . . . [that] exerts a definite oxidizing action on fats." The chemical restores the missing aroma but, unfortunately, not the missing vitamin A.

The handbook of the Food Protection Committee of the National Academy of Sciences lists diacetyl as an additive that is being used today in butter, margarine, buttermilk, cottage cheese and baked goods.

A similar issue of deception is posed by the use of nitrated flour, which has a yellow cast, to suggest the appearance of eggs. The effect is achieved by treating the flour with nitric acid, a very poisonous substance which the FDA says has not been proved safe. Nitrated flour is illegal in standardized products, such as bread, for which the ingredients that can be used are specified, but it may be employed without restriction in other baked goods.

These substances, like the dyes, pose not only serious health problems but also the moral issues that have been pondered by scientists who are concerned about the expanding adulteration and nutritional deterioration of the food supply, not only in this country but generally throughout the world.

Dr. P. R. Peacock, of the Royal Cancer Hospital in Glasgow, Scotland, said:

"I think it is very pertinent to ask why foreign substances are put in foods. In the case of preservatives, I can understand that there are needs to add something to assure that the food will reach the consumer without deteriorating, and the consumer wants that. But is this true of artificial colors?

"Who wants to add artificial colors to foods? Do we, as physicians, as men of science, wish it? Certainly, we have no interest in advocating addition of artificial colors to foods, for, as Dr. Reding [a noted Belgian cancer specialist] pointed out, they add nothing of nutritive value. Does the consumer want it? It seems to me that the interests of consumers are to get food that retains its nutritive value, its taste, and its own color.

"Consumers might well, for example, refuse to eat pink peas. True, consumers buy a great many artificially colored foods, but is this not an artificial demand created by those who wish to market artificial colors? Is not the basic issue a desire by marketing interests to obtain certificates of harmlessness for these substances?

"Now, scientists might be able to furnish guarantees of one sort or another along this line after many years of study, but is there any reason to do all these studies and put off a decision for an indefinite time if the matter can be resolved now?

"*Human beings are walking colonies of cells, which, in the course of thousands of years of evolution, have learned how to metabolize or adapt to many natural substances with which they have come into contact. Today, chemists have produced hundreds of substances that never existed before, and it may take thousands more years of evolution to learn how our bodies will react to these new synthetic substances. We cannot consider the laboratory animals on which we do our tests as little men, and give certificates of harmlessness for men to substances tested on animals.* [Author's emphasis.]

"Even in tests on three or more generations of no matter how many different kinds of animals, we can never be entirely sure that the results would be the same in men. There are substances that will produce tumors in one species of animal but not in another. It is entirely possible that a substance judged harmless by any of our tests on laboratory animals may produce cancer in man.

"On the basis of these considerations, there would appear to be no justification, from the purely scientific point of view, for the needless addition of artificial substances to foods that are intended for human beings to eat."

7

Test-Tube Meat

PROBABLY NO ARTICLE in the American diet is as thoroughly tampered with as meat.

Beef, for example: In addition to being laced with pesticides, the average steak or roast probably comes from a cow born through artificial insemination, raised with an artificial sex-hormone implant in its ear, fed synthetic hormones, anti-biotics and insecticides, and shot with tranquilizers; even its natural pasturage is contaminated with radioactive fallout. If the animal survives the chemical onslaught, it is slaughtered—generally by an inhumane method—and sold as meat, which constitutes the primary source of protein in the human diet.

Cold meats and meat products are subjected to additional chemical treatments before they go to the consumer. Agents used in this processing include perservatives and curing agents, antioxidants, flavoring materials, coloring materials (including some of the coal-tar dyes), emulsifiers and refining and bleaching agents.

Even fresh meats, which are not supposed to be chemically tampered with after they leave the slaughter house, may, in some cases, receive a few licks of forbidden chemicals from unscrupulous butchers. Illegal though this is under Federal standards and some state laws, the cheating butcher and his surreptitious chemicals are difficult to catch. The consumer also must be wary about the number of sick chickens that are sold today in prepackaged containers that prevent the housewife from getting a good look at what she's buying.

But it's down on the farm, that outpost of twentieth century agricultural chemistry, that the real mischief takes place. Practically nothing that grows there escapes some form of chemical alteration. Along with all the things already done to beef cattle, they are expected soon to start getting still another chemical jolt. According to the esteemed *Farm Journal* (June, 1968) research is being conducted to force activated charcoal down the throats of cows to trap some pesticide residues, much in the way that filters trap tars in cigarettes; this would be fortified by treatment with the "enzyme-stimulating drug phenobarbitol". . . "your veterinarian can give you a prescription." Other drugs are used to slow down the metabolism of cattle so they will put on more weight with less food. Being a cow isn't very pleasant or rewarding (to the cow) these days.

Cows are not the only meat animals to receive medications of various kinds to interfere with their normal bodily functions. Poultry, lambs and swine also are dosed with chemicals.

Some 90 per cent of all the cattle that go to market each year, and 100,000,000 chickens, are estimated to be getting artificial hormones. The skyrocketing use of these powerful substances is indicated by the fact that only a few years ago estimates were that just half the cattle for market and 30,000,000 chickens were getting synthetic hormones.

Feeding antibiotics and tranquilizers to other meat animals is practiced almost universally in this country. Chickens and turkeys are dipped in antibiotics to increase their shelf life; and only recently the FDA gave permission for antibiotics to be fed to milk cattle. At the same time, numerous experiments on meat animals are under way with an arsenal of new and powerful medications that mean bigger profits for the chemical manufacturer, the packer and sometimes even the farmer. What they mean to the cow and the consuming public is seldom mentioned.

An idea of the stake the public has in this mass use of chemicals in its meat supply is suggested by an article in the magazine *National Livestock Producer*. It stated that the average American, if he survives his theoretical life expectancy of some sixty-eight years, will consume the meat equivalent of thirty-three hogs, ten lambs, eight steers and four veal calves. A scholarly study by the American

Meat Institute disclosed that all the frankfurters eaten by Americans this year would stretch to the moon and back, and there would be enough left over to encircle the earth five times, like a chain of satellites; in less fanciful terms, Americans eat five and one-half billion frankfurters a year!

The animals that supply this meat are subjected, virtually from the hour of birth, and probably before birth, to a bombardment of chemicals that produce radical changes in their basic physiology, and this continues until a few hours before they are slaughtered; in some cases it continues right up to the moment of death; there is, in addition, the frequent posthumous chemical treatment mentioned earlier.

The public is asked to believe that the meat from these biologically altered animals is not harmful to the people who eat it, and that nutritionally it is on a par (or even superior) to meat from untreated animals. The public also is asked to believe there is no danger from the chemicals that remain in the meat when it is eaten.

As usual, the critical question revolves around one point: the long-term effect of eating small amounts of poisons that in larger doses would be extremely harmful or fatal.

The most powerful substance given to meat animals is the artificial sex hormone diethylstilbestrol—better known as stilbestrol. This is a man-made chemical with an activity very similar to that of the natural female sex hormones; but it is more powerful than the natural hormones when taken orally because it is not broken down significantly in the liver. It is so potent that it has been called biological dynamite and, more fancifully, "queen of the hormones."

Like virtually every other additive, stilbestrol benefits the producer rather than the consumer. *Farm and Ranch* Magazine reported that sixteen cents' worth of stilbestrol in a cow's ear brings an extra twelve dollars' worth of beef, and when mixed with feed the cattle gain fifteen per cent faster on twelve per cent less feed; its use is said to be worth 675,000,000 pounds of beef annually.

Stilbestrol pellets were used in chickens from about 1947 until 1958. Directions called for inserting one pellet into the upper region of the neck, at the base of the brain, about four to eight weeks before marketing, during which period the chemical is slowly absorbed into the bird's system.

Male birds given this treatment rapidly lose many male characteristics; combs, wattles and reproductive organs shrivel, and the propensity for crowing and fighting disappears. These birds are called "caponettes" or "hormonized fryers." Results from stilbestrol are very similar to those obtained by surgically castrating the male bird. The popularity of the chemical method was due, primarily, to the ease and speed with which the "castrating" process could be accomplished, and the fact that the farmer needed no special training to use it.

The Delaney Committee's report described stilbestrol as "a potent and dangerous chemical, which cannot be purchased in drug stores for medical purposes without a physician's prescription." It could have added that a farmer can buy all he wants for the asking in feed-supply houses.

This accessibility is of particular interest in view of a warning from a noted endocrinologist that "stilbestrol is a potent drug and serious consequences may result unless it is used under constant medical supervision. Physicians who use this drug should be familiar with its indications, dosage, precautions, and particularly the possible detrimental effects. Extreme care should be taken to avoid overdosage. It is also desirable that the breast and pelvic organs be examined before treatment is instituted as well as during therapy."

Stilbestrol has caused a wide range of pathological changes in human beings and animals when taken in sufficient dosage. Doctors use it therapeutically in cases involving an estrogen deficiency. One witness, however, testified before the Delaney Committee that many gynecologists and obstetricians "are particularly against it, and in the big medical centers it is very definitely on the way out."

The substance is an acknowledged carcinogen, and warnings against its use in foods have been sounded by Dr. Hueper and the International Union Against Cancer. Dr. Hueper in 1967 (*Medical World*) said, "There can be no doubt that stilbestrol and other estrogens are also carcinogens for several species of experimental animals in which they induce not only cancers of the breast and uterus but also those affecting the kidneys, bladder, testis, and blood forming organs." He added that results may not be borne out in humans, "but the suspicion that estrogens might have such effects is provided by scattered observations" of women and men who developed cancers after receiving massive amounts of stilbestrol in an effort to control tumors. It is established that estrogens will accelerate the growth of some tumors already established, especially breast cancer in younger women.

Dr. Harold V. Burrows, author of *Biological Actions of Sex Hormones*, states that in women there is evidence that there is a connection between the administering of estrogens and the appearance of breast cancer. "Not only does the clinical evidence point to such a conclusion," he stated, "but now, with the lapse of time, cases are being reported in which cancer of the breast has followed prolonged treatment with estrogens."

Stilbestrol also is known to be capable of arresting the growth of children, bringing on excess menstrual bleeding, fibroids of the uterus, premenstrual tension and painful breasts. It has also caused impotence and sterility in men. In animals it has been shown to cause cysts and cancers of the uterus, cervix and breast, tumors of the testicles and leukemias.

Exactly how estrogens like stilbestrol work in the body is not known, but it is believed that they affect the pituitary or master gland, and they are known to change the entire blood picture. They also are believed to affect the body's enzyme systems, on which all bodily functions depend, and to interfere with vital functions in the liver.

An outspoken critic of the use of stilbestrol in food has been Dr. Robert K. Enders, chairman of the department of zoology at Swarthmore College and an unsalaried advisor to the U. S. Department of Agriculture and the Department of the Interior. He pointed out the extreme danger of having such a potent drug readily available.

"The chain of consequences that might arise from such use indicates that the availability of pellets which can be bought at any feed store may come to constitute a great hazard. Anyone who has examined the reproductive tracts in experimental animals fed on poultry waste (from stilbestrol-treated animals) shudders at this prospect. Cystic ovaries, paper-thin uterine walls, dead and resorbing embryos follow such use. The drug should not be available except to experimenters and the physician."

Dr. Enders added that if the use of stilbestrol and other hormones in the fattening of animals becomes widespread (as it has), "we may be able to paraphrase, and say, 'The vegetarians will inherit the earth.' "

The customary defense of stilbestrol is that little estrogen activity remains in the meat after the animal is slaughtered. This defense, as usual, overlooks the fact that stilbestrol has a cumulative effect, and it is so powerful that less than a millionth of an ounce is said to be a physiologically active quantity. *Modern Medicine* recently reported that a farmer who used stilbestrol pellets and paste for his chickens apparently handled the stuff with the usual lack of caution of the laity. The result: the farmer's 14-month-old son got big breasts, as did the child's two-year-old sister, and their mother had periods twice a month.

More important than the danger of an occasional accidental large dose of stilbestrol is the hazard of repeated small doses. Several researchers have found that the drug is more toxic in small amounts than in large doses. British investigators in the anatomy department of Kings College, London, concluded that, in animals treated with stilbestrol, the death rate was higher in those who received a daily dose of one-tenth of a milligram than in those who received a daily dose of one to five milligrams.

Dr. Malcolm Stokes, writing in the *Journal of Surgery, Obstetrics and Gynecology*, stated that "undoubtedly, single large doses of estrogenic substances are quickly excreted and are unimportant in regard to carcinogenic activity. On the other hand, long continued, repeated administration of relatively small doses may intensify tissue response to the hormone."

A researcher who has had much to say about the effects of small repeated doses of stilbestrol is the late Dr. Carl G. Hartman, director of physiology and pharmacology for Ortho Research Foundation, a branch of Johnson & Johnson. He was also consultant to the U. S. Department of Agriculture, a specialist in physiology and reproduction, and a former professor at Johns Hopkins and other major colleges.

He testified that "supporters of the use of stilbestrol always cite that the drug is used in medicine, with the inference that it is therefore harmless," and "they point out that large doses have been given patients without disaster. . . . They never mention the fact that small amounts, even minute amounts, given over a longer period may give results that differ from those where larger dosages are given under the supervision of a physician. Yet, the literature shows that extremely minute doses can effectively sterilize and injure laboratory animals where larger doses have no long-range effect."

In the minds of medical men, he said—"and I have talked to hundreds of them—estrogen is a means of stimulating cancer." He said he had not been able to produce it in monkeys, "but in other animals cancer has been produced, and you do not need to give it continuously.

"It was found in some experiments . . . if you give estrogen to a rat which is genetically noncancerous—that is to say, in a thousand you might find one case of cancer—in three months' time you can produce cancer. In seventy-five per cent of the cases they get cancer. We find if you give a little and then stop a while and then give a little more and stop a while and then give a little more, it is better than giving it continuously."

Shortly after chickens started being injected with hormone pellets, mink growers began feeding the offal of treated chickens to their animals and many of the mink became sterile. Dr. Enders said the number of minks so affected "was in the thousands."

He noted that one experimenter "fed minute quantities to mink—and when I say 'minute,' that is in the order of, say, ten to fifteen gamma a day, and a gamma being one thirty-five millionth of an ounce. What happens in these cases is that in these small doses an effect is built up that is quite different from the large doses that are given to human beings or to experimental animals."

Dr. Enders testified he had seen many minks that had been fed discarded parts of stilbestrol-treated fowl. " . . . they lost their hair, they were fat and puffy, you could put your finger in the skin and dimple it and the skin would not come back, there were scales around the external orifices because something was wrong with the urine, and . . . the few survivors were the most miserable animals I have ever seen for animals that were still breathing."

Q. Was there any effect on reproduction?

A. There just was not any reproduction.

Dr. Enders was asked by a member of the Delaney Committee what authority the Food and Drug Administration had to deal with stilbestrol. "I don't know, sir," he replied. "All I know about any of this is that, as I understand it, the use of this drug was based on what you might call ex parte hearings at which only one side was represented."

Stilbestrol also was considered for use in Canada. Experiments were conducted with women who had passed their menopause. After they ate the livers of stilbestrol-treated chickens for four days, tissue changes took place in their vaginal tracts (cornification of the mucosa of the vagina). It is against the law now to feed stilbestrol to food animals in Canada.

Endocrinologists point out that the balance between male and female hormones in the body is extremely delicate, and sex hormones, among other factors, determine and affect certain sex characteristics; the quantity and proportion may affect sex drive, development of sex organs, breast development, quantity of facial and body hair, height, voice pitch and similar characteristics. A significant imbalance between male and female sex hormones in the body is said to result in the individual's acquiring some physical characteristics of the opposite sex.

Among the hormone experts who have warned about the possible sexual repercussions stilbestrol-treated meat may have on human beings is Dr. Christian Hamburger of Copenhagen, who helped ex-GI George Jorgensen of New York become "Christine" and Charles McLeod of New Orleans convert to "Charlotte."

In 1957, Dr. Hamburger said that men who ate hormone-treated fowl may develop feminite characteristics. He said Danish health authorities prohibited the use of hormones for capons. After breeders inserted female hormones into the muscles of the fowl, some men who ate the treated capons became temporaritly impotent. The hormones were not destroyed in cooking, he said.

Curiously, in 1951 the FDA warned that the use of sex hormones without a doctor's order might cause cancer or sterility, stating that women might do "serious injury" to their reproductive organs by unsupervised use of female sex hormones.

The warning, issued in connection with the crackdown on two Los Angeles firms that were selling tablets containing the male sex hormone testosterone, cautioned men in particular not to take these testosterone pills.

In September 1958, hormones in meat were in the news again, this time with sound and fury. *Time* Magazine carried a story out of Rio de Janeiro with an inspired lead which stated that readers of a newspaper there were "shaken to their gonads by the blaring headline: TERROR IN BRAZIL—MEN FEMINIZED."

Time pointed out that the panic was caused by a charge that men had been feminized by eating beef of steers fattened with the aid of stilbestrol. One Sebastiao de Lima Serra of Aracatuba reportedly had suffered a "veritable metamorphosis, turning into a docile, falsetto-voiced creature of strange customs." Serra was said to have blamed his plight on hormone-treated beef, and *Time* quoted Rio's state government as proclaiming: "The necessary measures will be taken to end this evil."

As an indication of how people reacted to this knowledge, *Time* stated that before competent authorities could decide whether there was any evil to end, sales of beef had dropped 40 per cent in Rio, as much as 80 per cent in other cities, and the price of tenderloin had plummeted from 50 cents a pound to three cents. Millions of Brazilians took to a fish diet.

Time noted that hormone-fattening of meat is a common practice in the United States, but assured its readers that there was "probably" nothing to Senhor Serra's claim, explaining that *"nearly all* the hormone is metabolized" and *"virtually none* can ever be found in the meat *if* the hormone feeding is stopped (as required under U. S. regulations) 48 hours before slaughter." [Emphasis the author's.]

A similar reaction erupted in Italy in December, 1968, when a TV program informed Romans that their meat was treated with stilbestrol. *Variety* reported that "meat sales plummeted, newspapers launched an all-out campaign and the Ministry of Health began a special investigation last week after an RAI-TV current events program . . . revealed that a large percentage of veal sold in Italy is treated with estrogens, which cause loss of virility and possible cancer." The program stated that of 85 meat samples from various parts of the country only two were certified free of the drugs. The producer of the TV program, Emilio Fede, was "nominated for the Gold Medal of Public Health."

In contrast to this reassurance offered by *Time* is the statement by Dr. Hartman that men are "very sensitive to estrogens," and that researchers have demonstrated radical changes in their sexual capacity with tiny amounts of the substances. Dr. Hartman said:

"When you take the marginal cases, where the man has between fifty and sixty million sperm per cubic centimeter of the ejaculation, he is a borderline case. He may sire a child, but the chances are he will not."

These observations take on added impact when it is noted that one in every ten American marriages is infertile today, according to estimates by experts in the field. Since World War II alone, an estimated 100,000 babies have been born through test-tube methods, due to the infertility of American husbands; men are said to be the sole or contributing cause of sterility in about 40 per cent of the country's three million barren marriages.

Sterility has become such a widespread phenomenon in this country that, in 1952, the late Dr. Abner I. Weisman, then associate secretary general of the International Fertility Association, said that 15,000,000 Americans are barren, and more people in the United States face this problem than the total number who suffer from the country's six most widespread diseases. Statistically, this would mean that almost ten per cent of the American marriages are sterile.

Precisely what happens to stilbestrol when it is ingested is unknown. Only a small proportion can be accounted for, but studies show that it is not entirely broken down in the body. The *Journal of the American Medical Association* reported that hogs feeding in pastures occupied by stilbestrol-fed steers suffer "severe gonadal regression" because of the steroid content of the cattle's urine and feces.

Why stilbestrol causes cattle to put on increased weight with less feed is not known, but the FDA has said: "Hypertrophy (excessive development) of the liver, of the adrenal glands, and of the pituitary without specific cellular changes have been reported. These observations seem to indicate that there is a change in the endocrine gland metabolism. . . ."

Pointing to the effects estrogens have on the glands, Dr. Hartman observed that "whenever you tamper with one gland you tamper with all the others. When the ovaries or the testes are removed, the physiological effect is profound in the organism. If you give too much thyroid, you injure the ovary or the testes. We have to think of the body as a whole, and when you have an excess of one hormone over another you get effects which reverberate with the entire organism."

As justifiication for using stilbestrol as an implant and in feeds, it often is asserted that animals and even some plants secrete natural hormones, and they are able to metabolize and excrete them without adverse effects. They fail to note that stilbestrol is not a natural estrogen. It is a synthetic product.

Another consideration generally overlooked is the liver's role in detoxifying or deactivating stilbestrol. If the liver functions improperly because of poor nutrition or is damaged by the bombardment of poisons in the diet, then it will not be able to regulate the delicate hormonal balance in the body. The average woman has all the estrogen she needs; if more is added, the liver must deactivate it to maintain the balance. Still another burden is placed on the already overworked liver, and thus the hormonal balance may be jeopardized.

This is of particular significance because of the widespread liver damage among the population, and the likelihood that there will be more as the flood of chemicals in foods gains momentum.

What effect is this having on us as individuals and a nation? Is the man-made hormonal imbalance a factor in the increasing amount of impotence and sterility? An endocrinologist, pointing to the ability of stilbestrol to stimulate females at the same time that it reduces the male's sexual prowess, posed this tantalizing question: "Are we going to end up a nation of nymphomaniacs and impotent men?"

Both Dr. Hartman and Dr. Enders said that most of the weight put on chickens by use of stilbestrol implants was primarily fat and water. It is estimated that stilbestrol increases the weight of chickens about 20 per cent. Dr. Hartman said the fat of treated fowl differs chemically from that of normally fattened birds; "it is watery and inferior culinarily." He said the fat does not render like ordinary chicken fat "but leaves great strands in the pan." He explained that the excess fat raises the cost of the flesh part of the carcass, which has been purchased by the pound. Dr. Hartman said investigators at the State College of Mississippi found that the fat from stilbestrol-treated animals, when compared with ordinary fat, differed chemically "in certain fat tests, so that the molecules of fat are even different, entirely aside from the water content."

Dr. Enders said the stilbestrol produced no more breast in the chicken, but the skin of the animal became very nice and smooth because of the water and fat under it. "It increases the appearance of the fowl," he said, "it increases the attractiveness very, very, much."

On the economic side, he continued, "I agree with those endocrinologists who say that the use of the drug to fatten poultry is an economic fraud. Chicken feed is not saved; it is merely turned into fat instead of protein. Fat is abundant in the American diet, so more is undesirable. Protein is what one wants from poultry. By their own admission it is the improvement in appearance and increase in fat that makes it more profitable to the poultryman to use the drug. This fat is of very doubtful value and is in no way the dietary equal to the protein that the consumer thinks he is paying for."

Government officials repeatedly have insisted that stilbestrol-treated meat is as high in quality as untreated meat, but there are many indications that this might be a somewhat flexible interpretation of the facts.

The U. S. Department of Agriculture, in a release dated July 20, 1956, stated that its studies showed that stilbestrol could be used in cattle "without adverse effect on meat quality as measured by usual evaluation methods, including taste-panel tests." The previous year, however, Jack M. Curtis of the FDA told a group of health officials that when cattle were fed stilbestrol "usually the carcass quality is about one grade lower."

Experimenters at Kentucky University also found that cattle not fed stilbestrol had higher carcass grades and sales values than treated animals. "On the hoof," they stated, "the stilbestrol groups appeared to have extra bloom and finish when compared to the non-stilbestrol groups, but this was not borne out when the carcasses were studied."

A more revealing item appeared in the August 1955 issue of *Farm Journal*, which gave farmers this intrepid advice: "If you feed stilbestrol to your cattle, better not say anything about it when you send them to market. You might end by getting less money."

More serious than the question of quality and taste is how much stilbestrol remains in the meat of treated animals when they are marketed. Dr. Enders told the Delaney Committee that "it is surprising that the United States Department of Agriculture has not had this problem investigated more extensively, as it is basic to the issue." He said it cannot be claimed that the stilbestrol in the body tissues is inactive; this substance upon being removed and reinjected in another animal has "a profound effect on the pituitary."

For a long time it was assumed that when chickens with stilbestrol implants were killed, the pellets would be dissolved. Later it was found out that this wasn't true; part of the pellet had to remain undissolved until the time the bird was killed or it would have reverted to its male characteristics.

The danger of getting part of the pellet in food was frequently emphasized. Dr. Willard Machle, professor of occupational medicine at New York University and an official of the National Research Council, observed that in homes for the indigent and in many institutions it was quite possible that the remnants of a choice-cut fowl, such as the upper portion of the neck where the pellet was implanted, may have been used for soups, broths, or cooked for serving. "So I would say that a very definite potential hazard exists."

Others noted that since stilbestrol was not destroyed in cooking, if any part of the pellet was present in the fowl when used, it probably would be consumed in its entirety if made into soup. Dr. Hartman pointed out that "the liver and body fat store more of the hormone than any other organ, as has been known for twenty years—and people eat chicken livers."

The possibilities of getting part of the pellet were spelled out by testimony before the Delaney Committee. It was pointed out that the pellet may be walled off by tissue and not absorbed into the bird, or it may move elsewhere from the point of injection in the bird's carcass. Another possibility noted was that the market often changes abruptly and the farmer might market the bird without waiting the required number of days for the pellet to dissolve.

In nine lots of treated poultry entering the New York market, about 70 per cent of the birds had parts of the pellets still remaining in them, according to testimony before the Delaney Committee.

Of the original fifteen-milligram implant, two to four

milligrams remained. In at least half of the birds, the stilbestrol had been inserted one to one and one-half inches below the base of the skull, and a significant number of birds were said to have the pellet two or more inches below the spot where it was supposed to be inserted; this would mean it probably would have been consumed in the neck.

After spotting these violations, the FDA seized about 60,000 pounds entering the New York market and found pellet residues ranging from three milligrams to more than twenty-four milligrams.

Following the government crack-down, shippers tried to slip stilbestrol-treated birds past inspectors by designating them as "roasters," rather than capons.

The FDA seized the "roasters." In the necks removed from 200 birds, 95 per cent contained pellets estimated to average between five to seven milligrams. More than 50 per cent were one inch or more below the base of the skull. In one subsequent seizure, a pellet was found implanted in a chicken's back, along with several other violations. These pellets often migrate in the loose tissue under the skin, no matter where they are originally placed.

In some seized chickens, according to testimony, there were remnants of as many as four pellets; the farmers obviously believed that if one pellet was good, four were that much better. Dr. Theodore C. Byerly, of the USDA, testified there was "no way of controlling the man who implants pellets and saying he is permitted to implant one. He might implant twelve, if he so chose, though it is an added expense. It is remotely possible he might elect to do so. . . ."

The Delaney Committee, evaluating the difficulty of catching all violations, observed that the FDA has only a limited staff to cover the entire country, and that the agency could not possibly hope to sample and examine every interstate shipment. "Inevitably," it concluded, "many shipments of food must traverse state lines without any examination." Also emphasized was the fact that FDA has no jurisdiction over shipments that do not cross state lines.

After Americans had been consuming chickens treated with stilbestrol implants for 12 years, the FDA announced on December 11, 1959, a voluntary plan whereby they no longer would be marketed. FDA conceded that residues of stilbestrol were found in the skin, liver and kidneys of treated birds. Overnight it had become so dangerous to eat this meat that all treated birds were taken off the market at once at government expense—which is to say the taxpayer's expense—at a cost of $10 million. But the government noted that the action would not stop the use of stilbestrol in beef cattle, sheep and lamb.

Less dramatic but probably even more dangerous is the amount of estrogen activity that remains in treated meat when it goes to market. The FDA has admitted that steers fed 10 milligrams of stilbestrol per day produced meat that contained 0.6 parts per billion estrogenic activity when ready for market, but it characterized this amount as "of no significance." Other tests have been said to show stilbestrol present only in negligible amounts or just barely detectable by phenomenally sensitive testing methods. Other researchers, however, have pointed out that when the meat was fed to animals there was a definite estrogenic effect.

Since 1967, at least, there has been agitation to increase the stilbestrol dose in cattle feed from 10 milligrams daily to three times that amount (along with the permitted use of implants). It was said by researchers (Doanes, Oct., 1967) that the cattle made greater weight gains. Nothing was said about the people who eat the meat.

Stilbestrol contamination of meat has become so widespread that Dr. Clive McCay at Cornell, who was in charge of nutritional research for the Navy during World War II, reported that "rodents used in research, such as cancerous strains of mice, must now be fed with special diets to avoid reproductive failure due to stilbestrol." He continued:

"Special mixtures for such mice are now being marketed and these contain no meat scrap, because this product (meat) is the carrier of . . . stilbestrol. No one is certain how this stilbestrol gets into the meat meals, but it is there and has been during the past several years when steers have been fed stilbestrol."

In several instances the feed of small animals was contaminated by mixing machines that had been used to prepare stilbestrol pellets. In one case, guinea pigs got a heavy jolt that way and stopped reproducing, showing uterine discharges and other maladies.

Since the presence of stilbestrol in meat no longer can be denied, emphasis has shifted to the insistence that the small amounts present are safe.

Four eminent physicians, led by Dr. William E. Smith, the other three being Drs. Granville F. Knight, W. Coda Martin and Rigoberto Iglesias, presented their conclusions about the effects of the so-called small amounts of stilbestrol at a public symposium on medicated feeds in Washington in 1956. Only after trying repeatedly to discourage the four doctors from participating did Government officials reluctantly give them a place on the program. The effect was sensational.

The *Police Gazette,* never known for its subtlety, gave a colorful account of the background of the forum:

". . . despite the fact that top cancer experts have publicly warned that this hormone-producing chemical (stilbestrol) may be dangerous to humans, the U. S. Food and Drug Administration for some mysterious reason has turned a deaf ear to these grim warnings.

"Not only have FDA officials refused to take definite action, but they cooperated with the chemical industry in a recent public symposium which, in effect, whitewashed the users of medicated feeds.

"Here was a strange and terrifying situation.

"But before the symposium ended, the helpless consumer had the satisfaction of seeing the whitewash boomerang, leaving the FDA with a hot potato. . . .

"The symposium was dominated by chemical industry representatives and, furthermore," the *Police Gazette* reported, "the publicity for this so-called Government-sponsored meeting was handled by a New York public relations firm employed by a large chemical manufacturer.

"All the speakers listed on the program were in accord with FDA policies concerning the dangerous medicated feeds.

"For two days these U. S. officials and the chemical representatives had a lovefeast, extolling the 'benefits' of hormones as a means of stimulating weight gain for food animals.

"Then, on the third day of sweetness-and-light the atmosphere was rudely shattered by a report that rocked the symposium and sent the chemical boys into frustrated confusion. . . ."

The Smith group set the session—which began with a personal "Best wishes" message from President Eisenhower —on its ear by asserting that "in the case of market poultry found to contain up to 24 milligrams of diethylstilbestrol per bird, *one is dealing with an amount roughly equiv-alent to 342,000 times the daily dose necessary to produce cancer in mice.*" Twenty-four milligrams was the amount of stilbestrol found in the neck of one of the chickens seized by FDA inspectors in the New York market.

Before reaching this climax, the reluctantly invited phy-sicians had cited some other figures not calculated to calm the nerves of their hosts. Their report, citing experiments by the National Cancer Institute, pointed out that breast cancers can be induced in mice by as little as 0.07 micro-grams (seven thousandths of one milligram) of stilbestrol per day.

They concluded that "the cancer-producing dose of this drug approaches the infinitesimal. Claims that no appre-ciable quantities of it can be demonstrated in tissues of cattle to which it has been fed must therefore be carefully scrutinized as to the sensitivity and accuracy of the test methods."

They added that meat from a steer given the prescribed ten milligrams of stilbestrol had shown about fourteen times the amount of stilbestrol needed as a daily dose to produce cancer in mice.

Furthermore, the physicians continued, claims for the absence of stilbestrol in tissues were based on a method that had a limited sensitivity. The Smith group said "this means that a pound of meat, certified as free of diethylstil-bestrol, could contain nearly 14 times the amount of this drug necessary to induce cancer by a daily dose to mice."

It was at this point that the doctors hurled their bomb-shell about the market poultry found to contain up to twenty-four milligrams of stilbestrol per bird.

The report added that "intermittent administration of very large doses of estrogens is far less effective in induc-ing tumors than is a continuing exposure to extremely minute doses. *It is a continuing exposure to extremely minute doses that is to be feared from the introduction of estrogens into the food supply.*" [Emphasis the author's.]

Tumors have resulted in guinea pigs exposed to as little as eight micrograms (eight thousandths of one milligram) of stilbestrol per day, it was noted, and a pellet removed from a guinea pig one year after implantation still retained enough power to induce a tumor when reimplanted in another animal.

The report further emphasized that a prime consideration is the long period of time that elapses between the first exposure to a carcinogen, such as stilbestrol, and the eventual appearance of a tumor: "In animal experiments, exposure is customarily begun early in life and the majority of tumors arise when the animals are old. Experience in the results of. administration of estrogens to human beings has been largely limited to treatment of conditions arising fairly late in life.

"By comparison, the majority of human beings thus far exposed would complete their life span before passage of sufficient time to observe a carcinogenic effect of estrogens. The introduction of estrogens into the food supply, however, presents the problem of exposure of human beings from birth onward. . . ."

The National Cancer Institute reported that in the absence of long-term studies of the effect of stilbestrol-treated meat on human beings, the inferences drawn from many animal studies "well-documented by Dr. Smith's group, bring us as close to the clinical facts as we can come today." A member of the Institute stated: "It is my considered opinion that our food control authorities have not viewed these hazards in realistic or objective terms."

What has been the response to these various warnings? Researchers have been experimenting with giving even larger jolts of stilbestrol to meat animals. Prospects are that beef cattle will be given at least twice as much stilbestrol as they are getting now—unless the Government cracks down and uses the power given it under the new amendment to the food law.

(2)

Instead of trying to curb the use of chemicals in meat animals, the government has permitted their use to burgeon. In addition to stilbestrol, cattle and many other meat animals are getting tranquilizers; cattle often get especially heavy doses just before being shipped to market.

High-level shots of antibiotics also are given to cattle for "shipping fever." *Farm Journal* quoted an experimenter as saying that the drugs when given to cattle heading for market, "surely took all the snort out of them."

A scientific symposium held in 1967 estimated that more than 2.7 million pounds of antibiotic food supplements are used annually in the U. S. (*New York Times*). Several speakers at the symposium warned that the widespread use has led to increased resistance to the drugs. Many doctors have pointed out that this could have serious consequences for patients treated with antibiotics in severe illnesses.

In 1968 FDA began to tighten restrictions on the use of antibiotics in treating animals after federal investigators found residues in meat, milk and eggs long after the drugs were used, according to *Farm Journal*. For a long time it had been contended that these residues quickly disappeared. *Farm Journal* quoted an FDA scientist as having said, "These residues are a potential hazard to your health and mine."

The scientist said, "Many of us are sensitive to penicillin and streptomycin, for example. If we eat foods that carry residues of these drugs, we may get a serious reaction. And even if we are not now sensitive, we may develop a sensitivity by continued exposures to residues in our food. Then, if our doctor used one of these antibiotics in treating an illness, we might well have a severe reaction."

The *Journal* noted that health officials were even more concerned about the resistance that bacteria develop through continuous exposure to antibiotics. "We are very much concerned about recent discoveries that this resistance can be transferred from one species of bacteria to another," an FDA spokesman was quoted as having said. "Organisms have developed resistance that can be transferred from one species of bacteria to another."

The magazine added that "low levels of antibiotics in (animal) feed will probably not be affected, according to present FDA plans."

Antibiotics are given to dairy and beef cattle, poultry, lambs and swine; they are used to help put on cheap weight, boost production, treat disease, prevent disease, and as a preservative; they are used on fruits and vegetables to prevent blight and bacterial disease, and as "medicine" for sick food plants. At the same time, studies are being made with an eye toward using them as preservatives in vegetables, beef, ham and other perishables.

The word antibiotic means "against life." These compounds are chemical substances made from microorganisms and they have an antagonistic effect on other microorganisms. The majority are said to be effective chiefly because they inhibit the growth of microbes, although many actually destroy microbial cells. Their exact method of action is not known.

As usual, it is claimed that only negligible, insignificant or undemonstrable amounts of antibiotics appear in foods. The FDA's Jack Curtis said the feeding of low levels of antibiotics to meat animals has not resulted in the deposition of "any appreciable residues" of antibiotics in the tissues of treated animals. The *Journal of the American Medical Association* assured its readers that when fowl was preserved in an antibiotic dip, cooking destroyed "more than 99 per cent" of the drug. Stated another way, it might be said that even after cooking some residue remains.

The FDA said it would not permit the use of antibiotic dips now widely used for poultry until it was shown that the antibiotic residue was destroyed in cooking—which included frying. In the spring of 1959, the Government authorized the use of antibiotics to preserve fresh-caught fish. Antibiotics have been used to embalm poultry since 1955. The British have refused to permit the use of antibiotics to preserve fish because, among other reasons, "frying leaves minute traces," according to the highly respected British medical journal *Lancet*. Let us hope that frying fish and chicken in America destroys more antibiotic residue than frying fish in Great Britain.

It is known that antibiotic residue has appeared in 5 to 12 per cent of all milk samples tested by the FDA. The drug gets into milk from massive shots of antibiotics given to cattle suffering from mastitis, an udder infection; more than 75 tons of antibiotics—primarily penicillin—are said to be used annually for this ailment alone.

Farmers are not supposed to market milk from treated cows until seventy-two hours after the dose is applied, but the large number of violations shows the frequency with which the order is disregarded. From 1955 to 1956, according to samples tested, the *number* of violations showed an encouraging drop, but the *average concentration* of penicillin in the milk more than doubled; the highest concentration of penicillin in an individual milk sample in the 1956 tests was more than seven times that in the previous year's test results.

The large number of violations emphasizes how precarious the public's margin of safety is when a dangerous drug is placed in the hands of laymen who have no idea of its power and who are expected to exercise their sense of responsibility at the risk of losing money.

Despite the frequency with which FDA regulations are violated, the agency placed another dangerous economic tool in the hands of farmers by permitting use of the antibiotic aureomycin in the daily feed ration of milk cattle. *Farm Journal* stated that in order to get FDA clearance for the drug, a chemical company "showed by field trials that none of the antibiotic was detected in the milk *when fed at the recommended level.* [Their emphasis.] *But if you feed enough more than is recommended, it can show up in the milk."* [Author's emphasis.]

In many cases the amount of antibiotic residue in milk has been large enough to interfere with cheese-making because, as the FDA explained, the bacteria that produce cheese were knocked out by the penicillin.

The FDA has conceded that the "small amounts" of antibiotics appearing in milk "could conceivably" cause a reaction in a sensitive individual. The large number of persons who suffer from various allergies and possibly would react to small amounts of antibiotics makes this a threat not to be taken lightly.

The *Journal of the American Medical Association* has recognized the threat from small amounts of antibiotics appearing regularly in the milk; it states that while antibiotics combat the development of bacteria, "It is not so generally appreciated that their medical usage is attended by distinct hazard of sensitization. . . . To the individual who is or has become sensitized, administration of an antibiotic may cause serious illness or even death.

"A method of developing sensitization is by administering the agent in small repeated dosage, in a manner paralleling that of repeatedly ingesting food preserved with an antibiotic. [Emphasis the author's.] The use of antibiotics as food production adjuvants in such ways that they actually are consumed is therefore manifestly contrary to the public interest, and the Food and Drug Administration has formally so declared."

Almost ten years ago the FDA reported that serious reactions to antibiotics were increasing. A nationwide survey of nearly 3,000 histories of such cases was said to indicate that about one third were so serious as to threaten the life of the patient.

Effects of the indiscriminate use of antibiotics are further dramatized by the number of deaths due to the virulent "staph" (staphylococcus) germ, which has become resistant to antibiotics. The Public Health Service has called the staph menace a national problem. Many deaths have been attributed to it. One way doctors were advised to fight staph germs was by not giving antibiotics haphazardly and never in small "preventive" doses which are believed to encourage the development of resistant strains of germs.

Doctors have warned against the promiscuous use of antibiotics both in medicine and agriculture, pointing out that when they are needed in an emergency as a heroic measure, the patient who previously has had repeated small doses may not respond—or may have an adverse reaction, or even die.

Many doctors are convinced that the steady ingestion of antibiotics in foods, regardless of how small the dose, might be having adverse effects on natural processes of the body in addition to causing sensitization. One doctor refers to these drugs as "vitamin antagonists." Dr. Hartman pointed out that aureomycin—the antibiotic primarily used in animal feed—destroys bacteria in the intestinal tract, "and as a matter of fact, we depend on bacteria in the intestinal tract to make vitamins for us." Again, it is only logical to ask what effect antibiotics in feed are having on the health of animals and, consequently, on the human beings who eat their meat.

Lancet noted that there is little information about the effects on man of small and intermediate doses of antibiotics.

The questions posed by the use of these relative strangers to the food supply go unanswered, as far as their effects on humans are concerned, but there are up-to-the-minute statistics on animal weight gains and increased profits from use of antibiotics.

Another chemical treatment for cattle is a grub killer. The compound is applied internally to kill the parasites before they work their way from the animals' intestines through their hides. Directions state the product should not be used on producing dairy cows or beef animals within 60 days of slaughter. It is to be hoped that cattlemen who use the stuff follow directions more conscientiously than many farmers who apply stilbestrol, pesticides, antibiotics and other powerful chemicals with disregard to minimum safeguards.

One of the rare setbacks chemicals suffered was the disclosure in *Farm Journal* that a Department of Agriculture entomologist announced that the USDA "was withdrawing methoxychlor (a chlorinated hydrocarbon) from its list of chemicals recommended *for use directly on dairy cows*. He said that USDA would continue to recommend it for use inside the barn *as a residual spray*." [Emphasis theirs.]

The canny *Farm Journal* continued: "But the catch is this: The decision not to recommend methoxychlor's use on dairy cattle doesn't *forbid* its use [emphasis theirs]. Registered manufacturers haven't been asked to change their labels."

In the march of chemical progress down on the farm, chickens have not been neglected. Antibiotics in chicken feed are said to have stepped up egg production in low-producing hens from 26 to 57 per cent, and antibiotic dips have increased the shelf life of poultry from the normal seven days up to twenty-one days. Other supercharged chemicals also are pumped into poultry feed; some packages of the stuff now carry warnings that the birds should no be killed for food until two weeks after the treated rations are withdrawn—something else for the harassed agrarian-chemist to remember.

Among the ingredients in some chicken feeds is arsenic, a known cause of cancer in man. "Fortunately," said Dr. McCay, "the producers of arsenicals for poultry made a careful study of chicken livers and if one reads the literature he knows how much arsenic he is getting in his giblet gravy. In many cases this is not done and one has no way of knowing the amounts ingested.

"A few years ago when dogs were poisoned and paralyzed by residues of a compound . . . which was carried over in the mixer from poultry to dog feeds, no one could tell us how much of this toxic agent was stored in the livers of chickens and turkeys. Perhaps one should not worry, since the turnover in the use of these toxic compounds is so rapid that one would learn about one, such as arsenic, when his knowledge would be obsolete, because a new compound . . . would have entered the picture."

The FDA reported that "an ingredient" in poultry feed was the "probable cause of outbreaks of a mysterious poultry disease estimated to have taken the lives of several million birds between October 1957 and February 1958."

FDA attributed the disease to "the use of certain fatty

materials in the poultry feed . . . The fatty materials were
compounded in part from a black, tarry residue left from
fat-processing operations." The cause of death was known
among poultrymen as "water-belly"—an accumulation of
fluid in the heart sac and the abdominal cavity. Symptoms
appeared after the birds had been on the feed two weeks or
more.

The Government, noting that a survey was being made
to determine whether similar fatty materials were being
offered to feed manufacturers, said the poultry losses that
occurred could have been avoided had the tarry residue
been tested adequately before it was used as an ingredient
of feed.

Who can say how many birds that died of the ailment—
or were suffering from it when they were killed—wound
up as somebody's Sunday dinner? Although the FDA
pointed out that the poultry losses could have been avoided, they failed to state what might have happened to the
people who unwittingly ate the diseased flesh from the
birds. It also is pertinent to wonder if the preservative
process of the antibiotic dip masked the diseased condition
of some of the flesh. (Antibiotics are used in some preservative processes to stop the spread of disease that may
still be present after death.)

Also pertinent is an item that appeared in *Farm Journal*
in October 1957, stating that "Leucosis—a cancerlike disease that's rated as the No. 1 killer of adult poultry—now
is showing up in *younger stock.*" [Emphasis theirs.]

Pointing out that researchers had found "serious infesta-
tions" in birds from eight to twelve weeks old, the article
continued: "The trouble is that there's no solution for the
disease. USDA research scientists in Michigan are working with a vaccine that looks hopeful for one type of the
cancer that hits chickens, but there's no commercial product on the market yet."

Farm Journal added its own postscript with this conclud-
ing paragraph: "Strangely, the disease didn't come to
growers' attention by killing birds. Federal and State inspectors in processing plants were the first to notice it—
they were condemning more birds because of abnormal
organs."

This disclosure raises more vital questions that urgently
need answering: Is there a parallel between the rising incidence of "cancerlike" diseases in young chickens fed toxic

substances and children who are being raised on poisoned foods today? Also, how many chickens in early stages of disease are being marketed and eaten? With FDA's limited staff, would it be possible for even the most conscientious and diligent inspector to examine every bird that goes to market?

And so it goes, down on the farm.

What happens on the. consumer level was suggested by an interview *US News & World Report* had with FDA Commissioner George P. Larrick. Mr. Larrick outlines the problem so well that he deserves to be quoted verbatum:

Q. Is there a lot of diseased poultry on the market?

A. Yes, that is true.

Q. How can the individual protect himself?

A. The first thing the individual can do would be to get behind the bill that is being considered in Congress to require inspection of poultry. . . . The second solution is for the prudent housewife to look at the bird. If it's skinny, has any sores on it, if the giblets or any of the organs appear to be abnormal, she should reject it.

Q. You never see the bird any more; all you see is a few little pieces of meat wrapped in cellophane—

A. Yes—that's the problem. The housewife used to be able to watch her own sanitation for herself. Now she's got to hire an inspector to do it for her. . . .

Q. Would you guess what percentage of the poultry that is bought in stores is diseased?

A. Probably a very small percentage but significant.

Q. Does the fact that a chicken is diseased make it dangerous to the human being?

A. Most diseased poultry is handled so that it will not be dangerous. There is a disease of poultry in this country called ornithosis. You may recall that parrots and parakeets had a disease some time ago that was transmissible to man. Well, that same disease—or a form of it—is being found now in chickens, turkeys and ducks. And there have been some very serious outbreaks of the disease in the workers in the processing plants. We have never found a case of it transmitted to the consumer of the poultry or the woman who handled it in the kitchen. But there have been some very serious outbreaks in poultry plants, and particularly in turkey-processing establishments.

Q. Is this what is called "parrot fever"?

A. Well, it is the same as parrot fever, but it is also called ornithosis or psittacosis.

Q. What does it do to you?

A. Symptoms are similar to those of a severe upper-respiratory ailment. It's amenable to treatment with some of the antibiotics. Untreated, it may cause death.

Mr. Larrick did not speculate on any possible relationship between the amount of sick poultry turning up and the increasing use of chemicals in their feeds, nor did he offer any other explanation for this phenomenon. But he did repeatedly emphasize the need for a law that would require the inspection of poultry *after it went to market.*

The entire emphasis down on the farm is turning out quantity as cheaply as possible. Quality and nutritive values are virtually never mentioned. The aim is do it cheap, do it fast, make it big. Dr. Jonathan Forman, the former editor of the *Ohio State Medical Journal,* observed that we are putting "emphasis on tonnage and bushels, giving our domestic animals fattening feed instead of food that would have made them strong, muscular and healthy, and presumably of higher nutritive value when their flesh is eaten by man.

"This is not all presumption, for we do know that the vitamin-B content of the muscles of a pig can be influenced by the food he gets. We know, too, that the typical pig ready for market is a sick animal—the victim of obesity—who would die long before his time if we did not rush him to market for the city people to eat."

(3)

After meat has undergone its harrowing exposures to chemicals on the farm, it frequently is subjected to still further chemical treatment in processing or adulteration before reaching the consumer.

To list each formidable-sounding chemical used in curing and preserving cold meats would serve little purpose, unless the reader were a chemist; virtually all are poisons, and they are permitted in small amounts on the usual theory that this is safe procedure. Worthy of mention, however, are a few of the more commonly used compounds, especially those ingested frequently by children. In this category are sodium nitrate and sodium nitrite, widely used in lunch meats; the nitrates are used extensively in frankfurters.

John Cullen, former Canadian food-inspection official, said: "These chemicals, which of themselves have no color, serve to fix and hold. and accentuate, the natural color of the meat. This leads the buyer to believe that the product is of better quality than it actually is, and in this way he is deceived." He said their addition to meat is "highly objectionable not only on account of the deception, but on account of its being injurious to health."*

Many cases of poisoning from these substances, when used in larger amounts than legally permitted, are on record. Several cases of severe illness occurred in New Orleans several years ago when wieners that were supposed to contain no more than 200 ppm nitrites were found to have up to 6,750. A preparation used in corning beef and freshening hamburgers contains 8 per cent nitrites, 4 per cent nitrates and glucose; 3 cc. of this extract fed to adult male rats by stomach tube reportedly caused their death in thirty-five minutes from blood disorders; when the extract mistakenly was substituted for maple sirup on a dining car, several people became seriously ill.

Nitrates and saltpeter have been added to the beverages of boarding-school students in the belief they would inhibit sex interest. Saltpeter can cause gastric distress, nausea, vomiting and excessive urine discharges.

Boric acid, according to testimony of Dr. Lehman of the FDA, "is dusted on hams during the curing process to keep off what they call skippers, a fly infestation. It has been used also as a preservative in waxy covering for certain fruits and vegetables." He added that the FDA considers boric acid as "poisonous per se" and that it should not be used in food products.

Prevention Magazine reported that it wrote to the USDA to find out what synthetic sausage casings are made of. USDA was quoted as saying one brand of casings was made of synthetic resins, "modified by the addition of a small amount of harmless chemicals." Another brand was said to be made of "regenerated cellulose" consisting of "wood pulp and cotton linters, and plasticized by treatment with alkali." Materials of a third casing, *Prevention* wrote, "(you won't believe this we're sure, but it's there in

*"Don't Eat That . . . It May Be Poison!" published by Pure Food Guild, 1952.

black and white) are made of 'synthetic rubber modified by the addition of a small amount of harmless chemicals.'"

Prevention, stating that these revelations made its hair rise in horror, conceded that the casings are peeled off and not eaten; "But the meat has been packed in them for weeks (or perhaps months) before we buy it. How much of the synthetic rubber, resin, cellulose and 'harmless chemicals' have been absorbed by that meat before we make it into a sandwich?"

Sausage long has been celebrated as one of the mysteries of life. *The Economist,* a British publication, recently carried a dispatch from its Bonn correspondent, who discussed this exotic foodstuff from his homeland." It has always been fairly easy," he said, "in the very nature of the business [sausage business], to conceal from the ordinary buyer exactly what a sausage is made of. The trouble now is that the wider use of chemicals for preserving and coloring, along with the improvement of cutting and blending machines have made adulteration even less discernible. . . ."

What holds good for sausage in Bonn also holds good here. Sausage generally is made of inferior grades of meat; its casing is suspect as a carcinogen and frequently contains coal-tar dyes; the meat itself is preserved with powerful chemicals. In some cases, where not protected by Federal meat laws, it may be adulterated with illegal preservatives. But sausage is only one of many meat products that give the food adulterer an opportunity to practice his black art at the expense of the public.

Probably the most infamous of the surreptitious chemicals he uses is the powerful sodium sulphite. By Federal standards this chemical is illegal in meat but appears in certain other foodstuffs—which also holds true of the preservative sodium benzoate. "If the meat is of an unusually bright red color," says Mr. Cullen, "it is reasonable to assume that it has been doped and doctored with sulphurous acid or sodium sulphite. This is especially true in the case of hamburger that has been made from stale meat trimmings, pork kidneys, pigs' hearts, sheep hearts and other meat by-products including large quantities of fat."

He says it is a "great favorite with butchers and manufacturers of meat products generally . . . This preservative is very dangerous to health, especially when used in meat, because it will not only restore the color of putrid and almost black meat, but also because it will destroy the strong odor of putrefaction.

"Many butchers will contend that they use this preparation only because it arrests the spread of bacteria. Nothing, however, is further from the truth. Changes of the most dangerous character are continuously taking place in the meat, but the sodium sulphite obscures them and makes the meat appear to be fresh and of better value than it really is, and enables the seller to perpetrate an unscrupulous and deliberate fraud."

What does this have to do with meat in the United States? Over the years many butchers in this country have been caught using sodium sulphite in retail stores. A few years ago the state food commissioner of Connecticut warned market owners there that "continuation of the fast-growing practice of adding sulphite to hamburger to conceal decomposition would lead to court prosecution . . ."

Another state official, warning about violations, said sulphites do not inhibit the growth of organisms which produce poisons that cause food poisoning; consequently meats treated with the substances may look and smell all right, and, at the same time, contain toxic substances and be undergoing putrefaction.

The chemical doctoring of meat continues virtually until the consumer's teeth bite into it and end the opportunity for further treatment. One manufacturer offers a product that "imparts a charcoal flavor to the meat, especially valuable for institutional sales," *Consumers' Research* notes. "This additive will tenderize low-grade meat cuts, which are simply dipped in the magic liquid for about 45 seconds."

Another company offers a new liquid tenderizer for meat cuts intended for freezing, with the idea of "turning lower-price cuts into new profits." The supplier of "steaks" of this type claims they "never, never taste tenderized," that his product "transforms low-cost beef into mouth-watering steaks" which "eat like high-priced steaks, but can be served at just a fraction of the cost. . . . Join the ranks of profit-minded food executives."

In days past a man sat down to enjoy his Sunday dinner with little more to think about than whether the roast or chicken was properly done and seasoned to his taste. Now he must concern himself with calculated risks, human failure and some stranger's sense of responsibility—or lack of it—set against his desire for the highest possible profit.

8

Emulsifiers—
Whose Laboratory,
Which Tests?

FEW CHEMICAL ADDITIVES outrank the so-called emulsifiers as a bonanza to the food processor—and few are more suspect of causing damage to humans than some of these widely used compounds.

Emulsifiers have many uses in foods: they promote smoothness and keep incompatible ingredients like oil and water from separating; they may also be used to give stale baked goods a deceptive appearance of freshness; and they act as substitutes for more costly and nutritious natural ingredients such as eggs, milk, butter and vegetable shortening.

Some emulsifiers, in only moderate doses, have been shown to be extremely poisonous to animals; others have not been adequately tested.

Yet tens of millions of pounds of emulsifiers are used annually in foods. These compounds have a variety of names: softeners, surface-active agents, wetting agents; some are very close chemically to detergents used in laundering and cleaning.

Two main categories of emulsifiers are used in foods. To the chemist the first is composed of mono- and diglycerides, the second of polyoxyethylene monostearate and related compounds. More familiarly, they are known as the glycerides and poly compounds. The former are artificial fats derived from glycerides; the latter are derived in part from ethylene oxide, which has been aptly described as "a stranger in the food world."

In 1937 it was found that when small amounts of the

glyceride compounds were mixed with shortening and incorporated into baked goods their use resulted in "more tender" bread, buns, cake and other sweet goods. Thereafter, shortenings containing these products were marketed. Subsequently it was found that by increasing the ratio of glycerides in shortening, a very soft loaf of bread could be produced. This led to their being called "bread softeners."

In 1947 the polyoxyethylene monostearate type of bread softener appeared on the market to compete with the glyceride compounds in baked goods, ice cream and other foods. Their biggest manufacturer was a chemical company that produced explosives.

After people had consumed millions of pounds of these new softeners, evidence built up that they were not safe for use in food. Gradually they were outlawed for use in most breads, salad dressings, mayonnaise and, more recently, ice cream—foods for which standards (establishing ingredients and amounts that can be used) are fixed by Congress. They also were banned from use in meat products under the Federal Meat Inspection Act.

Following the bread hearings in 1952, Charles W. Crawford, then FDA Commissioner, was quoted in *The New York Times* as having said the polyoxyethylene monostearates would make "good paint removers."

At the time of the Delaney Committee hearings it was estimated that Americans were eating ten million pounds of the poly materials annually. A committee member said this represented ten million pounds of chemicals that were being used in place of the fats and oils that contain vital food nutrients.

Although the poly compounds have been eliminated from a few food products, they are still widely used in prepared cake mixes, cakes, hard candies, various chocolate confections, soft drinks, dill pickles, multivitamin drops, peanut butter, pressure-dispensed whipped cream, whole milk with vitamin D dispersed in it, sweet rolls, doughnuts and other products.

It should be borne in mind that unless barred by specific state law, they can be used anywhere, in any product as long as they do not cross state lines. It also is worthy of note that labels generally state only "emulsifier added," so the consumer has no way of knowing which type is used—or the amount.

In various legal actions the manufacturers of the poly compounds have tried to get their product back in use in bread. So far the courts have ruled against them.

Various hearings and legal skirmishes have given considerable publicity to tests conducted on the poly compounds. These tests suggest how thin the public's margin of safety often is when human health, life and death depend on animal experiments. The tests also dramatize and illuminate some of the fancy scientific footwork that can take place in the usually dark corridors of food-chemical testing procedures.

In testing for the toxicity of chemicals, standard procedure calls for feeding large amounts of the substance in question to animals to determine the type of injury to look for when smaller amounts are fed in chronic-toxicity studies.

Claims that the poly compounds are harmless are based primarily on experiments carried out by Dr. John C. Krantz, Jr., professor of pharmacology at the University of Maryland School of Medicine. Dr. Krantz testified before the Delaney Committee that he was hired by a manufacturer of the poly emulsifiers to conduct toxicity tests on the products.

He said his experiments covered ten years and included studies with nearly 3,000 animals—monkeys, rats, dogs, rabbits, mice and that "an occasional study was made in man." As a result of these impressive experiments, he testified, "A great amount of data is available to show that prolonged feeding of these compounds at relatively high levels is not harmful."

However, other tests conducted elsewhere did not produce such optimistic results. Some of these tests were carried on by Swift & Company, which produces mono- and diglycerides. Swift's motive in conducting the tests was questioned but not explained. Would it be cynical to suggest that the poly products were cutting into Swift's sale of glyceride compounds?

Dr. Edward Eagle, a physiologist and toxicologist with Swift, testified before the Delaney Committee that he performed experiments with several of the poly compounds. The injuries they brought about were horrendous, covering almost every part of the animals' anatomy. They ranged from retarded growth to premature death; one group of weanling hamsters fed 15 to 25 per cent of one of the compounds was said to have died within two weeks.

Dr. Eagle presented photographs of "six very large stones" taken from the urinary bladders of hamsters. He said the stones were larger than the normal bladders of the animals. In other words, he explained, "the bladder had to be stretched at this time tight as a drum to accommodate it . . ." Other random injuries listed included kidney stones, blood in the feces, hemorrhage from the genitourinary tract, liver damage, thickened bladder walls, extensive diarrhea, atrophied testes, etc.

How to reconcile the incredible difference between the findings of Dr. Eagle and Dr. Krantz, both highly qualified scientists? The Delaney Committee began to ask questions, among them, how much of the poly chemicals had each experimenter fed his animals?

Dr. Eagle said he fed the materials in amounts up to 25 per cent of their diet. He said that might sound like a lot, but the FDA was on record as having said that any substance proposed for use in food should be tested at a level of one hundred times the amount proposed for use in food.

"Now these materials are proposed [for use] at levels of 1 per cent," said Dr. Eagle, "and 100 times 1 per cent is 100 per cent, which reduces it to an absurdity. So, if on the basis of that 25 per cent, even 25 per cent is not an extremely high level."

Furthermore, he continued, "the FDA states . . . that in order to prove the nontoxicity of any substance, it has to be fed to animals at a level of 5 per cent with no harmful effects. These materials cannot be fed to animals at 5 per cent with no harmful effects."

Dr. Eagle said there were no toxicological data on man for the poly compounds, "but it has always been felt . . . that the most sensitive animal is man. If you can cause harm to any animal with anything, that material is not good for man . . . any material which is toxic to a rat or a hamster or a rabbit is unsafe for man."

And what did Dr. Krantz have to say about this? He testified that he had fed his animals the poly materials in amounts ranging from 2 to 5 per cent of their diets. Why such modest amounts? Well, he said, he tried to estimate how much of these products a man actually would eat in his diet and then he took from twenty-five to one hundred times the largest amount. He said he also varied the amount of the particular compound tested according to how much of that particular product would be ingested; the more toxic the product, the less would be eaten, he concluded, and thus the less he fed the test animals.

It also turned out there was a difference in the animals used in the two tests. Dr. Eagle got some of his most striking results by using hamsters. Hamsters are known to be especially susceptible to the effects of the poly compounds; it is standard procedure to test with the animal known to be the most sensitive to a product in order to establish maximum damage. Why didn't Dr. Krantz use hamsters?

"I have not worked with the hamster," Dr. Krantz said, except to inject some materials into them, and I didn't like them as experimental animals, and discarded them altogether in my laboratory." For most of his tests he used only rats, he said.

A committee member asked Dr. Krantz if he had been paid for conducting the tests. He said he had, and he also was a consultant to the firm.

Q. Had you been employed by some person who had indicated a desire to show that these products are harmful, would it have been possible to have changed the methods employed to reach a conclusion different from that which you did reach?

A. Sir, I only know one way of doing an experiment, and that is to bring in all of the possible conditions, and then run adequate controls and let the chips fall where they will.

Q. The reason I asked that question was, because it has been indicated here before, we have gotten such a contradictory mass of evidence that I wondered if it was possible for scientists to go about it in a different way and arrive at a different answer.

A. What has happened in many of these cases, if you will permit me to make this comment, is that people have manipulated diets, they have left out factors, they have added factors, they have made synthetic diets. . . .

The bewildered Delaney Committee tried to unravel its confusion by calling other witnesses who had experimented with the emulsifiers. Among them was Dr. B. S. Schweigert head of the division of biochemistry and physiology of the American Meat Foundation, who had conducted his tests with the help of Dr. Anton J. Carlson at the University of Chicago. While their experiments did not turn up quite so sensational a catalogue of biological horrors as did the Swift tests, they did disclose extensive damage to several internal organs.

Dr. Schweigert testified that short-term tests with hamsters fed some of the poly compounds at 5 per cent of their diet, showed "definite deleterious effects" after ten weeks. He said no experiments had been conducted with lower levels.

Whether the poly compounds should be added to foods is a problem that involves not only their safety and degree of toxicity, he said, but also whether they contribute anything nutritionally to the food. "As far as I have been able to ascertain, they would reduce the caloric value of the food . . . so that . . . aside from the question of safety, then, the problem of the nutritive value of the product also must be considered.

Dr. Schweigert pointed out that it was also necessary to remember that some people eat relatively large quantities of a single food. "Some older people or young children . . . might not have as great an ability to prevent deleterious effects of a chemical as some people who do not eat so much of it or are generally in a better state of health or perhaps are middle-aged," he stated.

Dr. Carlson, also testifying about the poly products, said much work should be done on a great many species of animals before these chemicals could be considered safe. The outcome of such long-time work could not be predicted, he said. because "the subclinical injury, serious injury, we have no certain methods to detect. Small amounts of injury in certain percentages of the people may go undiscovered for generations. This is a serious problem involved in the changes of such fundamental things as that type of food for man."

Dr. Carlson also defended the use of testing certain poly compounds although they were not actually used in foods, pointing out that such testing serves as a guide to possible injurious consequences from chemically related compounds that *are* being used In view of the test results of the poly compounds, he flatly said, "We should not yet introduce them in human food," adding that the number of foods they were used in accentuated the problem.

Another witness who testified about tests on the products was Dr. Robert S. Harris, head of the nutritional bio-chemistry laboratories at Massachusetts Institute of Technology. Dr. Harris said the tests there were financed, half by the Shortening Institute and half by M.I.T., and that they were done at his personal request after he attended the bread hearings that lead to fixed standards for bread. His only motive, he said, was to test a vitamin theory of his in relation to the use of the poly chemicals; he emphasized that he had no personal interest in the outcome.

Dr. Harris said his tests showed no vitamin K deficiency among rats fed the poly substances; but some of the animals lost their tails and others died prematurely; those that survived suffered such ailments as kidney and bladder stones, liver damage, impaired growth, diarrhea, poor food utilization and other adverse effects.

Dr. Harris was asked if he could explain why the results of his tests, which paralleled findings of the Schweigert-Carlson studies, were so radically different from those of Dr. Krantz.

The primary difference, he said, was the amount of the substances fed to the animals. He said the 25 per cent dietary level he used was not excessive, because it represented only fifty times the expected exposure of the population. If these compounds are used extensively in the food supply, he added, "I don't think that a level of fifty times the expected exposure for a substance that is to be used in staple foods is a high level at all. . . . I might add that I feel that maybe this level should be increased above twenty-five times when this substance is to be used in staple foods and foods that will be consumed from day to day."

Many things could influence the outcome of feeding tests on animals, he explained: the amount of the compound given, the number and species used, whether the material was fed by mouth or into the stomach by tube, the animals' diet, length of time the tests were continued and many other factors.

Many toxicity tests in the past were unreliable, Dr. Harris testified, because the animal groups studied were too small, their diets were inadequate nutritionally, routine observations were not extensive, the histopathology (tissue studies) was improperly done, and other factors.

"Toxicity tests require the combined skills of the nutritional biochemist, the toxicologist, and pathologist," he said. "Since none of these is fully qualified to carry out these studies alone, they should be conducted by a team of experts." This is an ideal which has been met so rarely that it casts serious doubt on most of the tests purporting to prove the safety of chemicals now in use.

Finally, said Dr. Harris, animal tests can at best be only guides and *"no toxicity tests on animals ever give absolute proof of the harmlessness of a compound in human beings."* [Emphasis the author's.]

Complete testing of a compound costs $25,000 to $50,000, he said. "Though large, the sum is insignificant, for we are dealing with human health and the human life. *It is likely that some of our chemically treated foods are partly responsible for some of the illness of the American people; whether the incidence is great, no one knows. It is also likely that chemicals in foods have caused deaths, but again we do not know how frequently."* [Emphasis the author's.]

Dr. Harris made the significant statement that at the time he ran his tests a proposal was before the FDA to permit use of the poly compounds as optional ingredients in white bread and flour without restriction. But after results of his tests were made known, he said, the proposal was changed to exclude the laurate (poly) type of compound.

"Possibly," he added, "if more work were done on some of the compounds still included in the revised proposal, they too might have been shown to be harmful to animals and the proposal would then be restricted still further."

This suggests that, had it not been for Dr. Harris' chance experiments, the poly compounds probably would have been included in the bread standards as adopted, and that he was not satisfied that the emulsifiers still permitted to be used in bread had been proved conclusively safe.

The standards provided for the use of mono- and diglycerides, and they are still in use.

In a sideswipe at the glyceride emulsifiers, Isaac Fogg, president of Atlas Powder Company, said the two types of emulsifiers were "used substantially for the same purpose"

and were in competition; also that "twice as much mono-
and diglycerides generally is needed to do the same job"
as the poly compounds.

"Manufacturers of mono- and diglycerides devoted their
case at FDA almost exclusively to testimony designed to
exclude Atlas products from the proposed bread standards," he charged, "while seeking to mask the true bread-
softening effects of their own emulsifiers. . . ."

Citing previous testimony about tests on poly emulsifiers
by Swift's scientists and the American Meat Institute
Foundation, Mr. Fogg declared: "Although the Chicago
record shows that mono- and diglycerides are the end result of a chemical process and are surface-active agents
like Atlas products, I think it is significant that while one
of these competitors spent considerable time and money
testing Atlas emulsifiers, he admitted to comparatively little
knowledge of safety tests on his own mono- and
diglycerides.

"Many of the questions our competitors have sought to
raise about the safety of our products apply to mono- and
diglycerides as well. These questions, as I understand it,
have to do with the effects of surface-active agents on the
absorption and digestion of other foods in the body. If
such questions are valid as applied to our products, they
are equally applicable to all types of surface-active agents."

Mr. Fogg then made a revealing statement about the in-
tramural aspects of competitive practices among companies
selling chemical additives and the government's role as an
impartial observer:

"It happens that the two giant manufacturers of glycerides are also the principal producers of emulsifying
shortening. Through a system of patent licensing they had
developed for themselves and their licensees an exclusive
business in the addition of chemical emulsifiers to shortening. The food industry's growing preference for Atlas
emulsifiers has posed a definite threat to the monopolistic
position of these vast concerns."

Stating that Atlas was asking to reopen the bread hearings so they could prove there had been discrimination,
Mr. Fogg continued:

"Essentially, we are requesting that mono- and diglycerides be subjected by FDA to the same criteria, standards, and tests as our products—a comparison which has
not been made in the bread hearings to date. Moreover,

we have specifically suggested to FDA that all competing surface-active agents, including both mono- and diglycerides and Atlas emulsifiers, be subjected to tests by an impartial research group, with both the testing body and method determined by FDA. . . .

"It is not in the American tradition . . . for a government agency to favor one product over another without subjecting both to the same scrutiny. . . ."

Mr. Fogg's remarks about the unknown effects of softeners were underscored by warnings that appeared elsewhere. *Baker's Weekly* (June 25, 1951) discussed a "not for publication" study of the Food and Nutrition Board of the National Research Council.

The report cautioned that there was insufficient scientific information to justify their use in foods "at this time," and there was no conclusive proof "that their effect will be harmless, especially when used in a variety of foods consumed over a long period of time. . . . On surface-active agents generally, including the mono- and diglycerides, they feel that additional research is necessary in order to judge the accumulative effect of such materials as found in various types of foods."

An earlier report of the American Medical Association's Council on Foods and Nutrition noted that the "widespread" addition of surface-active agents into foods was viewed by the Council "with considerable apprehension. . . . Available knowledge of the possible toxicity of these substances is fragmentary; particularly is evidence lacking as to chronic toxicity. The employment of these agents in the processing of such basic foods as bread and bakery goods, as well as other foods . . . could lead to the ingestion of considerable quantities of these materials of uncertain toxicologic action. . . ."

Another critic of the softeners was the American Institute of Baking, which advised against their use as early as 1945. When Dr. William B. Bradley, scientific director of the Institute, appeared before the Delaney Committee in 1951, he was asked whether the use of softeners—aside from the question of toxicity—was in the interest of consumers.

"I do not see that it performs a function useful to the consumer," he replied.

He pointed out that the poly softeners did not keep bread from going stale but merely kept it soft. A loaf of bread that contained them would be soft, he said, but it also could be "somewhat stale," adding that softeners do not retard the staling process "at all."

The committee, turning its attention to the glyceride compounds, focused on one called Esterine, manufactured by Swift & Company.

Q. What recommendations were made to bakers by the manufacturers of Esterine?

A. At one time it was claimed that Esterine could be used to increase the absorption of the doughs, in other words, to provide a means of getting more water into the dough. . . .

Q. Putting more water in?

A. Yes, sir.

Q. Saving money for the baker?

A. Well, it could. If he doesn't bake it out, it could.

Dr. Bradley was asked if the reaction product of the wheat starch with the monoglycerides was digestible by the enzymes of the intestinal tract. He replied:

"I do not know. I know that in the test tubes . . . that product remains undigested, but whether it is digested in the alimentary tract or not, I do not know."

He then was asked if he had reached a conclusion with respect to the value to consumers of the use of the mono- and diglycerides as bread ingredients.

A. Yes, sir.

Q. What conclusion have you reached?

A. I think that it is of no value to the ultimate consumer.

Q. Would you repeat that, please?

A. I think it is of no value to the ultimate consumer.

Several other witnesses testified that the use of emulsifiers had made it possible to replace natural ingredients of high nutritional value—fats, oils, eggs and milk—in baked goods containing these chemicals. A U.S. Department of Agriculture official lamented that this substitution could work to the disadvantage of the farm economy—but others noted that it also might not be so good for human beings, either.

9

White Bread—
Enriched but
Still Impoverished

(1)

THE AVERAGE LOAF of commercial white bread sold today is primarily the product of chemical ingenuity, clever mechanical technology and advertising guile.

It is subjected to a bombardment of chemicals, stripped of virtually all nutrients, given a few synthetic vitamins, shot with emulsifier to keep it soft and, with a final touch of Voltairian irony, sold to the gullible public as an enriched product.

Bread and most other commercial baked goods are more closely allied with the test tube than with nature. Several years ago Emanuel Kaplan and Ferdinand A. Dorff, of the Baltimore City Health Department, listed the chemical fate of the various ingredients used in common bakery practice. Their report, "Exotic Chemicals in Food," was presented at a meeting of Food and Drug Association officials and published in the *Quarterly Bulletin* of the Association of Food and Drug Officials of the United States. Some of its highlights were these statements:

Let us quickly consider the chemical treatment of the various ingredients used in bakery practice. The flour is derived from seeds probably treated for plant disease protection with organic mercurials or similar agents and the seeds are planted on soil influenced by fertilizers. Selenium (an exceedingly poisonous mineral substance) may be extracted from the soil. In milling, flour is treated with improvers, oxidizing agents such as persulfate, bromate, io-

date and nitrogen trichloride, which affect protease activity
and gluten properties.

Bleaching agents such as oxides of nitrogen, chlorine and
benzoyl peroxide convert the yellow carotenoid pigment to
colorless compounds because of alleged consumer desire
for white bread. Vitamins and minerals are added in com-
pulsory "enrichment." Mineral salts may be added to sta-
bilize gas-retaining properties of flour gluten. Cyanide or
chlorinated organic compounds may be employed in fumi-
gation of the resulting flour in storage.

The water used may be chemically purified by means of
alum, soda ash, copper sulfate and chlorine. In the refining of sugar, lime, sulfur dioxide, phosphates and charcoal
are employed. The salt may contain iodide and agents such
as calcium and magnesium carbonates to promote "free-
running" and prevent caking.

Ammonium salts and other chemicals are employed as
yeast nutrients. To help feed the yeast diastatic enzymes
in the form of malt preparations may be used. Chemical
leaveners may contain sodium bicarbonate, alum, tartrates,
phosphates, starch, and cream of tartar. Fluorine is a possible natural contaminant of the phosphate. The shortening
is a refined, bleached, deodorized product, possibly hydrogenated to change liquid oil to plastic fat and if so, containing traces of nickel; or the shortening may be glycer-
inated and may contain antioxidants.

Oleomargarine, if used, may have added color, vitamin
A, neutralizers, interface modifiers and preservative; or the
margarine may be packaged in a preservative-treated wrapper. Mineral oil is frequently used as a dough trough or
pan lubricant. The eggs may be liquid, dry, or frozen
whole eggs, yolk or white, treated with sugar, glycerine,
preservative or interface modifier.

. Milk or milk products may contain neutralizer and antioxidants. Special pastry shells may be treated with alkalies
such as ammonium carbonate, which incidentally through
excessive use denature the protein and render it indiges-
tible. In pie making, the fruits employed probably contain
sulfite and perhaps added citric acid, vitamin C or other
antioxidant. Artificial coal tar color may be used.

Stabilizers and thickeners such as gums and treated
starches may be employed as fillers. Synthetic flavors used
contain glycerine, alcohol or substitute chemicals as solv-
ents for a variety of alcohols, aldehydes, esters, acids and

ketones, and may contain saccharin. Spices may be natural spices subjected to fumigants or solvent-extracted spice essences. Mold inhibitors such as calcium propionate may be employed and the final product may be contaminated on the store shelf with insecticidal powders such as sodium fluoride.

The report could not note the deluge of new chemicals that have come into common use since it was published a decade ago; it also could not take into account the fact that virtually every ingredient would be contaminated by residue of DDT and other powerful new pesticides that now drench the earth.

Among the ingredients mentioned in the report, the hydrogenated oils, whose use is increasing, deserve elaboration. These have been closely linked to heart disease. Production of hydrogenated oils now amounts to one billion pounds annually.

Hydrogenation turns liquid oils solid, so they may be stored longer without turning rancid, and are less subject to absorption of extraneous tastes and odors. Dr. Jolliffe says that diets high in saturated fats (including hydrogenated oils) result in high levels of blood cholesterol. It is believed that this substance is deposited in the arteries, bringing on heart disease.

The most common ingredient in baking is white flour. In the diet of the average American, white flour, refined white sugar and saturated (non-liquid) fats make up more than half his food intake, according to many nutritionists. This means a diet composed primarily of carbohydrates, without compensating protein to build and maintain the body.

The fate that befalls an innocent wheat berry more fittingly belongs in the annals of crime than in a treatise on foods. "We throw away the germ and the vitamins and a great deal of the valuable proteins and retain essentially the starch," noted Dr. Carlson. "Then we call that bread or flour enriched when as a matter of fact it is still impoverished. . . . If we had to depend on white bread, as the people in the Orient depend on polished rice, we would be a sicker people than we are."

The starchy, anemic part of the wheat grain that survives the milling process is an excellent vehicle to hold the chemicals and water that go into it. The *Medical Press*, a prominent British journal for physicians, observed that among the changes chemical adulteration has brought in foods is the baking of loaves of bread which are very large for their weight, containing "as much water as can be persuaded to 'stand up.' "

The baking industry as a whole has been content to sell the public a counterfeit product labeled bread, concentrating on high-pressure advertising to proclaim its nonexistent tastiness and nutritional properties. Among the few exceptions has been Pepperidge Farm in Norwalk, Connecticut; the success of their product proves that the public is willing to pay premium prices for quality if it understands the advantage in nutrition and taste.

While the baking industry cannot be blamed entirely for the widespread use of white bread, it has done little to re-educate the public to the advantages of whole-wheat bread made from freshly ground wheat. It has compounded this disservice by producing a whole-wheat bread lacking in taste and quality. Almost anyone who has eaten well prepared home-made whole-wheat bread is forever spoiled for eating ordinary commercial breads.

In re-educating the public to the taste and nutritive qualties of whole-wheat bread, one of the primary obstacles to be overcome is tradition. As far back as the days of the Roman Empire it was a social distinction to eat white bread; only the lower classes had dark bread. Dr. Carlson recalled: "I have seen educated American women, college graduates, crying when they saw the Russian Cossacks eating that black bread, which is whole rye, and it is the thing that keeps the Russian going. We ignorant Americans cry and think that is terrible."

A second obstacle to overcome is the common belief that there is little if any nutritional difference between white and whole-wheat bread. The baker is delighted to maintain this canard because white flour will keep much longer than whole-wheat. Several scientists have noted that bugs avoid bleached flour because it doesn't have enough nutrition to keep them alive. "Only humans eat it," said Dr. Carlson.

Samuel Lepkovsky of the College of Agriculture at the University of California in Berkeley, and author of *The Bread Problem in War and in Peace*, noted that "instead of being alarmed at the decreased nutritive value of white flour as shown by the inability of insect pests to thrive on it, the production of white flour was hailed as a great forward step."

For more than twenty-five years flour was bleached and "matured" with nitrogen trichloride, a gas known as Agene. But in 1946 the late Sir Edward Mellanby, a distinguished British physician and nutritionist, discovered that dogs fed bread made with Agene-treated flour developed "running fits" or "canine hysteria."

Not until 1950 was Agene legally banned for use, and it was not until 1955 that the ban was enforced—some ten years after the substance was found to be a powerful nerve poison for dogs.

With the prohibition of the use of Agene, the government repeatedly emphasized that industry voluntarily quit using the substance before it legally had to, citing this as an example of industry's sense of responsibility to the people. Much also was made of the fact that there was no proof that human beings had been injured by consuming Agene-treated flour.

Having demonstrated their sense of responsibility by voluntarily renouncing Agene only after a substitute gas was found, the flour millers announced that its replacement would be chlorine dioxide. The 1948 edition of the authoritative *Lockwood's Flour Milling* had this to say about that substance:

Chlorine dioxide (Addage process)—The use of chlorine dioxide is more powerful than nitrogen trichloride (Agene); the quantities used are one-third to half those of nitrogen trichloride. Chlorine dioxide not only oxidizes the flour pigment but also has a valuable bleaching effect on the coloring matter of bran, which makes it particularly valuable for bleaching low grade flours.

Use of chlorine dioxide was approved over the protests of many U.S. nutritionists. The FDA lists the gas as a poisonous substance, permitting it on grounds that it is "probably safe as normally used." The late Leonard Wickenden, a noted chemist, cheerfully pointed out in his book *Our Daily Poison* that "No one has yet discovered that it gives dogs running fits so it is considered quite safe."

While Agene and chlorine dioxide generally are called bleaches, their primary purpose is to age flour artificially.

Aging is considered necessary to give some flours the right consistency, but to avoid costly storage and waiting for the process to take place naturally, they are given a shot of gas.

One of the first great crusaders for replacing white flour with whole-wheat was Sylvester Graham. Lepkovsky says Graham had an unusually good understanding of the nutritive properties of bread, noting that whole-wheat bread was almost a complete food and in addition could cure digestive disorders such as constipation and diarrhea; he also warned that removal of the bran by bolting (separating it from) the milled flour reduced the nutritive value.

Lepkovsky quoted a J. B. Orr as recalling that during the Napoleonic wars the men from northern England and southern Scotland who lived in the country and had plenty of whole-wheat grain, milk, eggs and vegetables were big, powerful and energetic men who made the best infantry soldiers of Europe. During the Boer war a large percentage of the recruits from this district were short, frail weaklings who could not be used as soldiers.

"A commission was appointed to investigate the cause of this striking change in the physical condition of these men, and the most probable explanation found was that many people who had moved off the land and had gone into the slums of the big cities where their eating habits had changed, and they were depending too largely on white flour and sugar."

In Denmark, during World War I, grains were not refined. As a result of this improved nutrition the death rate reportedly decreased substantially: cancer, diabetes, high blood pressure and heart and kidney diseases dropped sharply, and the general health of the population was greatly improved. Similar improvements in health were observed in England during World War II, when grains were only slightly milled.

As far back as April 1919, the U.S. Public Health Service issued a warning that pellagra, beriberi and other deficiency diseases in the South had been traced to the refining of grains. But the millers applied such pressure that six months after the warning bulletin was issued the same public health officials backtracked by issuing a "correcting" bulletin, asserting that white bread was wholesome if balanced in the diet by an adequate consumption of the so-called protective foods: fruits, vegetables and dairy products.

This introduced a technique that has been widely used since then by apologists for the food industry. In effect they were saying that it didn't hurt to eat a deficient food if enough other nutritious foods were eaten to compensate for its shortcomings.

The fallacy of the claim is apparent. People don't look upon bread as a frivolous food; they buy it for nutritive values. In many families it is a major part of the diet, especially among lower-income groups who depend upon it for a filler as well as a nutritional base. These people know nothing about protective foods that are supposed to be eaten as a crutch for the ailing white loaf, and the wrapper never carries a warning to that effect.

The correcting bulletin on bread marked a black milestone in the Government's retreat from its obligation to protect the people from avaricious commercial interests. It was to serve as both policy and formula in subsequent clashes between public and industrial welfare.

Despite spirited opposition to white bread by many doctors and health officials, the milling industry laid down a massive propaganda barrage which buried its opponents. Anyone who attacked the nutritive values of white bread was denounced. Industry was aided in this campaign by organized medicine and the Government.

On May 7, 1930, the millers won a tremendous victory when the United States Department of Agriculture issued a release signed by a dozen eminent nutritionists in and out of government. The nub of this release was its conclusion:

> Bread, either white or whole wheat, is always an economical source of energy and protein in any diet. The form may be left to the choice of the individual when the remainder of the diet is so constituted as to contribute the necessary minerals, vitamins, and any necessary roughage.

This followed the established pattern noted previously. All it said was, in effect, that the deficiencies of white bread would not become apparent if the rest of the diet compensated for them.

This technique of misleading the public about the nutritive value of milled grains is still in effect, along with the parallel technique of assailing anyone who attempts to interfere with profits from the sale of impoverished foods.

(2)

By the time World War II erupted, opposition to white flour and bread had been virtually stilled. But, as pointed out by Lepkovsky, it was apparent under the impact of war that the nutrition of the army and civilians would play a major role in the struggle of survival and "the nutritional poverty of white bread as compared with whole-wheat was so great as to demand attention."

This led to the fortification of white bread.

The fact that it was found necessary to fortify bread with additional vitamins and minerals should have been proof that the previous claims about its nutritional values were misleading. Unfortunately, however, this self-evident fact was buried under a new propaganda barrage that a good product was being made even better.

To understand what is involved in fortifying bread, it is helpful to observe what happens to the grain in milling:

A grain of wheat, or berry, as it is called, is composed of three principal parts: the outer shell or husk, the endosperm or kernel and the germ from which the grain reproduces itself. When the grain is planted the husk protects the seed while it germinates, and the endosperm—a carbohydrate—feeds the germ until it gets a foothold and takes nutrients from the earth and air.

The modern steel flour mill is a devilishly clever device; it removes the husk and the germ of a grain of wheat, leaving only the endosperm; it is the endosperm from which flour is made.

The flour that emerges is little more than pure starch, containing only about seven to eleven per cent low-grade protein; when mixed with water the flour becomes an easily shaped paste. The miller loves white flour because of its long-keeping qualities and unattractiveness to bugs. But a secondary attraction is that he can sell the removed bran as feed for animals, and the wheat germ as a food supplement for human beings and animals.

Dr. Carlson testified that "It is a tragedy to me . . . that we mill the best of our ingredients out of our grain and that the best part is fed to hogs and cattle while we eat the poorest part."

In the discarded parts are nutrients essential to human health and life. The husk (itself made up of three layers) is composed of minerals and vitamins, including the essential B vitamins. The germ, along with its high protein and mineral content, is rich in vitamin E and the complete vitamin B; this is one of the few sources of vitamin E, which is known to play an essential part in animal reproduction and is believed to be important in human reproduction. Recent studies suggest that vitamin-E deficiency may be a factor in heart disease.

Vitamin B, once thought to consist of a single vitamin, now is known to consist of at least ten separate vitamins, and it is believed there are others—perhaps many others —still unidentified. These are known as the B complex. The vitamin B complex is necessary to the function of every cell in the body, and when it is lacking, affections of the liver, the cardiovascular system, the nervous system and the digestive system occur.

An extreme vitamin B shortage can lead to beriberi and pellagra, once rampant in the southern United States, but in less acute form these ailments—still widely prevalent— are often diagnosed as other forms of illness.

Because of misleading propaganda, people in the United States seldom think of themselves as suffering from vitamin and other dietary deficiencies due to poor nutrition. But the fact is that a large proportion of the population does not eat enough of the right foods, and many people are on the border of deficiency diseases from improper diet.

The late Dr. Tom D. Spies, one of the most famous and highly respected physicians and nutrition researchers in America, has pointed out: "Investigation of the diets of large groups of people correlated with laboratory studies and direct examination has led to the startling observation that the margin of safety against deficiency disease is narrow rather than broad, that the presence of nutritional inadequacy is widespread and not limited to the lower economic group. As information is increasing, it is found that relatively few people in the United States consistently eat diets that are adequate in all respects. . . ."

Most of the investigations of Dr. Spies, who was chairman of the Department of Nutrition and Metabolism at Northwestern University Medical School and Professor of Nutrition and Metabolism at the celebrated Hillman Hospital in Birmingham, Alabama, centered around vitamin B deficiencies. He and other researchers have expressed concern about the frequency with which a deficiency of this essential vitamin complex is encountered.

The wheat germ is one of only four known sources of the complete vitamin B, and few if any other sources contain as much vitamin E. As already noted, bleaching destroys the flour's carotene content, which is a source of vitamin A. Between the ingenious milling process and the heat generated by modern mills made of steel (which replaced stone mills) virtually all vitamins and most of the minerals—including calcium and iron—are removed in processing.

Dr. Lionel Picton, who has championed whole wheat, noted that in 1864 18 ounces of bread made from whole wheat contained 540 units of the complete vitamin B, and before fortification 18 ounces of white bread contained just 70 units.

Daily consumption of whole-wheat bread in 1840 is said to have assured 1,200 units of natural B_1 while today's average daily intake of *fortified bread* assures only 200 units, mostly synthetic.

Although the nutritional shortcomings of white bread were not corrected by the fortifying program, it was an ingenious solution to the baking industry's problem. The millers could answer their critics, claiming they were doing their part to improve the nation's health, while they continued the profitable practice of milling most nutrients out of the grain and added a slight charge for a few synthetic vitamins pumped into the bread.

Despite the opportunities for propaganda and advertising that enrichment offered, the baking and flour interests at first were only lukewarm toward the program. Only when convinced it would be national suicide not to improve the diet did they lend their reluctant support. Later, however, they realized the commercial advantages to be gained and became enthusiastic supporters of the "new improved loaf."

The enrichment program had only the half-hearted support of nutritionists; many openly opposed it. There was never any real question about the nutritional superiority of whole-wheat over white bread, even when the latter was "enriched." This fact was established by numerous experiments on both sides of the Atlantic.

At a meeting of the National Nutrition Conference, Dr. John Murlin of the University of Rochester disclosed that dogs fed the six synthetic vitamins proposed for use in "enriched" bread "remained deficient, but the deficiency cleared up at once when the dogs were fed yeast, indicating essential but as yet unknown factors in the vitamin B complex."

This confirmed warnings by other researchers that enrichment would add just part of the B complex to the diet, and while thiamine was necessary to the diet, they said, so were other factors in the B complex; they added that an adequate diet could be compared with a chain whose strength was determined by its weakest link.

Many investigators pointed out that splitting the B complex was strictly a laboratory maneuver, never occurring in nature. Several researchers warned that giving only a couple of synthetic single B vitamins, rather than the entire B complex, might create imbalances with adverse consequences.

Dr. Marion B. Richards, a British investigator, demonstrated that overloading a diet with vitamin B_1 could produce a deficiency of vitamin B_6, producing symptoms of deficiency because the B complex had been unbalanced. Dr. Richards concluded by warning that attempts to improve the diet with indiscriminate additions of large supplements of single synthetic B vitamins might bring on ailments more serious than those they were designed to correct.

Dr. Richards' countryman, Dr. Picton, found it unfortunate that "enriching" was always referred to as adding vitamins to the bread. "It is perhaps a pity that they did not phrase it 'restored to,'" he said wryly, "for then the public might have asked, 'Why ever was it taken out?'"

Lepkovsky noted that the British turned the question of "enrichment" into a national debate that spilled over from the scientific world into the trade and lay press and was hotly debated on all sides. In Canada, he said, the medical men and nutritionists early appreciated the superiority of whole-wheat over "enriched" white bread and Canada's leading scientists "took a definite stand against fortification of white flour. They insisted that the way to get the vitamin B complex in bread was to so mill the wheat that these vitamins would be retained." Canada subsequently made it illegal to "enrich" bread. Great Britain adopted the practice for a while and dropped it.

The American performance on the "enrichment" program, Lepkovsky observed, "seems below par. Unlike the

English, the Americans have not discussed with any degree
of thoroughness the relative merits of whole-wheat bread,
white bread and 'enriched' white bread."

Perhaps the most outspoken critic of the "enrichment"
proposal was a United States Health Service official, who
delivered this blast: ". . . to me it seems a little ridiculous
to take a natural foodstuff in which the vitamins and minerals have been placed by nature, submit this foodstuff to
a refining process which removes them, and then add them
back to the refined product at an increased cost. Yet this
seems to be the thing that is being proposed. If this is the
object, why not follow the cheaper, more sensible, and
nutritionally more desirable procedure of simply using the
unrefined, or, at most, slightly refined natural food?"

Within a year, however, he had seen the error of his
ways and was a vigorous advocate of the enrichment program. Apparently it no longer seemed ridiculous to him to
remove some twenty natural vitamins and minerals from
bread, replace them with four or five synthetic ones at
higher cost and call the product "enriched."

In spite of the voluminous evidence that pointed to the
folly and irresponsibility of fortifying bread, the Food and
Nutrition Board of the National Research Council announced on January 29, 1941, its recommendation to
enrich flour and bread. Lepkovsky said:

"The Council on Foods and Nutrition of the American
Medical Association accepted the 'enriched' white flour
because 'thiamin is the component which makes whole
wheat most significant in the diet at the present time.' No
attempt was made to justify this sweeping statement. The
council pointed out the presence of factors other than
thiamin in whole wheat not present in white flour, but this
objection to white flour was conveniently sidestepped by
calling these other factors 'plus values' which the Council
assumed, without any supporting evidence, were furnished
by the rest of the diet. Yet they recognized that the 'rest'
of many poorer diets might not furnish these 'plus values.'

"Finally, they emphasize the high nutritional qualities
of whole wheat and recommended undermilled flours.
Thus the Council on Food and Nutrition straddled the
issue of whole-wheat flour versus 'enriched' white flour and
failed to give the country the leadership so ably given to
England by the British Medical Council. Moreover, direct
experimental evidence proved that the 'plus values' were

not present in the diet of large sections of our population."

In May 1941, Lepkovsky continued, the National Nutrition Conference for Defense met at Washington to discuss nutritional problems created by the war emergency. " 'Enriched' white flour was accepted without discussion."

Lepkovsky found it difficult to see how in the face of the "impressive evidence of the nutritional superiority of whole-wheat bread, backed as it is by so many feeding tests," the AMA's Committee on Food and Nutrition could recommend "enriched" white flour.

In May 1941, the enrichment formula for bread was established. The formula returned three—later four—of twenty known (and probably others not yet identified) elements that were removed from whole-wheat bread and was launched under the banner of "enriched."

The program at first was adopted as a voluntary wartime measure, but became mandatory in January 1943.

Once more the Government made the public guinea pigs in a mass chemical experiment.

Numerous experiments since the program was adopted have confirmed the nutritional inadequacy of "enriched" bread compared to whole wheat. In one experiment carried out by Dr. Estelle Hawley, Associate Professor of Pediatrics and Nutrition at Rochester University, one group of rats was fed "enriched" commercial white bread and another was given bread made with the Cornell formula. The latter, formulated by Dr. Clive McCay at Cornell, consists of *unbleached* flour enriched with natural food products: wheat germ, soy-bean flour and a high proportion of milk solids.

Rats on the McCay-Cornell formula thrived, as did their offspring through the fourth generation. Rats on the commercial white bread became sickly and starved-looking and produced stunted offspring; all died off and the strain became extinct before the fourth generation.

The McCay formula produced such a superior white bread that the entrenched bread interests screamed. This brought the FDA on the run to protest that Dr. McCay's bread could not be sold in interstate commerce as white bread. It was too good to be called bread. FDA wanted to call it cake. Only after much controversy was the loaf permitter to be called bread—if the ingredients were printed on the label.

Few nutritionists have had kind words to say about "enriched" bread, and those who have come to its support usually cannot be properly described as financially disinterested. Most nutritionists without commercial ties have been uniformly outspoken against it.

One of the more pithy attacks was launched by nutritionist Adelle Davis, author of many books in her field. She said about "enriched" bread: "Enriched—yes—enriched like *you* are enriched when a highway robber takes your money at the point of a gun, then returns to you a dime to buy streetcar fare home . . . So-called 'enriched' flour is my idea of outright dishonesty."

10

The Sugar Story

WHITE SUGAR REPRESENTS another victim of the food refiner's black art. Chemical wizardry has enabled him to strip natural sugar-producing crops of their original nutrients until there remains only a pure carbohydrate incapable of sustaining life.

The American people are among the heaviest users of sugar in the world, averaging more than one hundred pounds per capita—compared to consumption a hundred years ago of only ten pounds per person.

Sugar represents about 9 per cent by weight of the total food consumed. According to the American Medical Association's *Handbook of Nutrition,* "It is clear that the present large consumption of sugar is disadvantageous in that it means a smaller consumption of nutritionally superior foods. . . ."

Behind the conversion of the American diet into a huge sugar bowl is a long and complex story, not without intrigue and drama, that involves national and international economics, pressure politics and an undercover clash between nutritionists and commercial interests.

It is not pertinent to this book to go into the fascinating but extraneous economic-political history of sugar production, except to note that it is a major industry in the United States; sugar interests maintain powerful lobbies in Washington, and much of the national economy is based on the tremendous growth and consumption of the commodity. Under the U. S. Sugar Act of 1937, sugar is one of the most planned products in the whole United States economy —the planning being based on annual consumption which at the time of the act was about 100 pounds per capita.

Behind the phenomenal growth of sugar consumption is a national sweet tooth that has been exploited by a relentless campaign of propaganda and advertising based on duplicity and half truths.

Americans have been educated to believe that sugar is a "quick-energy" food that is good for a quick pick-up. This theme has been so skillfully instilled in the national consciousness that countless numbers of people, already overweight and suffering the accompanying afflictions, managed to feel virtuous as they nibble their favorite sweet.

To the nutritionist, refined sugar represents "empty calories"—it supplies none of the protective or body-building elements necessary to sustain life. No vitamins, minerals or proteins. Further, it requires greater expenditure of body energy to utilize it than the energy it produces.

Carlton Fredericks, nutritionist, who had a popular radio program on WOR in New York, is an outspoken foe of sugar. He cites experimental evidence by Dr. Russell Wilder, a Mayo Clinic physician, who found that increased use of sugar leads to a vitamin-B deficiency; a diet that ordinarily would be adequate in B vitamins became inadequate when the intake of sugar was increased.

Is excessive sugar intake a factor in the widespread vitamin deficiencies among people in this country? The National Research Council's 1945 Bulletin of the Food and Nutritional Board, based on the correlated findings of 189 research reports and surveys from coast to coast, concluded: "All evidence is in agreement that deficiency states are common among the population of the United States."

Any good book on nutrition points out the harmful effects of refined sugar—too much sugar or too many sweets of any kind, in fact. Research has shown it to be an indisputable factor in dental decay. Many medical investigators are convinced that it is at least a contributing cause of many ailments.

The threat is increased because of the vast amount of sugar unsuspectingly consumed. Adelle Davis has pointed out that "our American diet has become largely one of sugar . . . it seems that the survival of every person unaware of nutrition is at stake: caught in this tide, the innocent victim is flooded by waves of sugar every time he entertains or is entertained, every time he eats at a restaurant, and often at every home meal and mid-meal. . . . This situation is not usually realized because many sugars are hidden. Persons may consume one or even two cups of sugar daily and still believe they have eaten 'no sugar at all.'

"Besides the obvious sugar added to such foods as cereals, coffee, and fruits, or consumed in candy, jam, or jellies, as much as one or two tablespoons or more of granulated sugar is obtained in each small glass of fruit-ade, ginger ale, cola drinks, cider, Manhattans, and highballs; every serving of cake, pie, gelatin dessert, ice cream, pudding, custard, or canned fruit with juice; or even a single cookie."

Many of these hidden sources of sugar are starches. The body can get all the starch it needs, along with valuable vitamins and minerals, from whole grains and fresh fruits and vegetables; but man's sweet tooth, which should direct him to these essential foods, has been perverted by concentrated sweets and processed foods that are almost wholly starches.

A particularly rich source of hidden sugar is soft drinks, as noted by Dr. McCay in testifying before the Delaney Committee. Dr. McCay said that while he was in charge of nutrition research for the Navy during World War II, studies were made on certain soft drinks, and it was found that all soft drinks consisted of about ten per cent sugar.

This discovery, he said, led to some even more startling disclosures:

"Since 1943," he testified, "we have devoted substantial research to the study of injurious effects of the class of soft drinks known as the cola beverages. During World War II . . . I made a study of food purchases by men at ship's service. Much money was spent for 'cokes.' The cola industry was given sugar certificates for all the sugar sold to the armed services. While studying these certificates I was amazed to learn that the beverage contained substantial amounts of phosphoric acid. . . .

"At the Naval Medical Research Institute we put human teeth in a cola beverage and found they softened and started to dissolve within a short period."

He added that one of his laboratory technicians "became so expert in judging the conditions of the surface of the molar teeth of rats that she could tell those that had had one drink of cola beverage amounting to two and a half teaspoonfuls. . . . We have published data indicating that the molar teeth of rats are dissolved down to the gum line if rats are well fed but given nothing to drink except cola beverage for a period of six months."

Dr. McCay noted that dentists at the Mayo Clinic, Rochester, Minnesota, had published photographs of patients' teeth that were believed to have been eroded by cola beverages.

Data have been published, he continued, "indicating that the cola beverages contain substantial amounts of caffeine. These cola beverages deserve careful consideration not only in relation to our national problem of poor teeth but in relation to our numerous cases of gastric ulcers, and welfare of our children.

"The acidity of cola beverages . . . is about the same as vinegar. The sugar content masks the acidity, and children little realize they are drinking this strange mixture of phosphoric acid, sugar, caffeine, coloring, and flavoring matter.

"Several other acids are used in other carbonated beverages and these all deserve careful study, since solutions even one-tenth as acid as the cola beverages are claimed to erode the enamel of teeth.

"Since soft drinks are playing an increasingly important part in the American diet and tend to displace good foods such as milk, they deserve very careful consideration."

Dr. McCay was asked by Representative A. L. Miller who had charge of passing on the contents of soft drinks.

"So far as I know, no one passes upon it or pays any attention to it," Dr. McCay replied.

Q. No one passes on the contents of soft drinks?
A. So far as I know, no one.

Congressman E. H. Hedrick asked if Dr. McCay had made any tests on the cola beverages with respect to the effect they have on metal or iron.

A. No sir; I have not done any metal tests.

Q. A friend of mine told me once that he dropped three tenpenny nails into one of the cola bottles, and in forty-eight hours the nails had completely dissolved.

A. Sure, phosphoric acid there would dissolve iron or limestone. You might drop it on the steps, and it would erode the steps coming up here. Spill a bottle of cola on them, and you could see it fuzz up—try it.

One committee member pointed out that a Washington doctor had prescribed a small amount of cola beverage for his baby. In view of Dr. McCay's startling discovery, he wanted to know how that came about.

"Well," answered Dr. McCay, "they probably have not read the literature about the cola beverages. It is a very restricted literature; it has not ever been able to get into the press, so what does the American public know about it? It is not declared on the bottle. They are as ignorant as I was in 1943 about the composition of the beverages. How would the public ever know if it cannot get into the press? There is no way for them to know."

The press, while sparing the public from such disturbing disclosures, has been outspoken and courageous in warning the public against food "quacks" who decry the use of processed foods. There is, virtually, only one major nutritionist who has encouraged the public to eat sugar, white flour and other processed foods, and he is frequently found spearheading these attacks.

Many experiments have pointed to a relationship between sugar and tooth decay. Tooth decay has been found to be decreased markedly when a reduced sugar intake is reinforced by good nutrition. One of the most damning experiments pointing to sugar as the primary culprit in causing tooth cavities was performed at Harvard.

Time Magazine (January 13, 1958) reported that biochemist Dr. James H. Shaw and his assistants had worked more than ten years in their laboratory at Harvard to find out how certain sugars promote tooth decay, and how to prevent it.

The project, according to *Time*, was bankrolled, curiously enough, by the Sugar Research Foundation, Inc., to the tune of $57,500. The Shaw group reported their findings in the *Journal of the American Dental Association*. Among them were the following:

Tooth decay is caused only by food remaining in the mouth—proved by feeding rats through stomach tubes. Even sugar, fed this way, causes no decay.

Sugar, in solution, causes little decay; granulated sugar (as sprinkled on fruits and cereals) causes much more.

Of the various kinds of sugar, fructose (from most fruits), glucose (from grapes and starch foods), sucrose (table sugar, from cane or beets), lactose (from milk) and maltose (from beer) are all precipitators of decay. So is a high starch diet, even when relatively low in sugar. It does no good to substitute raw for refined sugar; but blackstrap molasses causes a marked reduction in cavities. (Blackstrap molasses, along with being a source of jokes for comedians and a target of foes of food faddists, contains the concentrated vitamins and minerals that remain after the processing of white sugar.)

"Dr. Shaw's conclusion: 'We should cut down on our sugar consumption, particularly candy. We should be careful about sugar in forms that remain in the mouth because of their physical properties.' "

Time then concluded the article with this comment:

"Along with his findings, Dr. Shaw also reported that his work has stopped. Reason: the Sugar Research Foundation withdrew its support."

In a nation that has been encouraged by commercial interests to eat mountains of candy and other carbohydrate products and drink oceans of sugar-saturated bellywash, the number of cavities and dental afflictions is hardly surprising.

The extent of tooth decay in America came in for considerable attention before the Delaney Committee when Dr. Fred D. Miller, a dental authority from Altoona, Pennsylvania, testified. Dr. Miller, whose many professional honors and appointments include lecturing on his specialty at the University of Pennsylvania and Georgetown University, stated that dental decay is the most prevalent disease known to civilized mankind, and at least 98 per cent of the population of this country suffers from it.

He noted that the American Dental Association recognizes that there are 285,000,000 cavities in the teeth of American children, and in the teeth of the adult population another 235,000,000 cavities—a backlog of over a half billion cavities!

"We have in the United States about 78,000 dentists, who cannot possibly keep up with the velocity of dental decay, to say nothing of the other dental diseases which include the destruction of the bony support of the teeth and the diseased gum conditions," he said.

Dr. Miller testified:

"During World War II, I was on the medical advisory board in our community. In the first draft of the first million men, there were 188,000 men rejected because they could not meet Uncle Sam's dental requirement, six teeth above and six teeth below, opposing. During this time, I examined thirty-nine patients to determine if they should be accepted. Most of them were rejected—then Uncle Sam found out that if he stuck to his dental requirements he could not get an army, so he threw out all his dental requirements and took men if they had an upper and a lower jaw. That was necessary to get an army.

"In World War I, Army dentists made practically no dentures. In World War II, the peak month for the Army dentists alone was 102,000 dentures. . . ."

Instead of recognizing the damage that sugar and improper diet have done to the public's teeth, the Government has latched onto this scourge as a wedge to force into the nation's diet still another chemical—sodium fluoride, one of the most powerful poisons known.

No Government agency ever warned about the danger of sugar or urged a reduced intake. This would step on the toes of a powerful commercial interest. To prevent tooth decay the public is harangued to fluoridate its water supply.

The cavity-preventing qualities claimed for fluoridation are far from proved, and its toxic side effects are virtually untested, especially on persons with metabolic ailments.

Practically every community that has had access to the facts on fluoridation has rejected it. But frequently health officials, using Government funds, have rammed it down the throats of communities, citing misleading statistics about its benefits and false statements about its toxicity.

This is not the place to go deeply into the controversial issue of fluoridation, but some pointed questions have been raised in Congress about the Public Health Service's unexplained about-face to support the use of this chemical and the methods used to promote its use.

The reader should be aware that wherever fluorides are injected into the water supply, foods canned or otherwise processed there will have still another chemical added (in concentrated form, due to the cooking) to their composition.

As the cavity-causing properties of sugar led to fluoridation, its weight-producing effect has set the stage for another possible biological disaster. And once more the public is cast in the role of guinea pig. To reduce the caloric content of soft drinks and some confections, manufacturers have been using the artificial sweetener cyclamate as a sugar substitute.

Recent FDA studies, according to *Medical World News* (November 15, 1968) have shown that many humans who ingest cyclamates convert it in the body to cyclohexylamine —the latter produced chromosome breaks when fed to laboratory animals. It is pointed out that it isn't known for certain what this means for humans. The FDA has been very cautious in making pronouncements or interpreting the findings. But a high FDA scientist was quoted as having said, "It's a big one. This is potentially one of the biggest things we've had around here for a long time." His words recall the thalidomide tragedy—how thousands of children were born with deformities after their mothers were given the drug during pregnancy.

Medical World News also stated: "A prominent British government investigator who has been working closely with the FDA on cyclamate research said that he was surprised and 'slightly amazed' when told of the latest FDA findings on cyclohexylamine. . . .

"Any effect on chromosomes is a major item," said Dr. G. B. West of the British Industrial Biological Research Association, "and the low dose . . . discoveries of the FDA study are right in the danger zone. These findings should be borne in mind by everybody researching cyclamate."

Like other scientists, Dr. West was cautious about relating the FDA animal studies to man. But the article stated:

"Meanwhile, in England, private-label foods containing the artificial sweetener cyclamate have been banned from the shelves of at least 27 department stores and 270 supermarkets. The three major retail chains that own the stores said their restrictions are in part based on the results of two recent Ministry of Agriculture studies on the toxicity

of the sweeteners. A spokesman for the retailers said that
the government report raised enough doubt to justify their
caution."

Meanwhile, as this book goes to press, the cyclamates
are being used in the United States to sweeten oceans of
soft drinks and mountains of desserts, and not only for
calorie-reduction in dietary products—cyclamates are
cheaper than sugar.

11

You Are What

You Eat

> . . . it appears to me necessary to every physician
> to be skilled in nature, and to strive to know, if
> he would wish to perform his duties, what a man is
> in relation to the articles of food and drink, and
> to his other occupations, and what are the effects
> of each of them to every one.
>
> Whoever does not know what effect these things
> produce upon a man cannot know the conse-
> quences which result from them.
>
> Whoever pays no attention to these things, or
> paying attention, does not comprehend them, how
> can he understand the diseases which befall a man?
> For, by every one of these things a man is affected
> and charged this way and that, and the whole of
> his life is subjected to them, whether in health,
> convalescence, or disease. Nothing else, then, can
> be more important or more necessary to know than
> these things.
>
> —HIPPOCRATES

(1)

DESPITE THE HUGE AMOUNT of evidence linking food directly to human health, it is the exceptional doctor who

ever bothers to ask his patients what they eat. Even more remarkable is the physician who is interested in how the food was grown and prepared.

In the medical world the science of nutrition has been almost totally ignored, beyond the most elementary facts. Less than a half dozen medical schools even give special classes in the subject.

At the same time, however, some of the most progressive medical researchers are learning to appreciate the scientific truth of the old saw, "You are what you eat."

This doctrine has touched off a bitter controversy. Medical science traditionally has accepted disease and sickness as natural to living creatures. But in recent years a revolutionary theme has been preached by a hard core of researchers in nutrition. They hold that *the birthright of all living creatures is health,* and sickness and disease are perversions of the natural condition. Further, they contend, proper nutrition is the key to health, and if people eat the right foods they will enjoy good health.

Dr. Tom Spies made this provocative statement: "All diseases are caused by chemicals, and all diseases can be cured by chemicals. All the chemicals used by the body, except for the oyxgen which we breathe and the water which we drink, are taken in through food. If we only knew enough, all diseases could be prevented, and could be cured, through proper nutrition."

Dr. Spies made that comment upon receiving the American Medical Association's highest honor—the Distinguished Service Award—in 1957.

As far back as 1952, at a meeting of the Southern Medical Association in Miami, he pleaded for a new concept in medicine. A *New York Times* dispatch noted that he made the point that " 'We are what we eat,' which means that more attention ought to be paid to the chemistry of disease." The article continued:

> We are chemically composed of the air we breathe, the water we drink, the food we eat, is Dr. Spies's guiding principle. . . . the 20 years of research that he and his group have carried on convince Dr. Spies that even diseases of the heart, cancer and the degenerative diseases are the result of chemical disturbances. . . .
> He is not content with the prevailing medical

acceptance of the traditional view that aş we age
we must expect to lose strength, keenness of vision
and alertness, and to look and act old. . . .

As the thesis "Man is what he eats" becomes more widely
accepted, there is increasing concern about the adverse
effect on health caused by the adulteration of the food
supply with chemicals and mechanical processing.

The *Medical Press,* a well-known British journal for
physicians, recently lashed out at the increasing use of
chemical in foods by stating: "We have started down a
long, steep slope of sophistication, processing, bedevilment
—call it what you will—the end of which we cannot fore-
see. Scarcely a single article of diet arrives on our tables
unembellished by the technologist's art."

It warned that unless the medical profession took a firm
stand, "Expediency will continue to triumph over caution
and common sense, and we may well be faced with irreversible results . . . we may well spend the next generation in
medicine trying to unscramble the harm that has been done
to the human organism by prevalent factory practices in
preservation, processing, and sophistication of foods."

Another voice of protest was that of Sir Edward Mellanby, the British investigator who discovered the harmful
effects of Agene. He objected to turning the bodies of millions of human beings into so many chemical research
laboratories. Dr. Mellanby noted that during the last fifty
years there has been "an enormous and not readily ex-
plicable increase" in the incidence of disease of the alimentary tract, particularly "a sudden and extraordinary rise
in appendicitis and peptic ulcer." He added that there were
still countries in the world today in which these diseases
were almost or quite unknown.

Probably the most dramatic proof of how the body is
affected by the quality of food ingested was furnished by
still another British medical researcher, Major-General Sir
Robert McCarrison, former chairman of the Post-Graduate
Medical Education Committee in the University of Oxford
and director of research on nutrition in India.

As a member of the Indian Medical Service, Dr. Mc-
Carrison's duties included supervision of a people known as
the Hunzas, in nothern India. He was amazed by the remarkable health and vitality of these people. Many of them

did physical work in their eighties and nineties and often lived to be over a hundred.

Dr. McCarrison later noted that in seven years he spent with the Hunzas "I never saw a case of asthenic dyspepsia, of gastric or duodenal ulcer, or appendicitis, of mucous colitis, of cancer. . . . Among these people the abdomen oversensitive to nerve impressions, to fatigue, anxiety, or cold was unknown. Indeed their buoyant abdominal health has, since my return to the West, provided a remarkable contrast with the dyspeptic and colonic lamentations of our highly civilized communities."

Dr. McCarrison puzzled over why the Hunzas should have enjoyed health so superior to that of their dyspeptic neighbors. The only difference he could find was in their diet. The Hunzas practiced a Spartan form of agriculture, returning all organic matter to the soil. Their food consisted chiefly of whole grains, raw fruits, vegetables, milk products from goats, and occasionally a small portion of meat. Neighboring villages were addicted to white man's foods.

To test his theory that foods made the difference, Dr. McCarrison began his historic feeding experiments.

Some rats were fed the identical diet of the Hunzas, while other rats were fed the food of less healthy Indian people. The results startled even Dr. McCarrison. In every case, the average health standard of the people whose diet was fed to the rats was mirrored in the health of the animals, including the percentage of specific diseases, and even mental condition and temper.

The rats that ate the diet of the Hunzas had the same astonishing health, vitality and gentle tempers; the animals grew rapidly, were never ill, had healthy offspring, and autopsy (at the age equivalent of fifty in a man) revealed virtually nothing wrong with their organs.

In subsequent experiments Dr. McCarrison removed essential components of a complete diet and was able to produce variations in disease—the same diseases from which humans tend to suffer. During the course of his experiments on some 2,243 rats fed on faulty Indian diets, he found and listed diseases of every organ of the body.

Among the ailments they suffered were diseases of the respiratory system, adenoids, pneumonia, bronchitis, pleurisy, pyothorax and infections of the nose; infections of the ear; infections of the eye; dilated stomach, growths, ulcer and cancer of the stomach, inflammation of the small and large gut; constipation and diarrhea; diseases of the urinary passage, such as Bright's disease, stones, abscesses, inflammation of the bladder; inflammation of the womb and ovaries, death of the fetus, premature birth, hemorrhage; diseases of the testicles; inflammation of the skin, loss of hair, ulcers, abscesses, gangrene of the feet and tail; anemias of the blood; enlarged lymphatic glands, cystic and suppurating glands; goiter and diseases of the special glands; wasting, enlargement of, and inflammation of the muscle, and inflammation of the outer lining of the heart; inflammation and degeneration of the nervous tissues, diseased teeth and bones; dropsy; scurvy; feeble growth, feeble appetite, weakness, lassitude, and ill temper.

"All these conditions," said Dr. McCarrison, "these states of ill health, had a common causation: faulty nutrition with or without infection."

Dr. McCarrison continued:

"I found that when young, growing rats of healthy stock were fed on diets similar to those of people whose physique was good, the physique and health of the rats were good; when they were fed on diets similar to those of people whose physique was bad, the physique and health of the rats were bad; and when they were fed on diets similar to those of people whose physiques were middling, the physique and health of the rats were middling."

As early as 1921 Dr. McCarrison wrote his classic *Studies of Deficiency Diseases*, which he said provided experimental evidence that "appeared to me to warrant the conclusion that food of improper constitution" was responsible for a large proportion of ill health in Great Britain.

In addition to lowering the standards of physical efficiency, Dr. McCarrison said, food which was faulty with respect to suitable proteins, minerals and vitamins—or all three—gave rise to many minor manifestations of ill health which defy a diagnostic label.

He pointed out that some of the conditions brought about by faulty foods were so subtle that they might not be noticed. But they would be present, he warned, perhaps disturbing the functions of the various organs and tissues of the body, and each alteration would contribute to impaired well-being.

Dr. McCarrison said that symptoms of subnormal health

are common enough in human beings, but since they conform to no stereotyped disease, have no microbe nor any
toxin associated with them, and cannot be accounted for
by any laboratory tests applied to them, "we are apt to
find nothing wrong with sufferers from them and to mistake their malnutrition meaning."

He said he emphasized these minor manifestations of
malnutrition because they represent the beginnings of disease, "and their recognition is, to my way of thinking,
vastly more important than that of the wreckages of health,
which even the man in the street can see, though his name
for them may be less sonorous than our own."

Dr. McCarrison's experiments in nutrition have been
famous in Europe and Asia for many years. In the United
States they are hardly known; most doctors are not ac-
quainted with them, and the FDA apparently never heard
of them.

As recently as 1949, the late Dr. Elmer M. Nelson, in
charge of nutrition for the FDA, testified in a court hearing:

> It is wholly unscientific to state that a well-fed
> body is more able to resist disease than a less well-
> fed body. My over-all opinion is that there hasn't
> been enough experimentation to prove dietary de-
> ficiencies make one more susceptible to disease
> [Washington *Post*, October 26, 1949].

Ten years earlier, according to Dr. Royal Lee of the Lee
Foundation for Nutritional Research, Dr. Nelson "with his
group of experts, testified in a similar court hearing that
neither degenerative disease, infectious disease, nor functional disease could result from any nutritional deficiency."
Dr. Lee continued:

"For all these years, he has battled for the maker of devitalized foods, tried to stem the tide of public opinion
against the use of white flour, refined sugar, pasteurized
milk, and imitation butter by vigorous prosecution of any
maker of any dietary supplement designed to abate the
consequences of using such devitalized foods, basing his
arguments on the thesis that there were no such things as
deficiency diseases."

In addition to having overlooked the studies of Dr. Mc-
Carrison, Dr. Nelson apparently also overlooked the find-

ings of Dr. Weston Price, an American dentist who amassed a tremendous volume of evidence to demonstrate what happens when primitive people adopt the white man's diet.

In a foreword to Dr. Price's book *Nutrition and Physical Degeneration*, the late Dr. Earnest A. Hooton, Harvard's famous anthropologist, paid tribute to Dr. Price with the comment that "really gifted scientists are those who can appreciate the obvious." Dr. Hooton also made this pithy comment: "Let us cease pretending that toothbrushes and tooth paste are more important than shoe brushes and shoe polish. It is store food which has given us store teeth."

It has long been known that primitive people, prior to their contacts with civilization, had excellent teeth. It also has been established that teeth are a valuable indicator of general physical condition: excellent teeth and excellent general physique go hand in hand. Unfortunately, the converse of this is also true.

While his colleagues were experimenting with new methods for controlling dental caries, Dr. Price was conducting research to learn why the primitive had such good teeth, and how this knowledge could benefit his civilized brother.

He investigated groups all over the world: in the Swiss Alps, New Hebrides, Australia, Alaska and South America, among others. The climates, people and even the diets varied, but all shared one thing—excellent nutrition. These people, drawing from the sources nature provided, instinctively supplied all their body needs—just as did the Hunzas.

Through laboratory analysis, Dr. Price discovered that although the foods varied according to the area, the total intake of vitamins and minerals was nearly identical. These admirable physical specimens possessed unbelievable endurance, and cheerful, even dispositions; their jaws were wide and well developed, and their teeth stayed free from decay, just as their bodies remained free of disease. Cancer, tuberculosis, high blood pressure, kidney and heart diseases, polio, cerebral palsy and other degenerative diseases were non-existent. Every mother nursed her baby; a nonfunctional breast was unheard of. Mental health was as high as physical health.

In every instance Dr. Price was able to compare his people with people living nearby of the same racial stock; sometimes the healthy specimens could be compared to their offspring who had been exposed to the city man's diet of white flour, refined sugar and canned foods. The deterioration that had resulted was pitiful and obvious: faulty bone structure, crooked teeth, extreme tooth decay, high incidence of disease. Cancer was rampant among the very tribes that had stayed cancer-free on their native diets.

In both his observations on these people and through animal experiments, Dr. Price was able to demonstrate the devastating effects of bad nutrition, not only on the present generation but also—far worse—on their offspring. His book has scores of pictures testifying to the destructive results from the white man's processed foods.

Dr. Price urged a return to harmony with nature by choosing foods in their natural state: whole grains, sea food, dairy products and vegetables, all untampered with by man. He also recommended organ meats. Dr. Price gives this warning:

". . . we cannot distort and rob . . . foods without serious injury. Nature has put these foods up in packages containing the combinations of minerals and other factors that are essential for nourishing the various organs. . . . Our modern process of robbing the natural foods for convenience or gain completely thwarts Nature's inviolable program . . . the robbing of the wheat in the making of white flour reduced the minerals and other chemicals in the grains, so as to make them sources of energy without normal body-building and repairing qualities. Our appetites have been distorted so that hunger appeals only for energy with no conscious need for body-building and repairing chemicals."

Still another outspoken critic of processed foods is Dr. H. M. Sinclair, an Englishman who is a leading nutritional authority. He has specialized in nutrition since his days as a medical student when he became convinced that "what was and is perhaps the most serious problem in medicine arose from alterations in our diet from the processing and sophistication of foods."

Dr. Sinclair, head of the Laboratory of Human Nutrition and vice president of Magdalen College at Oxford University, repeatedly has warned about the danger of processed foods and their relationship to the degenerative diseases, especially in their less obvious forms. He recalled that former Surgeon-General Thomas Parran, of the United States, once said that "like an iceberg, nine tenths of the effects of our malnutrition—and the most dangerous part—lies under the surface. One tenth is obviously and easily detected."

In a 1957 World Health Day address, later reprinted in the *British Medical Journal* (December 14, 1957) Dr. Sinclair recalled that in his days as a medical student "my clinical teachers could not answer why the expectation of life in this country of the middle-aged man is hardly different from what it was at the beginning of this century or even a century ago.

"That means that despite the great advances in medicine —pneumonia almost abolished, tuberculosis comparatively rare, the magnificent advances in surgery, endocrinology, and public health—a middle-aged man cannot expect to live more than four years longer than he could a century ago—and indeed in Scotland the expectation of life is now actually decreasing."

Dr. Sinclair said falure to increase man's life span was due to the "dramatic increase" of certain chronic degenerative diseases, which he blamed in large measure on food processing, with special emphasis on the destruction of certain vitamins.

Another telling indictment linking food to health was furnished by the "Medical Testament"—a document issued in 1939 by a panel of doctors in County Cheshire, England, who took a long, hard look at disease as both cause and effect. The Local Medical and Panel Committee of Cheshire (known for its cheeses and grinning cats), representing 600 family doctors, appraised its success under the National Health Insurance Act in fulfilling the dual object of "the prevention and cure of sickness." The testament concluded:

"Our daily work brings us repeatedly to the same point: This illness results from a life-time of wrong nutrition."

These doctors also noted that many primitive peoples remained healthy and free from disease on varied diets. They said that to spell out factors common to all these diets was difficult and an attempt to do so might be misleading, since knowledge of what those factors are was still far from complete. "But this at least may be said, that the food is, for the most part, fresh from its source, little altered by preparation, and complete."

The document added that in order for people to be

healthy there should be "no chemical or substitution stage" in food between soil and table.

Warnings about inadequate foods and deficiency diseases are not likely to be taken seriously by Americans because they have been so thoroughly indoctrinated in the belief that they are the best fed people in the world—a claim that has validity only if no distinction is made between quantity and quality. We are long on quantity, short on quality.

It will be recalled from Chapter IX that Dr. Tom Spies noted that the margin of safety against deficiency diseases in this country is narrow, that nutritional inadequacy is widespread and not limited to the lower economic groups.

This observation has been confirmed by many other nutritionists. Dr. Granville F. Knight, former president of the American Academy of Nutrition, observed that today good health is far from being the rule in America. "We are dealing with many nutritional cripples," he stated. "Inadequate food intake over several generations may help to explain not only the widespread incidence of allergy and dental caries, but the frequency of many other degenerative conditions as well."

(2)

In any discussion of the relationship between food and health, it is necessary to mention briefly the way foods are grown. This is an extremely controversial subject, but there is growing evidence that much of the poor health Americans and other highly industrialized people suffer may be caused by the way their foods are grown, as well as by the processing.

Despite the evidence, the FDA and the AMA have joined hands with commercial interests in a concerted campaign to attack this view. The AMA magazine for laymen, *Today's Health* (September, 1958), stated: "Extensive research conducted by the Federal Government has shown that the nutritional value of crops is not affected by the soil or the fertilizers used." Dr. Elmer Nelson of the FDA was reported in the article as saying that unless the necessary soil elements were present, crops would not grow or produce. "Thus," said Dr. Nelson, "the quality of the soil on which food is grown has a definite effect on the quantity of the crop, but very little on its quality."

It has been easy to convince people that one food

product is just as good as another because both probably look the same. But there can be a vast difference in the nutritional content of two similar products; they can differ in minerals, vitamins and perhaps other qualities not even identified at this time.

Many years ago Dr. Carrel pointed out that food still looks like it always did but it no longer contains the nutritive qualities it formerly did. "Mass production," he stated, "has modified the composition of wheat, eggs, milk, fruit, and butter, although these articles have retained their familiar appearance."

He added: "Chemical fertilizers, by increasing the abundance of the crops without replacing all the exhausted elements of the soil, have indirectly contributed to change the nutritive value of cereal grains and of vegetables. Hens have been compelled, by artificial diet and mode of living, to enter the ranks of mass producers. Has not the quality of their eggs been modified? The same question may be asked about milk, because cows are now confined to the stable all the year round, and are fed on manufactured provender.

"Hygienists have not paid sufficient attention to the genesis of diseases. Their studies of conditions of life and diet, and of their effects on the physiological and mental state of modern man, are superficial, incomplete, and of too short duration. . . ."

The claim that soil has virtually no effect on the nutritional value of crops has been so thoroughly disproved that it is hardly worthy of serious consideration. Josué de Castro, chairman of the Executive Council, Food and Agriculture Organization of the United Nations, notes that it has been demonstrated that "the proportion of iron in lettuce varied from 1 to 50 milligrams per hundred, according to soil conditions."

The Middle West is known as a goiter belt because of the widespread deficiency of iodine in the soil, a condition that is remedied by adding iodine to salt.

Further proof is provided by a U. S. Department of Agriculture publication (No. 369). It states that many cities are located near truck farms with deficient soils, and "large quantities of truck crops and fruits are shipped to these cities from the localities where nutritional disorders due to mineral deficiencies in the soils have been noted in both humans and animals. Although many factors other than the poor quality of food probably are responsible for dietary difficulties, this factor is believed to be an important one."

Probably the most revolutionary studies on the soil and the implications it holds for human health were done by the late Sir Albert Howard early in this century. He was knighted for his contributions to formal agricultural practices and honored by his British colleagues, but when he began his original experiments he was treated as an outcast.

While serving as an agricultural aide in India, he began to ponder why modern farming had to depend on artificial fertilizers, powerful sprays and other chemical paraphernalia to grow crops, when the natives were able to grow crops without chemicals, and had been doing so for thousands of years.

He studied the natives' methods and concluded that the secret was fertile soil, and the key to fertile soil was to return to the earth all living matter. This became known as the compost or organic method of farming.

Sir Albert's experiments convinced him that fertile soil contained elements that defied chemical analysis, but that they conferred immunity to disease and insect attack to plants grown in such soil—a finding made several decades before medical researchers isolated from the earth antibiotics which were to become famed for their incredible ability to kill infections.

Sir Albert's advocacy of natural farming methods posed a direct threat to the chemical industry and traditional farming methods based on the use of chemicals, and lead to sharp attacks on other advocates of organic methods. The latter were equally critical of chemical farming, pointing out that chemical fertilizer (NPK) consists of just three major soil elements: nitrogen, phosphorus and potassium. When only these three components are put in the earth they stimulate growth but deplete the soil of its vital trace elements and organic matter, turning it into crusted hardpan, subject to wind and water erosion. This has been called "mining the soil."

Sir Albert was convinced that it was the missing trace minerals that were responsible for most animal and human health. He held that the chain of health was: fertile soil—healthy plant—healthy animal—healthy human.

To test his theory he conducted animal-feeding tests. Oxen were fed organically grown crops until they were in fine fettle and then exposed to animals infected with hoof-

and-mouth disease, an illness ordinarily considered highly contagious.

"Nothing happened," he stated. "The healthy well-fed animals reacted to this disease exactly as suitable varieties of crops, when properly grown, did to insect and fungous pests—no infection took place."

Sir Albert's findings were later confirmed by many other tests. Crops were grown without the use of poisonous sprays or other chemical aids, and in many cases animals suffering from ailments ordinarily considered incurable by medical treatment were returned to full health by being fed organically grown crops.

Several researchers compared crops grown chemically with organically grown crops and reported that the latter had more vitamin and mineral content. Several feeding experiments with people have produced some remarkable results. Dr. Lionel Picton, under whose leadership the "Medical Testament" was written, related in his book *Nutrition and the Soil* that a Mr. Brodie Carpenter, upon taking up his duties as resident dental officer in an English boarding school, found the children's teeth in deplorable condition. Gradually the incidence of cavities dropped remarkably and the children showed an equally marked improvement in general health.

In 1939, the year of Mr. Carpenter's arrival, only 50 per cent of the children had no cavities, 32 per cent had 3 to 5, and 18 per cent had 6 or more. Within six years the respective percentages had jumped to 97, 3 and 0. Mr. Carpenter checked with the headmaster, to learn that a new gardener and matron had been hired in 1939. The gardener didn't believe in artificial manures, and had started growing all the vegetables with humus, and the matron believed in serving fresh salads.

An example nearer home is provided by Walter E. Clark, director of North Country School at Lake Placid, New York, which has a student body of fifty boys and girls. Mr. Clark said that after the school converted to natural growing methods, in 1948, the children showed a remarkable increase in health and decrease in tooth decay.

(3)

One of the foremost champions in this country of the soil as the basis for health has been Dr. William A. Al-

brecht, professor emeritus and formerly chairman of the
Department of Soils at the University of Missouri College
of Agriculture, and an international authority in his
specialty.

Dr. Albrecht has repeatedly warned that the nation's
soil fertility is sinking to a dangerously low level. He has
repeatedly cautioned that this imperils the nation's health
because the fertility of the soil determines the amount of
protein that goes into crops. In the last ten years, he said,
the protein content of corn has dropped ten per cent.

Dr. Albrecht has warned that "it has not yet been recognized that a soil may be speedily exploited of its protein-
producing power while its capacity for delivery of carbohydrate bulk holds on long afterward.

"We have moved more and more to those plants which
let them build up the vegetative bulk, carbohydrate, lets
them fill themselves with starch instead of protein, and
the human diet has come down. . . ."

The tremendous volume of crops and farm products
which is being rolled out today is produced primarily at the
cost of soil fertility, Dr. Albrecht notes. He said that 70 per
cent of the production of major crops represents exploitation and only 30 per cent results from fertility applied to
the soil.

He said he is not so much concerned with bushels and
tons of food produced as with "whether feed and food have
nutritional value of a complete order rather than fattening
value, which is *so easily produced on almost any soil.*"
[Emphasis the author's.]

This is in direct conflict with the Government's standard
of quantity as the measure of successful agriculture. Its
only criterion is the amount produced: the number of
bushels per acre, the gallons of milk per cow, the number
of cattle shipped to market. To achieve today's massive
farm output many agricultural tricks are used; the earth
is being soaked with massive shots of chemical fertilizers,
hormone preparations and other chemical growth aids.
Crops have to be juggled. Hybrid seeds are used. When
insects and plant diseases inevitably appear, they are blast-
ed with poisons, antibiotics and other test-tube preparations.
Then the harvest of poisoned and nutritionally inferior
crops is preserved with the host of additives already discussed.

Dr. Albrecht has emphasized that production of huge

crops is not proof of soil fertility; rather it represents exploitation of the earth's nutrients. He says "we must soon face the dilemma of feeding ourselves on paved streets, because the rural community is about to be the dead victim of a parasitic, technical soil exploitation that has failed to appreciate the biological aspect of the soils in the creative business of feeding all of us."

Turning to the problem of disease, he noted that protection begins in the soil where the "lowly microbes" produce antibiotics which are moved up through plants, to animals and to man at the top of the "biotic pyramid." Instead of poisonous sprays to protect plants, he advocates restoring fertility to the soil.

In experiments at the University of Missouri it was demonstrated that by increasing soil fertility it was possible to give plants 100 per cent protection from insects, without use of sprays. At the same time, adjacent plants, suffering from infertile soils, had 100 per cent attack.

Dr. Albrecht testified before the Delaney Committee that "using spinach, we had two rows of bugs, then no bugs, two rows of bugs, then no bugs. Not because we sprayed but because we got a different condition in the soil under it."

Just as correcting soil deficiencies gave plants protection from insects, supplying trace elements that were lacking in the diets of people and cattle suffering from Brucella infections helped them to recover. The experiments were conducted by Dr. Albrecht, in conjunction with Dr. Francis M. Pottenger, Jr., and Dr. Ira Allison.

Cows suffering from Brucella infection (called undulant fever in man) were found to lack in their tissues certain trace minerals present in healthy cows. Brucella disease is considered highly contagious in cows, and its victims usually are slaughtered. But when cattle were fed the elements in which they had been deficient, they recovered, became immune to the disease and reproduced calves.

Some 1,800 human patients then were given the trace elements fed to the deficient cattle. The majority reportedly were relieved of their symptoms in three to six months. The report stated that, typical of the type of symptom in many deficiency diseases, the patients initially complained of such varying symptoms "as to be too baffling for accurate diagnosis." Among the symptoms were aching back, shoulders and joints; allergies, arthritis, anorexia, fever, constipation, enlarged spleen, mental depression and up to two hundred others.

"Very significant," stated the report, "was the observation that almost every patient's previous dietary habits indicated possible malnutrition long before symptoms of brucellosis or other conditions inviting the physician's attention had ever appeared. . . ."

In other experiments reported by Dr. Albrecht it was demonstrated that soils and proteins can control animal reproduction. Lambs and rabbits were made potent or impotent, sexually eager or reluctant, at the researcher's will, merely by feeding them crops grown on soil that was fertile or deficient in certain trace elements. The soil was so sensitive to the elements that went into it that its fertility was reflected even by the health of the animals providing the manure used as fertilizer.

As the link between the soil and human health becomes stronger, more researchers are seriously leaning toward the view of Dr. Spies that all sickness has its roots in malnutrition, and as more is learned about the makeup of foods it will be possible to prevent and cure disease merely by correcting dietary errors.

Dr. Albrecht pursued this hypothesis when he said, "Isn't it good nutrition that is used as the 'cure' for human tuberculosis?" He continued with these provocative words:

"While it has long been common belief that disease is an infliction visited upon us from without, there is a growing recognition of its possible origin from within because of deficiencies and failure to nourish ourselves completely. Fuller knowledge of nutrition is revealing mounting numbers of cases of deficiency diseases.

"These deficiencies need to be traced, not only to the supplies in the food and feed market where the family budget may provoke them, but a bit further, and closer to their origin, namely the fertility of the soil, the point at which all agricultural production takes off. These increasing cases classified as deficiencies are bolstering the truth of the old adage which told us that 'to be well fed is to be healthy.' "

12

The Law

That Does Not

Protect

(1)

AFTER SIX YEARS of futile effort to change the pure food law, the 1958 amendment finally was passed by both houses of Congress in the final frantic moments of the 85th Congress and signed into law by President Eisenhower on September 6 of that year.

The law as amended is primarily a measure designed to accommodate industry and protect profits rather than consumers.

The basic immediate benefit the new law gave the public was that from then on chemicals must be tested *before* they could be used in foods. At the same time, it permits in foods the use of poisons that were barred by the former bill, under a tolerance concept similar to that provided by the Miller Pesticide Act. This means it is now possible for unlimited numbers of poisons to be injected into foods. Instead of the hundreds now being used, there may be thousands.

Under the old law no harmful substance was supposed to be used in food, but to remove such substances FDA first had to detect them and prove harm. This law, barring the use of *all* poisons, was known as the "per se rule." The intent of Congress in 1938 in passing the per se rule was unmistakable; it wanted to strengthen the food law by eliminating existing loopholes that permitted the use of certain poisons. The only exceptions Congress provided were for poisons that were "necessary" or "unavoidable" in the production of foods—a test that authorities said was met only by the pesticides. *All other poisons were illegal per se.*

But the FDA and some courts refused to enforce this rule, accepting industry's argument that when poisons were used in small enough amounts they ceased to be poisons. Congress made no provision to permit poisons in foods under such conditions; this was an interpretation to benefit industry, and the FDA held that a new law was necessary so it could control the amount of such substances used. Instead of enforcing the law as it was written, the FDA worked vigorously to change the law to accommodate industry.

The crux of the new legislation was the relaxation of the ban on poisons. Any poison may be used now, if a dose can be found that apparently is not harmful to some animals. Such substances need not even be useful to consumers; it is enough if they are useful to industry.

Consumer groups protested that if certain additives did have to be used, they should not only have to be proved safe but also to benefit the consumer. This stand was backed by the National Research Council and the American Public Health Association's Food and Nutrition Section. They agreed that since there could be no absolute assurance that *any* given dose of a poison was completely safe for humans, there should at least be some benefit for those forced to take the risk. Industry hotly protested it was nobody's business who benefited as long as the additive was shown to be "harmless." Industry's proposal, these organizations pointed out, would permit replacement of nutrients with chemicals whose only value to consumers was that they apparently would not harm a rat or mouse.

Omission of a clear usefulness-to-consumers clause, objected Dr. William E. Smith, would "open the flood gates to legalize adulteration of foods on an unprecedented scale." In other words, he said, industry was willing to agree to the pretesting of additives for safety, but in exchange it would convert the pretesting arrangement into a device for adulterating food with anything from plastic to glue. "This seems a large price for consumers to pay for the much-needed pretesting arrangement long sought by FDA," he said.

Dr. Smith also questioned the wisdom of diverting huge sums of money and scientific energy to testing innumerable nonnutritive chemicals for safety when fundamental questions about nutrition remained to be solved. The consumer, he said, needs food for life and health, not protestations that he is paying his money for nonnourishing substances that some one else thinks will probably not harm him.

He then warned: "It is to our peril if the human digestive tract is legislated into the role of a sewer for disposal of chemicals that afford only commercial advantage."

The FDA supported the use of unlimited numbers of poisons in foods under a tolerance concept, but stated that such substances must have "functional value." This cloudy phrase subsequently was explained by the then FDA Commissioner George Larrick to mean that the chemical must be useful to somebody—either the consumer *or industry*. Presumably this clause was intended to keep chemicals from being tossed into foods as adulterants merely to replace more expensive nutrients or stretch products further; but even chemicals that served no better purpose than this would undeniably be useful to industry by increasing profits. It always could be claimed that the saving was passed along to the public.

Testifying before a Congressional committee, Commissioner Larrick gave an example of what "functional value" meant to him:

"For instance," he said, "we had a man walk in not long ago who was a bottler of grape juice. He said that in bottling grape juice the process is very slow because as the juice comes down the automatic fillers it foams, and they have to stop and they cannot fill bottles fast. By adding a tremendously minute amount of a chemical called a silicone they can stop that foaming altogether and they can do a more efficient manufacturing job. I think the saving they make in that connection is passed on to the consumer and serves a useful purpose."

Curiously, even while the FDA supported overthrow of the legal ban on poisons, Commissioner Larrick warned: "There is always a residual risk in permitting use of even small quantities of poisons in foods to be consumed by the young, the old, the sick and the well. . . ."

He also warned that while analytical techniques have improved over the years, and it is possible to measure in fractions of a part per million, even this is not the whole picture, "since testing methods are lacking for many of the complex new chemicals which are being used today in and around food materials and products."

The onslaught of poisons that can be expected in foods under the new law was suggested by Mr. Larrick when he said that under the tolerance concept there is "virtually no limit to the expanding list of chemicals that may find their way into our food supply."

Behind the FDA's paradoxical support of the same risk it warned against was the agency's conflict between its obligation to consumers and its loyalty to industry. The FDA wanted the pretesting requirement to protect both industry and the public. Like enlightened food executives, FDA officials realized that if some overzealous processor used too much poison and caused wholesale deaths there would be a public outcry that undoubtedly would lead to severe legal restrictions. At the same time, the FDA saw that by relaxing the ban on the use of poisons it would be relieved of the embarrassment it suffered in permitting their use in violation of the law.

The two provisions—pretesting and the tolerance concept—fitted together as if made for one another. Testing a chemical would cost up to $50,000, but if the substance turned out to be poisonous, the money need not be wasted; it still could be used in "safe" quantities in foods under the tolerance concept.

To pave the way for the change in the law, the FDA and industry scientists preached their strange doctrine about the alleged harmlessness of small amounts of poison. Common sense and scientific reason alike were ignored. The scientists bypassed the fact that these "small quantities" were going to be consumed in tremendous numbers.

What this means to the public is graphically illustrated by the fact that from 1940 to 1956 some 25,000 chemicals were considered for use in foods, according to *Public Health Reports*. Presumably any or all of these can be used in foods now if a dose is found that does not produce apparent injury in laboratory animals and if the proposed additive meets the FDA's vague test of "functional value."

While the new law does not contain the nebulous phrase, "functional value," its effect remains; it requires the FDA to fix tolerances for any poisons its experts say are "safe." The only restrictions are that the chemical must accomplish its intended physical or other technical effect; that no more of the substance can be used than is necessary to accomplish the intended effect, and that it cannot be used to promote a deception of the consumer.

Not even this limited protection is afforded the public from substances believed to be "harmless." The FDA considered it "none of its business" what use is made of non-poisonous chemicals, according to William W. Goodrich, assistant general counsel for the FDA. If industry wants to replace the shortening in prepared pie crust with plastic or glue, the FDA will not object—as long as the stuff has not been shown to be poisonous.

A feature of the new law is that the FDA is empowered to require the testing of any additive *already in use* when the measure was passed, if the substance is not generally recognized by experts as having been "adequately shown through scientific procedures . . . to be safe under the conditions of its intended use."

The statute exempts from testing all chemicals recognized by experts as "safe." It also exempts pesticides used on raw agricultural products and chemicals approved for use under the Meat Inspection Act, as well as certain other ones. These exemptions are made under what is known as a grandfather clause.

The law, instead of requiring suspect chemicals withdrawn until tested and proved harmless, permits them to remain in use while they are being tested over a 30-month period. Representative Leonor K. Sullivan of St. Louis noted that past experience showed that there also were likely to be additional extensions granted.

The third major provision in the new law is an anti-carcinogen clause. This provision, of manifest value to consumers, should have offended no one except commercial promoters of questionable food-chemicals; but the big chemical interests have highly skilled and highly paid consultants who can "explain" many things and "educate" many people. This clause was dragged in by its heels at the last moment. Despite continuous agitation by some of the leading cancer experts for such protection, the FDA fought vigorously to keep an anticarcinogen provision out of the law. Only after Representative Delaney threatened to block the FDA bill from coming to a vote, through his post on the powerful House Rules Committee, did the FDA reluctantly agree to include it.

Various cancer experts and consumer groups urged that

the law not only bar all carcinogens but also require all additives to be tested for cancer-causing properties. Dr. Smith pointed out that without such tests there would be little point in merely prohibiting carcinogens.

The measure that became the law states:

> . . . no additive shall be deemed to be safe if it is found to induce cancer when ingested by man or animal, or if it is found, after tests which are appropriate for the evaluation of the safety of food additives, to induce cancer in man or animal. . . .

This provision rules out any chemical proved to cause cancer in man or animal when *eaten.* It does not exclude chemicals that cause cancer in animals by other routes of administration than mouth, and leaves the evaluation of such carcinogens and whether they will be used in food up to the FDA. Pesticides and chemicals covered under the Meat Inspection Act are not even subject to the limited protection of the cancer law because of the grandfather clause excluding them from its coverage.

The new law also *does not call for specific tests* to show whether chemicals already in use, *or proposed for use,* have cancer-causing properties.

The FDA opposed making such tests mandatory. Commissioner Larrick testified that he saw no more reason to single out cancer production for specific mention in the legislation than to single out production of a host of other infirmities. He said no additive would be permitted in food unless shown not to produce cancer in man. He did not explain how he proposed to accomplish this, in the absence of tests to find out if new additives would cause cancer.

By opposing a requirement to test chemicals for cancer, Commissioner Larrick spared chemical companies the cost of doing the tests and weakened the anti-carcinogen provision. How a carcinogen, distributed to the public in food, could ever be proved harmful to man was not explained; once a carcinogen is in the general food supply how could it be traced statistically as a cause of cancer in man?

In the absence of specific cancer tests, the only chance of catching a carcinogen is by stumbling on it in other research—too late to help those already exposed to it.

The difference between ordinary toxic chemicals and

carcinogens makes the lack of tests even more untenable. The effects of many poisons may be reversed, espcially those that are not cumulative; but damage from carcinogens is irreversible. The new law thus protects consumers from a form of damage that possibly can be corrected, but offers only limited protection from a far more serious injury that cannot be reversed.

As an unlimited number of new poisons are admitted to foods without tests specifically for cancer, the consumer can feel little security upon learning that about 25 per cent of all chemicals tested specifically for cancer-causing properties have been found to be carcinogenic. Cancer tests also are not required of chemicals already in use, although, as Dr. Hueper and others have warned, long use of a substance is no guarantee it will not cause cancer.

The need for cancer tests on food chemicals is underscored by the insidious nature of carcinogens; as we have emphasized, once they have started their daily work, the damage cannot be undone by subsequently outlawing their use in foods. Many studies testify to the delayed effects of these biological time bombs.

In 1938, Dr. Hueper said, it was discovered that vineyard workers in the Moselle Valley had an epidemic of chronic arsenic poisoning. From 1940 on, an increasing number of arsenic cancers of the skin was observed among the workers "because they ingested rather large amount of wine contaminated with large amounts of arsenical insecticides. Now they have among their vineyard workers not only skin cancer but lung cancer and liver cancers." (The use of arsenic on tobacco is suspect as a cause of lung cancer; more than 80,000,000 pounds of arsenic are used annually in pesticides.)

The public's precarious margin of safety from the cancer hazard inherent in the inevitable increase in food chemicals was dramatized by Dr. Machle, when he warned that there is "no method by which we can secure reasonable proof that a material is not carcinogenic for man, inasmuch as it may take fifteen or twenty years for known environmental agents under conditions of severe exposure to produce a cancer in an individual."

How easily a researcher could control the results of his tests if he wanted to prove the "safety" of a chemical was testified by Dr. Machle when he said the action of carcinogens fed to animals could be suppressed or enhanced in many ways, including the presence or lack of certain substances in the diet. The risk is emphasized by the different ways different species and even different strains of the same species react to chemicals. It also has been noted that instances have occurred when profound effects have been discovered in one laboratory and missed in another.

The public's margin of protection is further narrowed because the new law requires the FDA to approve additives on the basis of test data furnished by their proponents, or show cause for disapproval within 180 days—just about six months. Cancer experts have pointed out that this is far too short a period to evaluate or verify such technical data. Then industry has the right to go into court and capitalize on the ignorance of a lay judge. William W. Goodrich of the FDA once observed that court decisions as to whether or not to use chemical additives should not be decided by which side has the cleverest lawyer.

In addition to its time problem, the FDA is handicapped by lack of facilities to do the job it now is called upon to do. Congresswoman Sullivan noted that the FDA is "terribly understaffed, overburdened, poorly equipped . . . It does not have enough chemists and inspectors to begin with; it lacks modern laboratory equipment; its inadequate laboratory facilities, furthermore, are spread out all over town because of the lack of its own building."

These formidable obstacles failed to discourage Commissioner Larrick in his support of the new legislation which placed an even greater workload on his department, although in 1955 he complained that the chemical industry is giving "our chemists and pharmacologists such a backlog of work that they cannot catch up. The emergence of new chemicals demanding entry into the food supply is running far ahead of the scientific knowledge needed to be sure of their safety."

The new law contains no specifications as to what "safety tests" shall be done on chemicals proposed for use in foods. The tests to be performed and their interpretation lie entirely within the discretion of the FDA. In view of the agency's vigorous opposition to having a mandatory cancer test in the bill, and Mr. Larrick's reluctance to single out cancer for special attention among diseases, it is unlikely that industry will be required to test new substances for cancer—although the FDA does have that power. Cancer tests are expensive and require several years.

The vagueness of the new law has been sharply criticized by *Consumer's Research*. It charged that the drafting of the new law was largely determined by the pressures of industry legal experts, who were able to see to it that the new law is so constructed that (a) no one but a lawyer, "one of great ability, and time for close study, can possibly understand its provisions and (b) the loopholes that have been provided are so large and so numerous that many sorts of chemical additives that the food industry wishes to use can get by, if only those who favor them take care to employ the right experts to 'prove' them harmless.

"Fortunately for the food industry, and most unfortunately for the consuming public, the great majority of research agencies available for testing the poisonous qualities of additives will be those that are likely to turn up with an answer favorable to the interests of industry. There is no provision in the new law for making the laboratories' tests completely independent of any direction, control or pressure by the manufacturer of the food or additive—who rightly should cease to have any control whatever over the work, once he has signed an order to the laboratory to begin its work ... nothing appears in the amendment which will provide for the toxicological competence and skill and the technical and scientific *independence* of the testing.

Consumers' Research also objected to the fact that under the law the Secretary of Health, Education and Welfare is left to decide not only which opinion, among conflicting ones, he chooses to accept, but which experts have the "right" kind of training and experience.

"Such a provision, with its wide opportunity for decision by a political officer on a personal rather than a firm legal and scientific basis has no place in a law that affects the health and safety of 170 million consumers," the article stated.

It went on to say that it is contrary to sound principles of public administration, where technical and scientific principle are involved, to leave the final judgment of the frequently conflicting opinions of qualified experts to a political officer who is subject to many pressures.

"No secretary of a government department has the capacity to make such tremendous decisions wisely; literally the life and health of millions of persons will depend upon the way he exercises his scientifically untrained judgment, and who talks to him without a public record of the interview before he decides . . . The harm is in permitting a political official to accept or disregard the advice, as he may choose."

Consumers' Research pointed out that the food industry even scored "another triumph" in a simple matter of nomenclature. The amendment originally was to deal with chemical additives. Now it is called the *"food* additive amendment of 1958." A small matter, it might seem, notes the magazine, "but a vitally important one when one realizes that the aim was to get the public's mind off *chemicals* and to bring in the implication to the nontechnical public that the additive is itself a food, not a *chemical added* to food.

"The food industry correctly feels that the change from *chemical* additives to *food* additives will set many a consumer's doubts at rest and greatly reduce the public's resistance to use of chemicals as modifiers of the appearance and texture properties of foods and beverages and as preservatives (a fast-growing trend)."

A criticism Dr. Smith leveled at the bill was that the unlimited use of chemicals would increase the likelihood of mistakes. "Since the number of such mistakes will inevitably increase with the number of approved adulterants," he said, "there seems little justification for legislation obliging consumers to be guinea pigs for an unlimited series of sales-eager but biologically foreign substances of no nutritive value."

In direct opposition to the unlimited expansion of the number of chemicals in foods supported by industry and the FDA, he suggested that additives essential to provide food for the nation be specified and limited to as small a number as possible. Then those remaining could be so thoroughly tested that there could be confidence in their harmlessness.

The advantage of this, he pointed out, was that it would provide the necessary number of chemicals for industry without unnecessary multiplication of risks consumers must accept. This was the same principle followed in 1938 when the large number of dyes in use was cut to nineteen that were certified for use in foods. The moral was provided earlier in this book when it was brought out that the dyes were originally "proved safe" by testing procedures then available, but with improved testing procedures available today it has been shown that all but one of the dyes are poisonous—and at least ten will cause cancer.

(2)

Good faith is a built-in part of the new amendment to the food law. Good faith is supposed to compensate for the remarkable vagueness, ambiguity and weakness of the legislation. This good faith is extended not only to those who administer the law and evaluate the tests purporting to show the "harmlessness" of poisons proposed for use, but to industry and its hired scientists who do the testing.

It is this implied good faith that stands between the American people and possible disaster of incalculable proportions. The law which was supposed to protect the people against *any* poison in their food has been destroyed, and in its place stands a small band of political appointees who have the right to determine how many poisons the American people will consume, and in what quantities, each day of their lives.

Since good faith has become the invisible foundation on which the nation's welfare, and perhaps its survival, rests, it is only prudent to see how much of it the people can expect—both from Government and industry.

Revealing testimony was offered along those lines by Dr. Smith during Congressional hearings on the new food law in the summer of 1958. But as early as 1954, when he was chairman of a symposium on cancer prevention at the Sixth International Cancer Congress at São Paulo, Brazil. he indicated in a speech on cancer control that all was not well in the world of commercial science.

"Delays and obstructions have impeded advances in knowledge of preventable hazards," he said. ". . . little progress can be anticipated from termination of studies when potential risks begin to appear. Some of the most active scientists in the field of industrial cancer hazards have had their studies terminated or been obliged to leave their laboratories soon after describing findings that associated hazards with certain products. . . . "

These charges were not spelled out until Dr. Smith offered explosive testimony, in July 1957, before the House Subcommittee on Health and Science during hearings on the need for a cancer clause in the new law. He laid the groundwork by pointing out that the FDA was "well aware" of the cancer problem relating to foods and of resolutions adopted by the International Union Against Cancer and the American Cancer Society to exclude *all* carcinogens from foods and to test all additives for cancer-causing properties. Despite this knowledge, he said, the FDA supported legislation that failed to contain any provision to exclude carcinogens or require cancer tests of additives.

"This failure is not accidental," he testified. "During the past three years I have corresponded with the FDA about the need for such provisions. I am told that the FDA prepared that bill with the knowledge and approval of food industries, but without consulting the chairman of the Congressional committee that investigated the use of chemicals in food."

Dr. Smith then offered this bombshell:

"In 1950, the National Cancer Institute of the United States Public Health Service established a program for study of environmental chemical factors in cancer. Within a few years, a Dr. A. J. Lanza, then director of the Institute of Industrial Medicine at New York University, told me that he had been retained by a group of chemical industries to call upon the Surgeon General and object to studies conducted under this program. He stated that his objection had been successful, and that all field studies by the National Cancer Institute in this program would be stopped. They were.

"A few years later, I showed this same gentleman data indicating a cancer hazard for men employed in another industry that had retained him as a consultant. He advised me to keep out of this problem, and shortly thereafter notified me that my appointment as associate professor of industrial medicine at New York University would not be renewed. It was not renewed."

In addition to himself, Dr. Smith testified, he knew of three other research physicians who lost their jobs with chemical companies because of their interest in the cancer-causing properties of chemicals. He named Dr. Hueper, who he said was fired as assistant medical director of the Du Pont Company in 1938, after confirming with animal experiments that beta-naphthylamine (used in making certain food dyes) had caused bladder cancers in many hundreds of humans who worked with it; Dr. Robert Collier Page, who was general medical director for Standard Oil

Company of New Jersey; and Dr. Arthur Vorwald, director of the Saranac Laboratory, in 1951.

Dr. Smith charged that government, university and industrial research in the field of cancer control had been obstructed, while apologists for carcinogens were in great demand; scientists who advocated caution in the use of carcinogens "are apt to end up without a job."

His sensational testimony triggered a storm of protest and denial. Dr. Page, in a letter to a Standard Oil Company executive, claimed he had never been fired by the company and "I am presently enjoying my capacity as a consultant to Jersey Standard. . . ." He did not state when he was retained by the company as a "consultant." The Public Health Service claimed it had not curtailed field studies of cancer-causing chemicals and had even extended them. Dr. Lanza categorically denied Dr. Smith's charges.

Dr. Smith counterattacked by producing a letter written to him two years earlier (1955) by the official in charge of the specific Public Health Service program to which he had referred. The letter stated that Dr. Lanza had intervened with government officials and succeeded in stopping a program of research on lung cancer in the chromate industry. "It is my belief," wrote this official, "that through the intervention of Dr. Lanza, not only the interest of American industries with cancer hazards to workers employed in these industries, but of the American people at large, and of the American medical profession, was seriously damaged."

Dr. Smith's documentation of his charges included another letter from Dr. E. S. Ross, chief medical director of the Brotherhood of Railroad Trainmen, who recalled a 1955 meeting with Dr. Smith and the medical director of Du Pont "who was, I believe, a Dr. Fleming. I recall he said that Dr. W. C. Hueper had been discharged by that company shortly after showing that beta-naphthylamine induced cancer."

While all of industry cannot be condemned by a few unfortunate incidents, there has been a disturbing pattern of what Dr. Smith called "hopeful ostrich" attitudes toward cancer. This is expressed by ignoring the problem as much as possible; as long as chemicals are not tested for carcinogenicity, the question of whether they will cause cancer does not arise. Not testing also saves considerable money and time. The general attitude is that if the problem is ignored, perhaps it will go away—or drop dead. The "hopeful ostrich" attitude was emphasized by Dr. Francis Ray's testimony that "very few companies have carried out tests for cancer. The usual tests are acute toxicity tests. . . ."

The greatest optimism of all is the FDA's official attitude, which, in effect, holds that merely because a chemical causes cancer in some animals under some conditions it does not necessarily mean it will cause cancer in man. This free-wheeling attitude can be contrasted with Dr. Hueper's attitude that just because a chemical has not produced cancer in an animal "is not an adequate guarantee" that it is innocuous for man.

It would seem that where the safety of 175,000,000 people is at stake the more cautious attitude would be the accepted standard. But this is not the case, and the American people are forced to play Russian roulette with their lives, as far as carcinogens in food are concerned.

When food additives in use or proposed for use have been subjected to cancer tests, they have flunked their exams in a disturbingly large number of cases, as previously pointed out.

Dr. Smith observed that when someone has spent money developing a new chemical that he wants to sell for use in food, it is understandable that he would be reluctant to lose his investment, even when animal tests disclose that his compound induces cancer. "The Aramite decision," he said, "provides a convenient device for the developer of a carcinogenic food additive to go ahead and sell his product but it leaves consumers to take the risk."

Industry has enthusiastically espoused the "safe dose" concept for carcinogens. Its attitude, generally, was reflected by a witness who testified that "I see no reason to reject a compound considered as a food additive for the sole reason that it produces a skin cancer in a hypersensitive mouse." He didn't mention what might happen to a hypersensitive human.

Equally as serious as minimizing the danger of carcinogens has been the suppression of facts about them from the public. Government and industry officials have leveled widespread criticism at the International Union Against Cancer for lifting the curtain of silence about the cancer threat from chemical additives at the historic Rome meeting in 1956. Dr. Hueper, because of his paper outlining the dangers to which the public was being exposed, was singled out for special censure; since then he has felt the lash of official censorship. On at least two occasions he has been prevented by Government officials in the Department of Health, Education and Welfare from delivering papers on carcinogens in foods before meetings of scientists. On one occasion Dr. Hueper was scheduled to address the Ninth Annual Midwest Cancer Conference in Kansas in the summer of 1957 on "Consumer Goods and Cancer Hazards," but the speech was canceled after former FDA Deputy Commissioner John L. Harvey protested that it leveled "serious charges at the FDA."

Mr. Harvey's communiqué to Marion B. Folsom, then Secretary of the Department of Health, Education and Welfare, also revealed the FDA's attitude about what information should—and should not—be made available to the public, when he stated:

"We think it is desirable that our agencies bear in mind the great concern over cancer and the coverage that will be given in the lay press to the program of the 9th Annual Midwest Cancer Conference. Our experience following the International Conference in Rome . . . indicates that remarks by a scientist intended for a scientific audience may well be picked up by the lay press writers and used to confuse and alarm the consuming public. . . . "

After the speech was canceled, officials of the Department of Health, Education and Welfare denied having exercised censorship, claiming the Hueper paper was disapproved on other grounds. Following this incident, Dr. Hueper was supposed to deliver another paper at a meeting of the IUAC in London in July 1958, but again his paper was disapproved by department officials.

The Government has been able to clamp down not only on scientists on its payroll, including many who are violently opposed to official policy on chemical additives and other environmental poisons, but it also has been able to exert pressures on many other doctors and health officials who do not work directly for it.

The number of medical people who look to the Federal Government for all or part of their livelihood was pointed out by Dr. James A. Shannon, director of the National Institute of Health, when he said that "thousands of doctors now depend on NIH grants for most of their support. The training of many researchers is financed by the Government. A majority of U. S. medical schools admit they would be in difficult straits without Government grants."

Dr. McCay of Cornell has raised "the problem of how all of us can defend those scientists who honestly try to protect the public interests but are constantly threatened with destruction if they take a position against fluoridation of water or against carcinogenic agents in foods. This need is especially evident among state and federal civil servants."

Dr. McCay said the right of the professor to express himself in the area of his specialty is usually respected in better universities. "However," he added, "these institutions are under never-ending pressure to conform to the wishes of those who donate money. This pressure grows from year to year as research expands and the operation of universities becomes more expensive." He emphasized that such pressures had never been exerted on him by Cornell officials.

The problem of trying to retain scientific freedom in universities becomes more acute as industries "own" increasingly larger shares of such institutions through grants, fellowships, scholarships, donations, subsidies and other direct and indirect handouts, bringing a rich harvest in "loyalty" from the beneficiaries as well as certain income-tax advantages. Many professors owe their jobs to these funds. They, like others who serve industry as consultants, are seldom unaware of the source of their bread and butter or supplementary income.

Professional men and research scientists—physicians, dentists, chemists and others—are also subject to varying degrees of control by their professional societies. Some of these organizations, like the American Dental Association, have life-and-death economic power over their members.

In November of 1958 it was announced by an Ohio newspaper that Dr. Jonathan Forman, an allergist of Columbus and an ardent foe of chemicals in foods, was forced to resign as editor of the *Ohio State Medical Journal* because of his outspoken opposition to fluoridation.

A commentary on the unhealthy lack of scientific independence in America today was the difficulty the Delaney Committee had in getting scientists to testify about the harmful nature of chemicals in foods. Many prospective witnesses would privately express their apprehensions about the situation, but they refused to go on record for fear of economic reprisal. Some of the men who courageously spoke up said they were sticking their necks out.

Another serious aspect of the problem is the control Government and industry have over research. Virtually all funds for such purpose must come from one of these two sources. If they are not sympathetic to the project, financial support can be withheld and the experiment most likely will not be undertaken. If the test comes out wrong—as did the sugar experiment at Harvard—the funds may be withdrawn, as they were in that instance.

Still another aspect of the problem is the failure or refusal to recognize or report adverse effects from certain hazards. Dr. Hueper cited a case in which the occurrence of occupational cancers caused by chemicals in a certain manufacturing process remained unreported for many years "although the circumstances favoring their discovery were most favorable."

When hazards are brought to light, industry often has shown less interest in correcting them than in trying to whitewash them with frenzied public-relations activity—an abuse especially prevalent among pesticide manufacturers. The late Dr. L. G. Cox, formerly of the Beech-Nut Company, testified before the Delaney Committee that few producers of pesticides would admit the residue problem existed, nor would they try to correct it, but they did raise a reported $119,000 for public relations "to offset unfavorable publicity against chemicals in foods." On the other hand, he continued, "it has been extremely difficult to raise funds from either the food industry or the chemical industry, for research projects on residue problems in canned or processed foods."

A chemical trade journal disclosed that producers of hydrogenated fats were anteing up $300,000 for public relations to counteract the adverse publicity given their product as a suspected cause of heart disease.

The form this public-relations activity takes is not spelled out, but some politicians who have taken excessive interest in promoting corrective food legislation have noted that their opponents in election campaigns appear to have unusually heavy financial backing. Certain other political figures in Congress, the record shows, seem to take extraordinary pains to promote the use of chemicals in foods and defend their use. Public relations appears to have many facets.

On numerous occasions the public has been the victim of various political pressures exerted on behalf of special interests in the food or chemical industries. In one case the FDA was ordered by Congress (Agricultural Act of 1938) to stop two years of experiments designed to learn the dangers of poisoning from lead and arsenic, commonly used as insecticides until largely replaced by DDT, and the test animals were ordered killed—a procedure *Consumers' Research* compared to the Nazi book burnings. In another case cited by *Consumers' Research*, the public was kept in ignorance for many years by Federal and state authorities about the threat of selenium poisoning from flour milled out of wheat grown on certain selenium-bearing soils in some midwestern states.

Each incident of victimization of the public, economically or biologically, for the benefit of commercial interests could be isolated and dismissed as trivial, unimportant or even "statistically insignificant." But when we evaluate the good faith of those who are responsible for the integrity of the food supply, the collective impact of this good faith is hardly reassuring. Former representative Usher L. Burdick put the matter bluntly when he charged that the Food and Drug Administration, the American Medical Association and "the big chemical companies" have joined in a conspiracy "to inject these poisonous chemicals into food, not for the safety of public health, but for the profits arising from the manufacture of the chemicals. An examination of the records leaves little in doubt as to the facts of this conspiracy."

Further, said Mr. Burdick, a former Federal prosecutor, although it has been a crime to adulterate foods since the Pure Food and Drug Act was passed by Congress in 1906, *"the law has never been enforced, so that today poisons are being injected into food without limit, while the people believe they are protected by this law."*

The 1906 law fathered by Dr. Wiley was one of the great legislative achievements of this century, but it was hardly on the books before the adulterers began trying to emasculate it. From the beginning, they had but one goal—to get Congress to legalize the use of small amounts of toxic substances in foods. This goal eluded them until the summer of 1958—two years after the government paid homage to Dr. Wiley by issuing a special commemorative stamp in his honor.

Dr. Wiley's story is a catalogue of the frustrations and heartbreak suffered by a man who dedicated his life to fighting efforts to undermine the pure food law. Illegal boards were created to override his decisions prohibiting the use of poisons in any amount in foods; techniques he developed to substitute natural processes for the use of chemicals in foods were relegated to the Department of Agriculture's morgue, legal victories were nullified by administrative edict and court decisions were interpreted to suit political and commercial expediency.

Gradually the adulterers' tremendous power proved too great. A series of ruthless measures left Dr. Wiley and his department virtually powerless, and he was practically forced to resign. In ensuing years, the policies that he fought so vigilantly became departmental policy, capped by the 1958 amendment legalizing the use of small amounts of poisons in foods.

When the 1958 amendment was passed, the New York Times (Feb. 24, 1958) quoted Dr. Arnold Lehman of the FDA as asserting that he had been setting "tacit tolerances" for certain additives in violation of the existing law. "What we have been doing all along has been pretty illegal, until Congress bailed us out," he stated.

FDA apparently took it on itself to decide which of the nation's laws to enforce and which to ignore—a power never conferred on it by Congress.

To justify the FDA's failure to enforce the law *prohibiting the use of poisons in any amount*, then Commissioner Larrick, in seeking the amendment to legalize the existing illegal use of poisons, said the 1938 law "was never a scientific one, and mainly on that account it has often been impractical of enforcement. To abandon it is a realistic step. . . ."

In contrast to the tolerance the FDA extended to powerful manufacturers who dumped tons of poisons into foods in open violation of the law, the FDA could be stern and uncompromising for what it considered more serious offenses. It has been particularly severe with small purveyors of health foods who were guilty of too much enthusiasm in claiming benefits for natural foods free of chemical adulteration. The FDA contended that by claiming healing virtues for such foods, the foods became drugs and should have contained directions for use.

At the same time no one is known to have been sent to

jail for permitting the use of forbidden pesticides in milk or using excess amounts of pesticides on other foods. No one has had to face stern justice for leaving in chickens 342,000 times the amount of stilbestrol necessary to start cancer in a mouse. Similarly, the use of toxic food dyes, in strict violation of the law, has been overlooked.

Inequities such as these caused Dr. Wiley, the fallen crusader, to ponder what the condition of the country would have been if the pure food law had been enforced. No poisonous substances would have been allowed in foods, he said. No soft drink would contain any harmful ingredients. No bleached flour would enter interstate commerce.

"Our foods and drugs would be wholly without any form of adulteration and misbranding. The health of our people would be vastly improved and their life greatly extended. The manufacturers of our food supply, and especially the millers, would devote their energies to improving the public health and promoting happiness in every home by the production of whole ground, unbolted cereal flours and meals.

"The resistance of our people to infectious diseases would be greatly increased by a vastly improved and more wholesome diet. Our example would be followed by the civilized world and thus bring to the whole universe the benefits which our own people had received.

"We would have been spared the ignominy and disgrace of great scientific men bending their efforts to defeat the purpose of one of the greatest laws ever enacted for the protection of the public welfare. Eminent officials of our Government would have escaped the indignation of outraged public opinion because they permitted and encouraged these frauds on the public. The cause of a wholesome diet would not have been put back for fifty or a hundred years. . . ."

And last but not least, the peril Dr. Smith warned against would never have become the law of the land in the summer of 1958. The human digestive tract would not have been legislated into the role of a sewer for the disposal of untold hundreds of chemicals that afford only commercial advantage.

13

What to Do

about It

WHAT IS THE SOLUTION to the chemicals-in-food problem? I don't claim to have the whole answer. The task I set for myself was to compile the evidence and present the problem as simply and clearly as possible, and in that endeavor I have been fortunate in having the help of some of the country's foremost physicians who are interested in the cause of good, wholesome foods. But after three years of constant study of this tremendously complex situation, I can offer some suggestions and observations.

The beginning point must be recognition that the problem exists, and that unless it is solved we are courting disaster. No progress can be made along those lines while it remains a sacred cow of the advertising profession, to be ignored or whitewashed.

If the over-all problem is considered by any officially appointed body, that body should be kept independent of the pressures of industry and Government alike; keep it away from bureaucrats and politicians with an ax to grind; keep it away from scientists who owe their livelihood to industry and are more interested in proving that various food chemicals are safe than in finding out if they are harmful.

Many of these chemicals and the hazards they pose could be stopped by honest legislation designed to protect consumers. There is no excuse for artificial sex hormones, antibiotics, coal-tar dyes, carcinogens, suspect emulsifiers and most of the other toxic substances in common use. They never should have been permitted in the first place and they should not be allowed now. Industry should not be given six months, a year, two years, thirty months or longer to find out if they are safe; by government decree these substances should be banned at once, and they should not be readmitted unless proved to be *both safe for all persons who must eat them and of direct nutritional benefit to consumers.* Few chemicals could qualify under this test.

The number of additives necessary to feed the nation should be reduced to an absolute minimum, as Dr. Smith recommended, and those remaining should be tested by every known means until there could be confidence in their harmlessness. Testing procedures should include cancer tests, and chemicals found to cause cancer in man or animal should be automatically and instantly eliminated. Why should the consumer be forced to take the slightest risk from chemicals that offer no nutritional value? Why should he be asked to accommodate commercial interest at risk of his own health and life?

Further, let us stop being brainwashed by propaganda about the so-called agricultural revolution that has "enabled science to produce an abundance of quality food." Frequently neither science nor quality is in evidence. In their place are biological tricks and chemical deceptions to mask the deficiencies that accompany the production of quantity in place of quality. We have been so seduced by misleading advertising that we do not recognize the nutritional shortcomings of our chemically soaked food supply, and our jaded taste buds no longer recognize its lack of taste.

An even more serious part of the problem is the pesticides. This is the only field in which American industry admits defeat, even makes a virtue of defeat, pointing with pride to the lethal nature of its product. The government has made no effort to find out it the nation can be fed without being poisoned. Instead it says there is no proof that foods can be grown without the use of poisons. It ignores the fact that hundreds of farms are producing food without use of chemicals. In place of experiment to see if natural farming methods are feasible on a nationwide basis, the government does everything possible to harass and discourage those who practice this method.

The fact that sprays are claimed to be necessary to grow food is not a warrant for their increased use; it is an indictment of the critical plight of American agriculture and the waning fertility of our once-rich soils. Poison sprays, rather than being a solution, are merely a delaying action, a final desperate maneuver to stave off catastrophe.

There is tremendous evidence that the problem could be largely controlled if entomologists would get back to being biologists instead of chemists. There are promising leads that control could be largely effected through encouragement of harmless insect species that prey on the crop-eating varieties and development of air-conditioned grain elevators and mechanical and electrical devices that have shown promise as pest killers. Even more important is the urgent need to restore the health of our soil.

Dr. Albrecht has spoken eloquently about the threat of our declining soil fertility and the consequent shift from high-protein plants to carbohydrate fillers that offer little more than bulk to deceive the hungry belly. It is to be the final mockery of our civilization that we are to starve to death with full stomachs?

Our agriculture problem suggests a Gilbert and Sullivan operetta. We use chemicals to produce more food than we can use, sacrificing quality to quantity. Then the surplus must be stored at tremendous cost. To keep it from being devoured by insects it must be basted with powerful poisons; we seem to prefer eating poisoned dead insects to healthy live ones. Instead of consuming our "surplus" grains, butter, eggs and other protein products in health-promoting whole-wheat breads and other baked goods, we put chemicals into them that offer little or no nutrition. We remove the best part of the wheat, feed it to animals, and what remains we add synthetic vitamins to make up for the removed nutrients; then we call this impoverished product "enriched." Finally, we spend millions of dollars on vitamins and drugs to make up for the nutritional deficiencies of our foods.

The health of the people will not be served as long as agricultural production is geared to economics instead of the demands of the body. Let us stop deluding ourselves about our state of health, recognize it for what it is and see if a change in diet can improve it. A nation must recognize that it indeed is in a precarious state when crime and bad health are among its biggest industries.

Instead of finding out if our monumental amount of bad health is due to the use of food chemicals and improperly grown foods, we ignore cause and concentrate on effect; we block out unpleasant facts with nonsense about better reporting, better diagnostic methods, more accurate statistics and other smoke screens. This is trifling with catastrophe, both biologically and politically.

Many ingenious arguments have been presented to justify the use of small amounts of poisons in foods. All are said to be based on the scientific method. Proponents of these poisons have been singularly successful in establishing that anyone who objects to eating them is considered mentally deficient. When I wrote a series of newspaper articles attacking the DDT gypsy moth program, many sympathetic readers called to offer encouragement or information. Almost to a man they began by assuring me they weren't crackpots; because they objected to being doused with poison they felt compelled to defend their sanity.

Dr. Wiley's argument that the nature of a poison is not changed by reducing the amount has never been successfully challenged. Regardless how small the dose, it is still poison. It is still antagonistic to the human organism. It is worth repeating still again that when poison is applied to to the human body, there is damage. The more poison, the greater the damage. The smaller the amount, the less the damage. The fact that the dose can be reduced until damage no longer is discernible does not mean it no longer takes place—merely that it no longer can be seen.

As long as it is profitable to inject chemicals into foods, someone will be repeating the now familiar argument that because some substances found in the human body and in nature are poisonous when isolated in the test tube, it is sound practice to use more of these substances in foods. As scientists who temper their learning with humility have pointed out, these substances were introduced into the body by nature for a purpose. They were formulated in a specific amount for a specific purpose. If a larger or smaller amount were needed, the amount would have been larger or smaller. Those who reject this idea as unscientific must be reminded that nature produced and sustained life, a feat man has not been able to duplicate. Man does not even understand what life is; a single cell is so infinitely complex that increased knowledge and understanding brings to the humble only greater respect for the mystery and beauty of life.

All of us owe a debt to science, but we must also be aware of its limitations and acknowledge the difference between science and scientists. Science is an objective dispassionate body of knowledge. Scientists are men with the same strengths and weaknesses as other men. They too have biases and prejudices.

The subject is much too broad and profound for more than cursory mention here. Like other men who have found themselves in untenable positions, scientists are able to rationalize what they do. No one goes home at night to rub his hands together and say, "Well, I poisoned another million babies today." The scientist who advocates the use of poisons in small amounts has been able to convince himself this is safe procedure. But this hypothesis is not a scientific fact. *It is a scientist's rationalization.*

I recall one scientist, the head of a nutritional foundation supported by the chemical and food industries. Asked to comment on some food chemicals I was writing about, he endorsed the use of every substance challenged and I quoted him as saying the substances did "no harm." Upon checking the article for accuracy, he made one change. "No harm" was made to read "no great harm." It was his rationalization that the products he earned his living by endorsing did the public no *great* harm.

The industrialist who manufactures and sells food additives must be considered apart from the scientist. He lives by a different set of rules. He's not against people, but he usually thinks of profits first; he has a different set of values. He is less likely to regard the public as a collection of individuals than as a lovely big mass of consumers that offer wonderful opportunity for commercial exploitation. And besides, don't his own scientists tell him these things are safe in small amounts?

The greatest threat industrialists pose is their ignorance about the biological dynamite they are tampering with. As Dr. Roy C. Newton, vice-president in charge of scientific activities for Swift and Company, warned, the chemical companies' propaganda obviously was prepared by persons who do not have full realization of the delicacy of balance of chemical reactions within the human body and the ease with which foreign substances can throw this delicate mechanism out of balance.

Because of the enormous power industrialists exert, they have been able to get control of the Government agencies that are supposed to regulate them. They are able to place their own men in key spots and dictate policy. A former key official of one of the biggest milling companies in the country was, until his recent retirement, a top official in the FDA. Where would his primary loyalty lie—to industry or to the consumer? Could he be expected to have the viewpoint of the consumer?

These political appointees have the power to overrule the recommendations of career men who have the technical training and knowledge to appreciate the hazard the public is being subjected to by the increasing adulteration of foods. The FDA employs some of the finest scientists in the country, many of whom are strongly opposed to the official policy of permitting poisons in foods, but their recommendations are overruled and ignored on the politically controlled policy level.

Another aspect of the problem is that some Government employees plan, upon retiring, to seek a job in industry. This often makes them reluctant or unwilling to enforce unpopular regulations.

It is the unsuspecting public that ultimately must pay the price of tolerant attitudes by officials toward law enforcement. There need be nothing insidious in this. The public can be dismissed as a nameless, shapeless thing without form, meaning or personality, incapable of pain or elation.

While it is conceded occasionally that extremely susceptible persons may react unfavorably to some of the poisons used in foods, this admission is countered by the assurance that there is no danger for the great majority of people. This means there is little or no protection for some people, especially those with allergies and susceptibilities. Who are the ones who will prove to be vulnerable? You? Me? Your children? Mine? None of us can know until it is too late. Then those who succumb will be written off as "statistically insignificant." Is there any man alive who feels statistically insignificant?

More and more we tend to emphasize the average and forget the individual. Mass conformity has become the order of the day. It is not enough that we are supposed to conform mentally, physically and spiritually to the standards of the average man; it is becoming increasingly hazardous not to conform biologically.

The wanton use of chemicals in food emphasizes the personal problem of the individual who fails to measure up to the national average. With an issue like smoking, for instance, each person can evaluate the risk for himself and decide whether or not to take his chances; with foods, we are all members of a captive audience. We all must eat. We all must get our food from the same general sources. If the Government will not protect us, we have no real protection.

As long as the individual cannot look to his government for protection, he must take such measures as he can to protect himself. This is not the ideal remedy or the ultimate solution, but it does offer some immediate protection.

The most important place to begin is by having the best nutrition possible. In addition to laying the groundwork for general health, it is necessary to help the body fight the unavoidable poisons in the diet and daily environment. One of the best general books on nutrition is Adelle Davis' *Let's Eat Right to Keep Fit*. Good nutrition, as she points out, means a diet high in proteins and low in refined sugar. It includes whole-wheat grains, unsaturated oils, fresh fruits and vegetables, salads, milk, butter, eggs and meat (especially organ meats: heart, liver, kidneys, etc.)

The hardest part of trying to follow a good dietary regimen is the difficulty of avoiding pesticides. It is virtually impossible to avoid all pesticides, but intake of these poisons can be considerably reduced by following certain precautions; this is especially desirable since the storage of DDT in the body is in direct proportion to the amount one is exposed to in diet and environment.

Most DDT enters the body from meat, due to DDT's tendency to concentrate in the fat; this is unfortunate because meat is our primary source of protein. An elementary precaution calls for removing all visible fat and not eating gravy made from drippings containing fat. The valuable nutrients in the meat drippings may be retained by chilling the liquid and removing the hardened fat. This fat-removing procedure can also be followed in making soups.

Another precaution is to buy lean meats and lean chickens; lean meats, while less tender, are likely to contain less DDT because of the lower fat content, and they generally are cheaper. Especially desirable are sirloin, round and the organ meats, rather than porterhouse, tenderloin and other fat, well-marbled cuts.

Even with visible fats removed, beef, pork, chicken, duck and goose contain a considerable proportion of fat distributed through the tissues in such a way that it cannot be separated and discarded. This is especially true of the higher-grade prime and choice meats; the feeding of cattle and hogs to produce deposits of fat and "marbling" of steaks, roasts and chops has been accepted practice for many years.

Because of the possibility that stilbestrol pellets may remain in the poultry neck, some people discard the neck altogether. Poultry dipped in antibiotic solutions is supposed to carry a marking to that effect and can be avoided by those who wish to take that precaution. However, if not involved in interstate commerce, this poultry may not be labeled to indicate that an antibiotic dip has been used on it.

If fish are not subjected to the use of antibiotics as preservatives, they are one of the few uncontaminated foods available. Widespread use of sprays, however, has led to the contamination of many fresh-water fish. When uncontaminated fish are available, they can be used frequently to supplement or replace meat as a major source of protein.

It is preferable to prepare meat and fish by boiling, broiling, roasting and baking, rather than frying, to help reduce DDT exposure and cut down on undesirable fat intake.

Fats used in cooking also are likely to contain considerable pesticide residue. Vegetable oils have the compensating feature of being valuable sources of unsaturated fatty acids, but that advantage is offset if they are wholly or partly hydrogenated. *Consumers' Research* recommends using a minimum of shortenings and ready-prepared foods containing them (mass-produced cakes and pastries, etc.) which have labels that refer only to "vegetable oil" or "shortening," without naming the oil used or stating whether it has been hydrogenated. These and other ready-prepared foods also may contain a variety of other undesirable chemicals.

It also is prudent to practice restraint in the use of all ready-mixed or frozen and other ready-for-the-oven and heat-and-serve foods, as they are commonly made with processed fats, as well as other adulterants.

A further precaution in reducing DDT intake calls for peeling all fruits and vegetables that lend themselves to such treatment, even at cost of losing valuable nutrients in the skins. Apple cider and other fruit juices made of the whole fruit, including skins, must be held suspect as being highly contaminated with pesticides, especially apples, probably the most heavily sprayed of all foods. The outside layer of celery should be scraped, and the outside leaves of lettuce, cabbage and similar leafy vegetables should be disposed of and the remainder thoroughly washed.

Chickens and eggs (primarily the yolks) generally are heavily contaminated by pesticides and other chemicals, and poultry is often diseased. This makes it prudent to avoid commercial poultry products when possible by buying from local farmers who use a minimum of these substances; such farmers are rare, but there are a few left. Some abstain from the use of chemicals to put cheap weight on animals because they are interested primarily in producing nutritious and tasty food for their own families. A few feel it is immoral to inflict such biological indignities on any living creature.

It is axiomatic that anyone trying to reduce his DDT intake will use no aerosol bombs. Many people use these routinely in their homes, even in the kitchen. Women have been made so sanitation-conscious through advertising that they fail to see the irony of presiding over a sterile kitchen, as they prepare foods laced with some of the most powerful poisons known. Goaded by advertising, many Americans have developed a phobia about killing bugs—all bugs, helpful and harmful alike.

At various times efforts have been made to compel producers of fruits and vegetables to mark their products with labels stating all poisons used on them. This has been fought vigorously by the affected interests. They maintain it would be inconvenient, expensive and, more important, consumers would not buy products if they knew they were eating these formidable-sounding chemicals. Instead of viewing this as a mandate to eliminate these poisons, they regard it as a warning to keep the consumer in the dark about what he eats.

The law requires all shipments of fruits and vegetables treated with chemical preservatives to carry small cards (3 x 5 inches) stating in small type the substance used; these cards, according to the law, are supposed to be displayed on the produce by the retailer. Several surveys, however, failed to turn up any merchants complying with the law. There are no indications that the FDA has enforced this ruling.

Produce growers recently made a vigorous fight to push through Congress a bill to repeal the card-displaying requirement. But before acting on the measure, the House Committee on Interstate and Foreign Commerce queried the various states' food and drugs divisions. The states overwhelmingly opposed the change and the bill was dropped.

Dr. Martin of the Kansas State Health Department noted that in hearings on the proposed measure "a great many witnesses expressed the fear that consumers would be frightened by the long, unfamiliar, unpronounceable names of the preservatives used and avoid the purchase of foodstuffs so labeled." He added:

"As the name of the chemical becomes more and more frightening, at the same time the chemical is apt to be more and more foreign to the human body, relatively new and untested by time, and to have a smaller and smaller margin of safety. The intelligent and well-informed consumer might therefore very much wish to avoid foodstuffs with an impressive label."

Dr. Martin pointed out that in the case of chemical additives, what the consumer doesn't know "may very well hurt him. It would seem desirable to have chemically treated and untreated foods compete with each other in the market place, with the buyer making the decision on the basis of his own information and the pressure of economics."

While the FDA has concentrated its efforts to insist on accurate labeling, it has been demonstrated that many inadequacies still remain to be corrected. Labels, for example, may state that a product contains emulsifier, but the consumer has no way of finding out the type or the amount. He also has no way of knowing if he is being cheated on the percentage of ingredients used. To state that a product is rabbit and horse implies that there are equal portions of each; but this is not very accurate if the proportion is one rabbit to one horse. As Dr. McCay pointed out, it does little good merely to list ingredients without quantitative values.

Labels also are likely to be taken up mostly by the name of the product and the manufacturer, leaving only a small, half-concealed spot for the required declaration of ingredients. Or, as *Consumers' Research* pointed out, "perhaps he will use for this statement of ingredients a size of type or a color of ink and background that makes the wording difficult, and in some cases impossible, to read." Another trick used to evade the labeling requirement is to slap a special sticker over the label.

The whole labeling procedure urgently needs overhauling and greater enforcement if the public is to have the protection it is entitled to. Since most people are not chemists, a long listing of chemicals used in a product serves little purpose. The consumer could buy more intelligently, exercising any knowledge gained about harmful additives, if the label were required to state not only the name of the chemical used but the specific purpose it served. Then *the consumer*—and not the FDA—could determine if the additive served a useful purpose; the buyer could make up his own mind if saving some fraction of a penny, or perhaps several pennies, entailed risking his family's health or life.

The only foods that do not require labels stating the ingredients used are so-called standardized products—those for which Congress has set "standards of identity." This means specific components that can be used and the amounts permissible. The chief groups of "standardized" foods include cocoa and chocolate, flour, corn meal, farina and macaroni, bread, milk and cream, cheese and processed cheese, mayonnaise and salad dressing, canned fruit and fruit juices, preserves and jellies, tomato products and, recently joining the list, ice cream.

A shortcoming of the "standards" procedure is that the consumer has no opportunity to see which chemicals someone else has decided are safe for him. Ice cream, for instance, contains as one of its optional ingredients the stabilizer sodium carboxymethyl-cellulose, which "promotes smoothness." Dr. Hueper has named this substance as a cancer-producing suspect. Standards for ice cream also permit the use of coal-tar dyes and artificial flavoring agents, neither of which would be stated on the container.

The consumer might well wonder why standards, if designed to benefit the public, should not encourage competition on the level of quality by setting only minimum amounts of nutrients that could be used, with the maximum amounts left up to firms in competition with each other. Why shouldn't progressive manufacturers be able to force standards up by educating the public to think in terms of quality instead of quantity?

In the more critical area of nutritional "short weight," due to refining and use of chemical additives, many people, as a rule of thumb, use as few factory-processed foods as possible. As with all rules, there are exceptions, but, generally speaking, the less processing foods are subjected to, the greater their nutritional value.

The rule Hippocrates laid down is as valid today as when he propounded it: foods should be as near as possible to the condition in which nature intended them. Equally important, they should be as fresh as possible.

Almost all processing of foodstuffs is designed to increase their shelf life, and chemicals are used to mask the consequent loss of vitality, flavor, texture, color and other desirable natural qualities. The more all these chemicals can be avoided, the better, not only because of the direct hazard they impose on those who consume them, but also because of the damage they inflict on foods and the consequent deficiencies in people who eat them.

Preservatives and heat do not merely "stop the clock" on food spoilage, as claimed; they interfere with the life processes of the treated foods and lower their nutritional value. Some chemicals may not directly cause cancer or other diseases, and may never be proved to do so, but they could be indirect causes of infirmities by depriving the body of nutrients which protect against bad health. As deficient foods are eaten, the body progressively has less capacity to fight off effects of poisons in foods and a cycle of accelerating deterioration is set in motion. This argues with renewed force for the lowest possible intake of toxic chemicals and the least change from the natural state of foods.

Probably the most important protective measure anyone with a small amount of land can take is having his own garden. This assures many advantages: a constant supply of fresh products, economy, convenience and a pleasant and productive form of exercise. Many people, by using natural farming methods are able to grow their own produce without the use of chemical fertilizers or sprays.

It is unfortunate that the public has been educated to so many false values about food. Women have been persuaded to be more concerned with the external appearance of most products than their quality and flavor. Food is no different from any other commodity. You tend to get what you pay for. It costs extra money to produce quality foods because labor and natural products replace the use of chemicals.

With our curious sense of value, food generally is the first commodity we cut down on when trying to economize.

A French physician, Dr. Gabriel Mouchot, pointed out that France is different in this respect because in France most people spend quite a lot on food, "and in general their food is good." In England (which is like the United States), he said, "food is always at the end of the list." Writing in *Medical World,* Dr. Mouchot noted that in England the people develop complexes and have duodenal ulcers and other ailments.

"In Normandy," he said, "you can be jilted and survive: if you are crossed in love, your duodenum will not bleed; if you lose money on the Stock Exchange, a few sleepless nights may follow, but certainly no ulcer. You can be a politician in France and keep your duodenum—even if you lose your reputation. Why should anxiety cause duodenal ulcer in Kent and Gloucester, but not in Normandy?" He suggested the health of the people might be better if, "instead of spending million of pounds on idiotic films, tobacco, football pools and what else, more were spent on decent unadulterated food."

In France most foods are grown by natural methods, just as they are in Russia. A small item in the news recently noted that Lysenko, the famous and controversial Russian agronomist and geneticist, recommended the use of more organic fertilizers in place of chemicals; when the agricultural bigwigs opposed him, Premier Khrushchev came to Lysenko's support. The latest five-year plan, which began in 1958, called for the doubled production of compost. This is another warning the United States would do well to heed.

In this country, farmers who would de-emphasize the use of chemicals have received no encouragement. Instead, they have run into official antagonism and harassment, often being forced against their will to use poison sprays. Despite this obstacle, the natural method of farming without chemicals has grown steadily in the United States in recent years. Many growers now carry on a brisk mail-order business, sending their products all over the country as the word spreads about the advantages of unadulterated foods. Postage increases the cost, but as more regional sources of supply develop, this cost should be reduced. Most of the big natural growers now are located in California, Florida, and Pennsylvania, but they are spreading in the Middle West and Southwest. In California some big markets are starting to carry a line of naturally grown products, and the demand for these exceeds the supply.

Throughout the country there are a few other meat and poultry producers who operate on a more limited scale, growing some of their own feeds and supplementing them with commercial feeds; although any use of commercial feed makes it virtually impossible to eliminate all contamination, these growers are making praiseworthy strides *away* from adulteration by using, on their own animals, no sprays, antibiotics, artificial hormones or other chemicals that contaminate meats and alter the biology of the animals.

Many "health stores" sell naturally grown products. Generally, however, these are found only in large cities. They carry many commendable products, but they also have much junk. There are quacks and frauds in their ranks, just as there are among chemical growers and processors who enjoy the favors of the Government.

The best source of naturally grown foods is the grower himself, who often advertises his wares in those publications orientated toward growing and consumption of natural foods. Among the publications listing these sources are *Prevention* and its companion magazine, *Organic Gardening and Farming,* published by Rodale Press, Inc., Emmaus, Pensylvania. The latter publication is devoted to instructions for growing foods and flowers without the use of chemicals.

This is an organized movement representing a ground swell of public indignation, which gains momentum as people learn that the Government has sacrificed them to commercial interests. It recognizes that the only real reform must come from strong food laws vigorously enforced, and that such reform will come only when the people become sufficiently incensed to demand that their legislators give them the protection that is their right.

While it may be comforting to expect the Government

to guarantee the integrity of those who supply the nation's food, realism dictates that there can be no substitute for personal vigilance.

It is the individual, in the final analysis, who must be responsible for the purity and safety of the food he buys. Every housewife can choose between pure foods and those bearing labels stating that they contain artificial colors, artificial flavors, emulsifiers and the whole galaxy of additives. If the housewives of the country begin to seek and demand pure foods without additives or pesticide contaminants (which should be clearly listed upon the label) and insist upon their right to such foods, the food industry will see that they get them.

Bibliography

A COMPLETE BIBLIOGRAPHY of all the material used in compiling this book would run to dozens of pages, covering official reports, Congressional hearings, press releases, newspaper clippings, magazine articles, books, pamphlets, speeches, correspondence and various other data that fill several file drawers. To print such a voluminous record would serve little purpose for the average reader. For persons who are interested in further pursuing the subject discussed briefly in Chapter XII—the relationship between the soil and its products and health—the following books are recommended:

An Agricultural Testament, by Sir Albert Howard, Oxford University Press, New York.

Natural Food and Farming Digest, published by Natural Food Associates, Inc., Atlanta, Texas.

Nutrition and Health, by Sir Robert McCarrison and H. M. Sinclair, Faber and Faber, London.

Human Nutrition and Physical Degeneration, by Weston A. Price, Paul B. Hoeber, Inc., New York.

Nutrition and the Soil: Thoughts on Feeding, by Lionel Picton, M.D., Devin-Adair Co., New York.

Our Plundered Planet, by Fairfield Osborne, Little Brown & Co., Boston.

Our Poisoned Earth and Sky, by J. I. Rodale, Rodale Press, Emmaus, Pennsylvania.

Soil Fertility and Animal Health, by William A. Albrecht, Ph.D., Fred Hahne Printing Co., Webster City, Iowa.

Studies in Deficiency Disease, by Sir Robert McCarrison, Lee Foundation for Nutritional Research, Milwaukee, Wis.

The Living Soil, by E. D. Balfour, Devin-Adair Co., New York.

Silent Spring, by Rachel Carson, Houghton Mifflin Co., Boston.

The Soil and Health, Farming and Gardening for Health or Disease, by Sir Albert Howard, Devin-Adair Co., New York.

The Web of Life, by John H. Storer, Devin-Adair Co.,
New York.

The Wheel of Health, by G. T. Wrench, M.D., Lee Foundation for Nutritional Research, Milwaukee, Wis.

Your Bread and Your Life, by Doris Grant, Faber and
Faber, London.

Recommended for persons interested in learning more
about gardening by natural methods (without use of poisons):

Encyclopedia of Organic Gardening, Rodale Books, Inc.,
Emmaus, Pennsylvania.

*Gardening with Nature: How to Grow Your Own Vege-
tables, Fruits and Flowers by Natural Methods*, by
Leonard Wickenden, Devin-Adair Co., New York.

Make Friends with Your Land, by Leonard Wickenden,
Devin-Adair Co., New York.

Organic Gardening, by J. I. Rodale, Hanover House, Garden City, New York.

Pay Dirt, Farming and Gardening with Composts, by J. I.
Rodale, Devin-Adair Co., New York.

Recommended for general interest:

Let's Eat Right to Keep Fit, by Adelle Davis, Harcourt,
Brace and Co., New York.

Tomorrow's Food, by James Rorty and N. Philip Norman,
M.D., Devin-Adair Co., New York.

About the Author

WILLIAM LONGGOOD *is a free lance writer. For 17 years he was a reporter and feature writer for* THE NEW YORK WORLD-TELEGRAM, *winning many awards, among them a Pulitzer Prize in journalism.*